HELP

Garret Keizer

A COMMON READER
Pleasantville, New York

HELP

THE ORIGINAL HUMAN DILEMMA

GARRET KEIZER

HarperSanFrancisco
A Division of HarperCollins*Publishers*

Some names and biographical details in this book have been altered.

HELP: *The Original Human Dilemma*. Copyright © 2004 by Garret Keizer. All rights reserved. Printed in the United States of America. No part of this book may be used or reproduced in any manner whatsoever without written permission except in the case of brief quotations embodied in critical articles and reviews. For information address HarperCollins Publishers Inc., 10 East 53rd Street, New York, NY 10022.

HarperCollins books may be purchased for educational, business, or sales promotional use. For information please write: Special Markets Department, HarperCollins Publishers Inc., 10 East 53rd Street, New York, NY 10022.

HarperCollins Web site: http://www.harpercollins.com
HarperCollins®, ▟®, and HarperSanFrancisco™ are
trademarks of HarperCollins Publishers Inc.

FIRST EDITION
Designed by Joseph Rutt

Library of Congress Cataloging-in-Publication Data
is available on request.

ISBN 0–06–056062–2 (cloth)

04 05 06 07 08 RRD(H) 10 9 8 7 6 5 4 3 2 1

FOR KATHY AND SARAH

CONTENTS

I'm very proud that I went to Spain because I feel like I have done something in this world to help people. And that's what I'm here for. That's what we all are here for.

Salaria Kea O'Reilly
Nurse in the Abraham Lincoln Brigade

"Help," he said, "is giving part of yourself to somebody who comes to accept it willingly and needs it badly.

"So it is," he said, using an old homiletic transition, "that we can seldom help anybody."

Norman Maclean, A River Runs Through It

THE DARK WOOD

The trooper was calling long-distance from Arizona to find out what I knew about Kathy B. besides her name, the Christian half of which happened to be the same as my wife's. I registered the similarity as soon as he said the words: *Kathy is dead.* I hated the sound of that, though I had heard something like it once before. Years ago, when Kathy B. was living nearby and slowly draining the reservoirs of my goodwill, she had called the office at the school where I taught and asked that I be paged because of "an emergency."

"Who is this?" the secretary had demanded.

"Kathy."

But it had not been my Kathy, and it had not been an emergency, though I might well have had an accident or a heart attack as I dashed out of my classroom and down the crowded hall to the phone.

I told the trooper I did not know much. There was a couple over in Island Pond with whom Kathy had sometimes stayed during her sojourns in northeastern Vermont; the trooper said he had already found their names after searching Kathy's campsite. It was they who had recommended that he call me. Yes, I was a minister, I verified, but only part-time, and I had never really been her minister. I had found her sitting on the church lawn one Sunday morning (gaunt and toothless, at first glance neither male nor female but with an ascetic's preternatural strength in her grip and in her stride) and had tried to help her for a few months thereafter. In fact, I was one of those who had helped her arrange the trip to Arizona. She had seldom attended my church.

"I just tried to help," I said.

If the trooper was thinking what I was thinking, that apparently my help had not been enough, his voice did not betray him. In fact, he sounded ready to credit me with more grief than I could feel when he told me that Kathy B. had taken her own life.

Two lines from two songs keep playing in my head these days, though it has been a while since either was a regular on my stereo. The one is from the folksinger Joni Mitchell, and it goes: "If you can't find your goodness 'cause you've lost your heart." The other, from an Australian group called Paul Kelly and the Messengers, is much like it. "I lost my tenderness," Kelly says. Then he adds, "I took bad care of this."

It would make a neat transition to say "me too," but the truth is that I have not lost my heart or my tenderness as nearly as I can tell and so far as people tell me. Not yet. I also have not lost my hair or any of my teeth, which another singer, James Brown, claims are the main things a man needs to hang on to. (I assume that is especially true if the man is James Brown.) But I have reached that age when things do start to fall off or out of a person: hair, teeth, muscle tone, and perhaps some of the altruistic energy of youth.

A quip often attributed to Winston Churchill asserts that a man who isn't a socialist when he's young has no heart, and a man who isn't a conservative when he's old has no brains. I would sooner lose my hair than allow myself to become a conservative (or brainless)—but I am extraordinarily fond of that quote, and I take it there must be a good reason. It may be the same reason I keep imagining the Mitchell line and the Kelly line playing over and over like a dire musical omen—and the same reason too that I heard the trooper's announcement with a sense of mounting resistance. I am too old, I said to myself, to be surprised by this news and too old to feel implicated by it. I am also too old to feel guilty for not feeling sadder about it. I did what I could to help her. I saw this coming.

And yet I was apparently not too old to wish, and to say that I wished—in regard to the trooper's search for any next of kin—"that I could be of more help." And even though Kathy B. was dead now, I still prayed that God would help her.

•   •   •

Help is what this book is about. You will notice that I am also at the age when one has little patience for a long prelude. Along with that impatience comes a sense, hitherto rare in my life, of limited possibilities. At twenty-five, we feel that we will always be able to get to certain things at some later date; when we are fifty even a bookcase starts to look like a graveyard. *If I start right now, and read twenty-five pages every day. . . .* But of course we do not start right now, and even if we did, we would be unlikely to keep the resolution. We know more vividly than ever before that we are going to have to make deliberate, fatal choices about which books we are going to read and, in a case like mine, which we will try to write.

For various reasons that will become clearer as we go on, I have decided that one of the things I want most to read and write about is what it means to help someone—and what it means not to help someone. They go together, of course, because, as most people discover sooner or later, you can wind up not helping even when you wanted to help and vice versa. Let Kathy B. stand as my Exhibit A.

I should say at the outset that I am not writing primarily about altruism. I am not exactly sure what altruism is, and I suppose I need not be overly ashamed of my ignorance if no less an authority than the psychiatrist Anna Freud wondered if such a thing as pure altruism even existed. I'll go Anna one better and wonder if pure altruism would be such a good thing if it did. I can imagine God as a pure altruist, but I have trouble imagining a human being purified of all self-serving without also imagining a human being who thought he or she was God.

I used to believe, in that way we have of conjuring bogus etymologies from the English sounds of foreign roots, that *altruism* meant "all true"—that is, the belief that all of us are "true," none better than the other. I happen to like that meaning better than the actual derivation from the French *alter,* for "other." Altruism is defined as a concern for others, which sounds like the basis of all virtue though it has been the pretext for much sin, for there is a risk of seeing "the other" as a little too other, as the lesser object in what the theologian Martin Buber spoke of (in his book *I and Thou*) as an I-It relationship.

The word *help* strikes me as belonging more to an I-Thou relationship (assuming I have grasped Buber any better than I have grasped

altruism) because the other cannot remain detached from the evalua-
tion of my acts and because help is always an action. The other gets to
weigh in on whether I was a help and on how much help I was. I sometimes think of an altruist as a sort of ethical Don Juan, racking up his
conquests, whereas a helper partners up with someone who gets to
have a say in what they call their offspring, if they manage to have any.

To put the matter more succinctly, Kathy B.'s suicide is powerless to
impugn the altruism of anything I did on her behalf. But it does have the
power to raise the question of whether or not I helped her. While she
lived, so did she. Only a *Thou* can turn around and ask you a question
like that.

Help cuts about as close to the bone of what it means to be human as
any subject I can think of. We are, almost by definition and certainly
from the beginning of our lives, creatures who require a lot of help. No
human newborn stands up on shaky legs to suckle its first meal. Nor
can we imagine a fully formed adult who could qualify as human without giving some form of help to another. Such a person, neither helpless nor helpful, would be less than a robot, more soulless than a stone.

Over the centuries we have tried to define our species in terms of some
faculty to which we can make an exclusive claim: language, tool making,
or sapience. We now suspect that dolphins possess the rudiments of language. If one is willing to count a chimpanzee's chewed-up leaf sponge as
a tool, we have to extend the membership of that club also. As for any
claim to sapience, at this point in our history, it is perhaps best not to go
there. Our ability to give and receive help may be our best alternative for
defining humankind. The poet Goethe seemed to think so:

> Noble let man be,
> Helpful and good!
> For that alone
> Distinguishes him
> From all beings
> That we know of.

And yet we can cite examples of helping within other species and
between other species and our own that cannot be explained entirely

by who's top dog or who fills the food dish. Perhaps our ability to recognize this interdependence, and to value it above any claim specific to ourselves, is what makes us human after all. Perhaps the only thing that humans alone can do is to be humble. That said, the only way I've ever known to express humility, without turning it instantly into a form of pride, is to give help graciously or graciously to accept it.

The centrality of help to human nature is expressed in the biblical myth of human origins. Eve is created as "an help meet," to use the English of the King James Bible, which in 1611 meant "a fit helper." Popular usage has tended to misquote this as "helpmate." Since Eve is fit to help Adam, we have to assume that he must also be fit to help her. He too seems to have been created to help. He helps the Creator by giving the animals their names, and a chapter before he is cursed with the punishment of toil, he is blessed with the work of tending the Garden of Eden.

Our pagan ancestors, who built great bonfires on the tops of hills to help the sun rekindle its warmth at the winter solstice, were thinking along similar lines. We may tell ourselves that we have grown out of such nonsense, but I think rather that we have fallen into a predicament in which the bonfires make more sense than ever before. We have now "developed" to a stage where, if we refuse to help nature and each other, we not only will cease to be human, we will cease to be. In that regard, environmentalists and humanitarians are engaged in parallel enterprises, and not merely in the degree of desperation. Both are helping to undo harm that would never have occurred had our posture toward nature and each other been more respectful, more *Thou*-ish, if you will. In contexts like these, the word *help* can begin to sound coy, as when a colonial power speaks of helping its former possessions.

As for the confusion of *help meet* and *helpmate*, it may not be confusion after all. It may be that the richest illustration we have of mutual assistance is sexual intercourse, where two partners help each other toward greater pleasure and by so doing enhance their own. Small wonder that altruism can sometimes appear sexy or that acts of charity can sometimes lead to crimes of sexual abuse. Small wonder, finally, that self-help literature can seem like so much masturbation.

No less than we use help to define the human, we use help to invoke the divine. "Our help is in the name of the Lord, the maker of heaven and earth," says one of the psalms. The Buddhist bodhisattva, who vows not to partake of nirvana "until the grass itself is enlightened," the savior and the guardian angel, the patron saint and the fairy god-mother—all make their appearance as helpers. "Heaven help us!" we pray; "God help you!" we threaten, invoking help even for those we should like to kick. God is love, according to one of the letters in the New Testament, but it would seem that love, whether human or divine, is help. The medieval English mystic Julian of Norwich says in her *Revelations of Divine Love*, "I saw that for us [God] is everything that is good and comforting and helpful."

Albert Einstein, who seems to have regarded God mainly as a figure of speech, is supposed to have said that one of the most important questions we can ask is whether or not the universe is a friendly place. Our individual answers to that question will probably depend in large part on how much help we received—and gave—as we were growing up. Our first awareness that there is even such a thing as a universe probably came when we understood our needs and our desires in relation to those people we could count on to meet them. Then followed the heady discovery that this helping business could be a reciprocal deal, that patty-cake wasn't just a game; it was a demonstration of *torah*. The desperate cry of "Mommy, help!" could be turned into "Help Mommy," said sometimes as a shout of exultation and other times as an importunate demand, as in, "How about letting me take a shot at stirring that gooey stuff in the bowl?"

Then too we discovered that we could refuse help. We could insist on accomplishing something by ourselves—"By self!"—though this insistence did not automatically mean (yet another epiphany) that we could actually do it by ourselves. Surely the revelation of our abilities to receive, give, and refuse help are among the most exciting and, shall we say, messy developments in the life of a young child, just as the suspicion that we may not have been able to help much of anyone can be one of the sadder conclusions for an aging adult. If we loved symmetry more than hope, we could say that help is like the swinging door of human experience: "I can help!" we exclaim and go toddling into the sunshine; "I was no help at all," we mutter and go shuffling to our graves. I'm betting that the story can be happier than that, more progressive than regressive, but I have a clearer idea now than I once did of what I'm betting against.

• • •

Of course, that is true not only for me but also for many in my generation. That is one of the things I have going for me in this book: I can talk about a subject like the misgivings of midlife and count on more readers nodding their heads than could any writer of any generation before mine. That kind of immediate connection will be true of some younger readers also, if for no other reason than that they have become sick and tired of watching the older majority constantly nodding its collective gray head. *There they go again.* The demographic bulge that has moved through the various life passages like a swallowed antelope down the length of a snake, that put the Beatles on the charts and menopause on all the talk shows, is now at the place where issues of help may weigh the heaviest on our shared digestion. That is because, with decrepitude looming, many of us are going to need more help, while an unfortunate few of us (those of my daughter's generation) are going to be strapped with giving it out of all proportion to the help they received. Help can sometimes be so burdensome that it amounts to the main thing we want help with.

But let us not get ahead of ourselves. Before we come to decrepitude and dependency, people my age will come and are gradually coming to occupy that pivotal point of greatest need in the generations before and after their own. With men and women in our society living longer and having their children later, it is not unusual for my contemporaries to be doing the college tour at exactly the same time as they do the nursing home tour, each on behalf of someone who is likely to need their help well into the next decade. While medical technology is making ever-deeper inroads toward everlasting life, a less sanguine branch of research suggests that children of baby boomers will belong to the first American generation to receive less education and to earn less money than their parents did. In other words, the children may require some extra help. The duration of that pivotal point may go well beyond that of a few years. In fact, "pivotal point" may prove to be the wrong metaphor. The Great Plains may be more like it.

Even if neither our children nor our parents need our help, we may still find that we think more about the nature of helping as we grow older. These thoughts are likely to be ambivalent.

On the one hand, a sense of impending mortality has the potential to make us more compassionate. "I shall pass this way but once" and all the rest of it, so I ought to be as helpful as I can. I want to have made a difference. Perhaps I want someone to remember me fondly. Perhaps I am acutely conscious of all I have to be thankful for after half a century of good fortune or all I have to atone for after half a century of screwing up. Perhaps I even have the sense that living for half a century in the richest, most environmentally spendthrift country on earth is itself something to atone for.

On the other hand, that same sense of impending mortality can make me hesitant to invest too much of my short, sweet life in caring for others—especially if I've done a bit of that already and have had occasion to do some bookkeeping on the emotional profit and loss. If Kathy B. came back to life and back to Vermont, would I still help her? Yes, I think so. But I'm not sure I would give her any money, and I would keep my eyes on the clock in a way that I would have considered morally beneath me back then. Why should I feel like a bad person for telling anyone "I can only give you twenty minutes" if Nature has said to me, "You only have about twenty more years, maybe less, and maybe not such good ones and maybe minus the company of those you love most"?

I shall pass this way but once: it can be the reason you open the door or the reason you slam it in someone's face.

There is a story we love—and ought to love, because it is one of the loveliest stories we know how to tell—about a person of great wealth or high position who comes to see the shallowness of his self-serving life and learns to give of himself for others. It is the theme of Dickens's beloved *A Christmas Carol,* and I suppose that in a certain symbolic sense it is the theme of Christmas itself. (The Boss's Son leaves the family mansion and moves out to the boonies of human woe.) Allowing for the inevitable variations, it informs stories of help and service ranging from the founding of Habitat for Humanity to Lady Godiva's daring ride. We love these stories for any number of reasons, some humane and some belonging to that darkly lit den where Churchill and his cronies smoked their cigars. We like the idea that wealth has its advantages, that celebrity has a heart (or that a show of heart can sometimes lead to celebrity), that revolution or even a more progressive tax code may not be necessary in the long run. Most of all, though, we like the idea that there is hope for all of us to be better people than we are. I like that last one too.

But there is another kind of story, harder to tell and harder to hear and, from the view of what sells, just about impossible to publish. This is the story of the person who started out where the other person winds up, who helped without stint and gave without counting the cost, only to come round to the dismal place described by Dante in his *Divine Comedy:*

> Midway in our life's journey, I went astray
>> from the straight road and woke to find myself
>> alone in a dark wood.

Alone, and perhaps a bit cynical. Alone, and perhaps preferring it that way.

I would hasten to add that this is not my story or the story I plan to tell in this book. For one thing, I could never claim to be so disappointed because I was never so dedicated as the kind of person I have described. But I *do* claim that person as my spiritual kin, and there is no shame in that or even humility because that person can in turn make a claim of kinship with some of the most compassionate and helpful souls who ever walked the earth.

> Why have I not found favor in your sight, that you lay the burden of all this people on me? Did I conceive all this people? Did I give birth to them, that you should say to me, "Carry them in your bosom, as a nurse carries a sucking child"?
>> *Moses, to God*

> You faithless generation, how much longer must I be among you? How much longer must I put up with you?
>> *Jesus, as recorded by Mark*

> Who has ever had a sadder experience? Christ was betrayed by one. But my cause has been betrayed by everyone—ruined, betrayed, destroyed by everyone, alas!
>> *Florence Nightingale,*
>> *to her aunt, Mai Smith*

Do you think I enjoy living here?

Albert Schweitzer
(in Africa), to Dr. Edgar Berman

Were I somehow able to invite all of my readers to get into my car
and go for a ride with me, I would offer my front seat to that heart-
sore helper whose own exasperation echoed the preceding words. I
would do so, first of all, because that is the recommended seating arrangement for passengers who are starting to look a bit green around
the gills and, second, because that is where I like to have those passengers who are closest to my heart.

If I think of this book as a drive with you, my reader, I have several
reasons. The first is that while I know where I plan to end up, I do not
know, at this point, all the stops I am going to make along the way.

I do know the major ones. I am able to draw us a rough map. I am
keenly interested, for example, in our shared sense that certain things
are required of us if we are to count as good people. For persons
grounded in religious or philosophical systems, those requirements are
supposedly clear, though the daily application is often anything but
clear. That in a nutshell is the substance of my next chapter, "The Dubious Samaritan."

I am also interested in the ways that our sense of obligation chafes
against our desire for independence. We wish to be good; we also wish
to be free, and if that tension is arguably human, it is definitely American. I asked that my publisher not inflate my claims or my credentials
by describing this book as "a cultural history of help," though I suppose that is something like what I will attempt in "The Dream We No
Longer Admit."

Since much of the help we give and receive comes by way of a profession, it seems we ought to spend some time with people who help
through their work. That includes people who get burned at their
work. That I chose to start out with the story of Kathy B. in lieu of one
more inspiring says something about my emphasis. "Those Who Have
Hands," my chapter on help and vocation, could also be called "Those
Who Get Hurt."

Farther up the same road, we will visit those amateurs who have intentionally risked getting hurt—hanged, gassed, or shot—in order to help their neighbors in times of oppression. The fascinating thing about these people is that the most heroic turn out to be homebodies. Their help is based in their homes. Of course, even in times of peace, the role of "domestic Samaritan" can be harrowing—for the simple reason that the people we love most are often the very people we find it most difficult to help.

To name one last stop, we will take a look at some of the daunting questions posed by the existence of poverty. That includes the inner poverty that always wants to save those questions for later. We are likely to find both types existing in an ugly symbiosis. In that case I recognize, as Dante did, that the only help for someone lost in his own dark wood may be a willing descent into his own hell. We'll go there too.

Along with these particulars, I am interested in where I live—geographically, psychologically, and culturally. That doesn't mean that the map I have sketched is so provincial as to fit on the back of a napkin. In the course of these pages we will visit Paraguay and Cameroon, the streets of the Lower East Side of New York and the plateaus of southeastern France. We will range just as far historically, at least as far back as Isaiah and Lao-tzu. But my favorite travels tend to be local and of the moment.

One of the things I like to do when I'm not working is what people in my region call running the roads, a natural enough pastime when you live in a place where dirt road leads to dirt road, forking and merging to your puzzlement and delight, like ideas in an essay. Some of these roads give out to broader views; others wind up in somebody else's dooryard, with the hounds barking and the geese charging and the cows gaping as if you had just landed from Mars, while a few lead to the discovery of a trout stream or an ice cream stand you never knew existed, though it turns out not to be such a long way from home.

Nevertheless, home remains the imminent destination, which is part of what distinguishes "running the roads" from going "on the road." In this book, home is a lighted window somewhere in a dark wood. "You mean you will come around to hope," I imagine you saying, which is true enough. But light in a dark wood not only gives an impression of hope, it also gives an idea of just how dark the wood really is. Denying that darkness helps no one, least of all a person in whom compassion is matched by intelligence. I will always have the double aim of corroborating my reader's experience of the darkness—of normalizing that experience, to echo something a midwife told me about her role in labor—and of assisting any reader resolved to hope against the odds.

These are sober aims—but then, I do most of my road running minus the traditional accoutrement of a six-pack of beer. I also try to "jog" the roads at least as much as I "run" them, mainly to avoid crashing into the larger beasts that are known to leap in front of a car. In other words, I have learned to take my time and pay heed to my peripheral vision. You can expect some surprises.

Not more than half an hour ago—I am not making this up—a great bull moose walked out of the field across from my house, crossed the road, and ambled up my driveway and along the other side of my garage, through the raspberry canes that grow under my apple trees and out of the view of my study windows. This is not a digression; it serves both to describe the kind of place where I live and to reveal something about me, for I no sooner registered my surprise at the animal (which out of the corner of my eye had first looked like a stray horse) than I began to wonder if he might become tangled up somehow in the brush and rubble beside the garage and need my *help*. Basically, you are in the position of riding shotgun with a man who cannot see a moose without feeling a twinge of responsibility. That is an equivocal boast.

There was a time when I might have said that the world was divided into two types of people: those who saw every creature in terms of how they might be of help to it, and those who saw every creature in terms of how it might be of help to them. What I'd say now is that this is a fair division as far as it goes but that both perspectives are entirely too self-referential. What I'd also say now, *right now*, is that the moose I just saw outside my window strode through the brush and over the stone walls as imperturbable as a whale. He needed my help about as much as God does.

"Teach us to care and not to care," T. S. Eliot prays in his poem "Ash Wednesday." Well, I don't know. I don't know if I want to be taught—or to teach others—not to care. But I should like to learn when caring comes down to an honest appreciation of those creatures and persons who flourish without my help. In short, I should like to learn to be more humble. Run the roads with Eliot's line, and it reads something like this: "Teach us to stop at the scenes of accidents, and teach us to drive straight by." Teach us to keep out of the way of the ambulance crews.

Turn that into a dogma, however, and you're dangerously close to a rationale for hit-and-run. If anything you read in the following pages should ever seem to turn back on itself, do not automatically assume that I am lost (though I may be). Assume that dogma is my idea of a dead-end road. As soon as I spot the chain, I'm into a three-point turn.

Finally, I think of this book as a shared drive because most of my attempts to help other people, along with many of their attempts to help me, have involved one or both of us getting into a car and taking a ride. That was certainly true with Kathy B., though in that case I was riding shotgun and a friend was at the wheel.

Sonny and I have come this way once before, out of Island Pond and across the Connecticut River into northern New Hampshire, when we moved Kathy B., lock, stock, and barrel, to a live-in housekeeping job over the border. That was the type of job she wanted, one with room and board included and an employer amenable to her various requirements, which included a vegetarian menu, several meditation breaks during the day, and a tolerance for flute playing at four in the morning. As usual, the inflexibility of her needs seemed to belie her claims of desperation—for example, that she had a crazy boyfriend in Island Pond of whom she was deathly afraid, though my parishioners had spotted the two of them strolling blithely down the sidewalk hand in hand, and she refused to let us report his alleged threats or move her to a temporary safe house. But she accepted our donations and the use of the church phone to check on the employment ads, and as happy as we were to oblige her, it is only fair to say that we were equally happy at the prospect of her finding gainful employment some distance from town.

Soon she found the position she was seeking, which turned out to be in a bizarre compound of attached dwellings and horse barns tucked into the side of a hill. The employer, a single, middle-aged woman of the type who in a movie either owns a cattle ranch or manages a lunch counter that serves cowboys, seemed to like the idea of having an employee who meditated. She apparently had a spiritual side herself. But by early fall, the arrangement was beginning to sour, and Sonny and I are driving back to undo our good deed.

Kathy had come into our lives less than a year earlier, when the lakes were icing out and the geese were flying north again, with a knapsack over her shoulders and a dog-eared copy of a book by someone who called herself the Peace Pilgrim packed close to the top. She said that she had spent decades wandering, following the temperate seasons from Arizona to Vermont and back again. Like the pilgrim, she seemed to combine Tolstoyan ideals with an uncanny talent for smelling out the kind of individual who operates on a high dose of Tolstoyan guilt. And like many of the quasi vagrants I had met before and have met since, she kept herself going in large part by hoping for a return to some better place, where the weather is good and the people are nice and, one gathers, the handouts more generous or less necessary. What set Kathy apart from those others I have known who spoke longingly of Canada or India as the lost paradise was that her frequent allusions to Arizona were matters of itinerary more than myth. That is to say, in spite of any impressions of mental instability, she seemed to know what she was doing. To use the dialect of cheap compassion, she had managed to find the life that worked for her. Of course that always included, as we would learn, finding individuals who would also work for her.

We moved her to New Hampshire on the day before Easter. Sonny had offered me the use of his new pickup to move Kathy's gear, of which there was quite a lot and none of which she was willing to put into storage. I found him and his friend Skeeter sitting at the kitchen table, already two beers into celebrating the resurrection. They invited me to join in, but I protested that nine in the morning was a bit early for me. At the last minute, Sonny volunteered his services as a moving man to go along with the offer of his truck. Skeeter agreed to help us load. When I warned the men about the allegedly dangerous boyfriend, Sonny responded with his usual refrain—what he would say to me, for example, when I inquired about the origins of the "free Christmas tree" he had found for the church or the "free disposal" of debris left over from a parish work project—"Oh, Garret, you have so many more important things to worry about. I wouldn't worry about this."

In an attempt to reassure me further, he added, "If there's any abuse or violence or anything like that, we'll just shoot him." He was only half joking. I was not reassured.

In many ways Sonny was no less a mystery to me than Kathy B., who by that time had become quite a mystery indeed as well as a real pain in the neck. He rarely came to church. He never used religious language. His ties to the parish were mainly those of blood. Still, he insisted—and insists even to this day—that I call on him in any kind of a tight spot, no explanations required, no payment accepted. So when I was asked some years ago to bless an eighteenth-century farmhouse where sinister forces were supposed to be at work, it was Sonny who walked beside me with the basin (actually my wife's bread bowl) as I shook an evergreen branch drenched with holy water into the gloom. True to form, when there were fifty-gallon steel drums full of Kathy's camping supplies to be moved down four flights of stairs on a Saturday morning, Sonny cheerfully took an end of each one—more specifically, the end that required him to walk downstairs backward. He describes himself as a sentimental guy. "A dog dies and I feel bad," he once told me. I can only imagine how he felt on the winter afternoon some twenty years ago when his tractor-trailer jackknifed on a snowy road and killed a woman in the oncoming lane. His wife was hosting a baby shower for mine when the call came through. We have never talked about the accident, though I have wondered if it has anything to do with his truancy from church or his looking out for me or with neither or both. In any event, I believe that he worried a lot more about me than he ever did about Kathy, and I must say that as I recall these scenes now, it is my sense of his love, rather than her need or our mission, that threatens to overwhelm me.

•   •   •

We make good time, and we try to keep our spirits up, though this
second trip has a lonesomeness about it, and a sense of futility, that the
first one didn't have. Then we were something like the ambassadors of
our congregation; now we feel a lot more on our own. Now people in
the parish and in town are saying that Kathy B. is a con artist. There
are even wild rumors that she owns a house in France, where she
doubtless spends delirious evenings gumming crusty baguettes by the
basketful. Yes, I know as well as anyone that she can be manipulative.
One of her accusations against her employer is that the woman filched
a hundred dollars of her money, part of a donation from our church,
though I soon learn from another priest that a year ago Kathy made
the same claim, and for the same amount, against an elderly couple
who had given her temporary shelter in a town in the next county. But
would she have to engage in these subterfuges if she were not truly
poor and pitifully alone? And can we be absolutely certain that they are
subterfuges?

Kathy has insisted that we move her to a remote campsite deep in
the Vermont woods, on a tract of land owned by another of her occasional benefactors, though as yet neither Sonny nor I know just how
deep it is. Sonny seems to believe that this is not really going to happen. I have already offered her money for a motel until we can locate a
seasonal residence for her to hole up in, and although she has refused
it so far, Sonny probably believes that she'll come around in the end. It
is now November, well past the first killing frost. He murmurs a few
words of protest on the way over, but I play the priest and sound my
old theme: respect for someone else's right to self-determination.
Sonny is too deferential, or else too naive, to reply that since we're
using his truck it isn't quite self-determination. Nor does he say, What
about *our* self-determination? He says he sees my point. He just can't
see this woman camping all by herself in the woods in November.
What he also can't see is that by the time we pick her up and cart her
back to Vermont, where she continues to refuse a motel, I'm about
ready to wring her neck.

I assume Sonny is feeling the same way as his brand-new pickup is
jounced and scratched on our moonlit journey through the woods.

First we go through a series of connected hay fields, then down a logging road, and finally along a forest track that does not seem to have been groomed for a while. An enormous buck deer freezes for a moment in our headlights; Sonny shuts them off and allows it to pass. Our bodies jostle together in the cab even though Sonny has now downshifted to first gear and is going at a crawl. He has to be up for work at four the next morning—for another trip back to New Hampshire, this time to his job in a paper mill. It is close to midnight now. But Sonny's obvious agitation is prompted by different concerns from mine.

When Kathy finally directs us to stop in a clearing at the edge of a cedar swamp, Sonny gets out of the cab, takes one look around, and explodes. This is the man who is always telling me to stop worrying, to have a beer and relax.

"How can I go back to town and tell people that I just dumped a woman in the woods?" he cries.

I feel as though he is about to give birth, maybe to the memory of the woman who died in that truck accident, maybe (though I cannot know it then) to the visceral inspiration for this book. The words seem to burst from his chest.

"Girl—you got to have a better plan than this!"

THE DUBIOUS
SAMARITAN

According to one of my wife's friends, whenever you find yourself in the same kind of predicament for the third or fourth time, God is trying to tell you something. Going on that assumption, I might have taken Sonny's outcry for an oracle, meant as much for me as for our exasperating passenger. *You got to have a better plan than this!* You have to come up with something that leads you to a better place than this dark wood.

I had been there before—because of God, guilt, or gullibility—and I have been there several times since. I cannot blame the predicament on my duties as a minister, though I have sometimes caught myself trying to do so. In fact, the most similar precursor to Kathy B. was a person I met early in my adulthood, when I was not even attending church, let alone standing behind a pulpit with enhanced obligations to practice what I preached.

I was newly married and just out of graduate school when I landed my first nominally white-collar job as an intake clerk for the state employment agency. My task was to interview a string of job seekers, ranging in skills and prospects from Stanford PhDs to certified welders (actually the only Stanford PhD I met was a certified welder), from teachers in search of temporary summer employment to vagrants in search of day jobs that promised to pay by sundown. There wasn't a single morning when I dreaded going to work or when, as befits the restless creature St. Augustine says we are, I wasn't thinking about finding different employment. A sense of my own wasted credentials and the daily sight of a workforce in flux proved too hard to resist. I was convinced I had to look for something better, preferably a position teaching English, and I eventually got what I was looking for or, should I say, what I deserved.

In the meantime, I ministered to the jobless in eight- to ten-minute increments of kindness, with a schedule if not an income very much like a doctor's, and spent my lunch hours and coffee breaks reading Camus and the English mystics, listening to organ practice in the nearby cathedral, or strolling the main street past stores and restaurants I had come to esteem or despise based on what I now knew of their employment practices. My co-workers were a lively assortment of lovers and dreamers, mostly young and in general bright enough to appreciate the irony of their situation, the way they had met the predicament of what you do with nothing but a bachelor's degree—or what you do without it—by helping other people ask the same question. We included a recently divorced mother just off the welfare rolls, a natty young bachelor hardly ever off the phone, a balding actor who would declaim the more boisterous lines of his current roles as he strode among our cubicles, and a pretty young woman named Marilyn, who spoke with the happy-hour wistfulness of someone who believes she will never be happy—in all, a *Taxi*-type sitcom cast of more or less compassionate people trying to make a living and to help as many people as they could to do the same. If I have lingered too long over this, it is because I am sometimes tempted to think of that job as the vocational equivalent of Eden, a place of innocent camaraderie and simple service that inspired an unaccountable craving for an irreversible fall.

It was on an afternoon there that I met Debbie Sunn. She had already visited the agency earlier that day. The woman who interviewed her the first time told me that Debbie had recently been deported from Canada, which struck me then and still strikes me as questionable, since I have never heard of Canadians deporting anyone. Unless the woman was a spy—and my initial impression was that of someone conspicuously trying not to stand out, with her drab overcoat, dark sunglasses, black Buster Brown hair, and the overall appearance of a gray snowman. She was in a bind, she told me. She had obtained a job referral on her first interview, a live-in companion position for an elderly person, but she had no carfare to the interview and no place to stay for the night. I gave her some directions and lent her some money, not an unusual practice among the staff, though some had an understandable policy against it. She got the job, and, as was also not unusual, she repaid the loan. In a little while she was back for another referral.

Perhaps for no other reason than that first transaction, she immediately became "mine" and remained so throughout the rest of my tenure at the agency. All of the other interviewers also had their regulars, so there was nothing strange about her attaching herself to me. In another year I left the job and the city. My wife had finished her master's, and both of us had landed jobs in a school district roughly a hundred miles to the northeast. Debbie remained in the Burlington area, where she continued as something of a regular at the employment agency—but she also remained my "client." I continued to assist her in searching for better positions, made small loans and donations, and in general tried to be accessible when she called. And that, I suppose, was a bit strange.

Over time I gathered various pieces of her story, though I never managed to put them together into a coherent narrative or to arrive at any reliable estimate of her age. I guessed she was no older than forty. She claimed to be in flight from her mother. She said she had been molested as a child by her uncle. She also claimed to have had a lobotomy, though I saw no scars and few behaviors to suggest that she was missing a part of her brain. She strenuously maintained that she was a certified EKG technician, more as a point of honor, it seemed, than as an employment objective. I never asked to see her certificate.

She said she was in close touch with her "doctors in Canada," never saying exactly what kind of doctors they were. I had my hunches. I doubted that these doctors would still maintain transnational contact with a patient they could no longer treat, but then, look what I was doing. In any case, Debbie's stated goal was to earn enough money to go back across the border and place herself once again under their care. Till that could be accomplished, she refused to receive any medical treatment in the States while insisting with equal vehemence on maintaining a health insurance policy, which, except during the brief respite of a janitorial job with medical benefits, she paid for out of pocket. I forget what occasioned her sole visit to an American doctor—I vaguely

recall her blacking out while mopping a floor—but during the examination it was discovered that she had "a lump the size of a grapefruit"
in her abdomen. All my pleas to have it treated met with refusal and
annoyance.

Nuts, you are saying, totally nuts, and perhaps not just the woman.
And yet a number of middle-class professionals found her stable
enough to take care of their elderly parents. Although that may say
more about the state of filial obligation in America than about
Debbie's state of mind, she was on the whole a reliable person, good-
humored if not especially warm, and certainly not abusive. The employment situations, however, were not without abuse. Their chief
benefit for Debbie, and for the others desperate enough to seek them,
was the free room and board, but the downside of a live-in job is that it
can easily become a form of incarceration. You cannot in good conscience leave your "patient," but your employer can and frequently
does leave you. He isn't always specific about when he might be back.
Still, for all her strangeness, I never knew Debbie to abandon a person
in her care.

Nor did I abandon her, though I doubted I was of much help. She
certainly wasn't taking any of my advice, such as forget Canada and get
a real job, your own place, and some appointments with doctors you
can actually see. Above all, get that lump taken care of. To this day I'm
not sure as to the exact nature of the lump, if it was an actual growth or
just a fantastic self-diagnosis of all the stuff in her body and mind that
needed attention. Whatever its exact medical nature, it eventually
killed her.

The classic conclusion to a case like this—what we tell our friends
at dinner or ourselves in the later hours of the night—is that we could
have been of more help if the person had let us. True enough, if not all
that consoling. Surely one reason for the enduring appeal of detective
stories in the Raymond Chandler mode—easily as big a reason as the
existential solitude of the hero or the metaphysical intimations of
"mystery"—is the often dubious character of the person who hires the
private eye. If the private eye stands for every man or woman who has
ever tried to get to the bottom of something, the client stands for
every person that man or woman has ever tried to help. Either the
client is withholding information that would make it easier for the pri-

vate eye to do his job, or else the request for help is itself bogus, a pretext for achieving some darker end. The situation is immediately familiar. The patient with the mysterious ailment, the student who never hands in homework, the sibling who always seems to need money—all of them are incarnated in the dame who's not on the level, who looks through her black mesh veil and says, "I need you to find out who murdered my husband," and no sooner are the words out of her mouth than you sense that something doesn't add up.

To be honest, I began to wonder if I was being played, a suspicion that tends to sharpen whenever money is involved, not that I ever gave Debbie that much. I began to have my doubts, nevertheless; my left hand began to wonder what her right hand was doing. Along with the fight-or-flight response we have to danger, most of us have what might be called the cynic-or-sucker response to need. As with fight-or-flight, our instinct is to act as if these were the only alternatives. So, just as a person under pressure can vacillate between cowardice and belligerence, a person in over his philanthropic head can begin vacillating between offering a cold shoulder and being a soft touch. Soon he is reacting more to his own perceived extremes than to the person he's trying to help. Anyway, that's where things were going with me.

Not long before Debbie died, she began to make tantalizing references to the temperature of my feet, as in, were they terribly cold up there in the North Country, and did I think I could make it through Christmas. With each reply I gave she giggled like a little girl. I put together the hints and guessed that I was about to be presented with a pair of socks, possibly homemade.

The box that arrived in the mail was enormous. Maybe it was the only one she could find; maybe she had spent the past five years knitting socks. Inside was a brand-new goose-down bed comforter. My wife said it must have cost several hundred dollars. A cynic would have reminded me that we had paid for much of it, but that hardly made it less of a gift. I remained stunned by her generosity, probably more by that than by the call that came soon thereafter. Debbie was dead. Her employers, a middle-aged couple whose elderly relative she had looked after, would pay for the cremation and a small stone.

We slept under that comforter for years; I hardly gave it a thought after a while, though it comes to mind now and again, usually by association, after I have thrown off the bedcovers and taken the day's first stand at the toilet. There is my face, looking ever older in the medicine cabinet mirror, and there by the window is the hanging ivy, which has been hanging there so long that I can forget it was a gift from Kathy B.

Not surprisingly, I experienced the same chain of association when the trooper called from Arizona, trying to locate Kathy's next of kin. There had been the same futile search with Debbie Sunn. Her two employers and I had been the only ones at her burial. If God was trying to tell me something through the parallels, I was not sure I wanted to know what it was. For one thing, it promised not to be an uplifting message. And to be honest, I tend to be skeptical of the "God is trying to tell us something" idea in cases like these. As I see it, God has been trying to tell us something since at least the Axial Age, and the message is both clear and generic, namely, that we are in this world to help each other or, in the words of the Torah, to love our neighbors as ourselves.

"But who is my neighbor?" a man asks Jesus, giving him the straight line that leads to the much-loved parable of the good Samaritan. According to Luke, the only one of the four evangelists to tell the story, the questioner is a lawyer "wanting to justify himself." I suppose that is intended as our cue to boo and hiss.

I confess that, the older I get, the more I sympathize with the lawyer—and by no means in spite of his seeming inability to think outside the box. That is what he seems to want from Jesus, some kind of a box with which to limit his obligations. That is how I once characterized him, and disparaged him, in sermon after sermon, and that is precisely the reason I have gradually come to see him as a basically good man who tends to put his money where his mouth is. Abstract compassion has no such need for defining limits. You know that someone is sticking pretty close to his laptop when he starts tossing around phrases like "thinking outside the box." *Thinking* indeed. When it comes to responsible *action*, the operative question is "Where on earth is the box?" Where in God's name are the boundaries for this? Which is to say, the operative question is the lawyer's question, or something like it.

Jesus replied, "A man was going down from Jerusalem to Jericho, and fell into the hands of robbers, who stripped him, beat him, and went away, leaving him half dead. Now by chance a priest was going down that road and when he saw him, he passed by on the other side. So likewise a Levite, when he came to the place and saw him, passed by on the other side. But a Samaritan while traveling came near him; and when he saw him, he was moved with pity. He went to him and bandaged his wounds, having poured oil and wine on them. Then he put him on his own animal, brought him to an inn, and took care of him. The next day he took out two denarii, gave them to the innkeeper, and said, 'Take care of him; and when I come back, I will repay you whatever more you spend.' Which of these three, do you think, was a neighbor to the man who fell into the hands of the robbers?" He said, "The one who showed him mercy." Jesus said to him, "Go and do likewise."

In one sense, the answer Jesus gives frustrates the lawyer's expectations. His reading of the Law of Moses allows no limits to neighborhood. The man who fell among thieves is the Samaritan's neighbor, if for no other reason than that the Samaritan laudably chooses to regard him as one. By the same standard, the Samaritan ought to be regarded as the lawyer's neighbor too. Our neighbor is wherever we are willing to recognize him. Kierkegaard provides what may be the best commentary: "To choose a beloved, to find a friend, those are indeed complicated tasks, but a neighbor is easy to know, easy to find, if we will only—recognize our duty."

In another sense, though, it would seem that Jesus does give the lawyer something like the boundaries he is looking for and most of us are looking for. It probably would not have been difficult for the lawyer to "justify himself" according to the standards of the parable. The good Samaritan certainly goes the extra mile, but he hardly goes the whole distance. There is, as we like to say nowadays, closure to his good deed. The duration of his commitment is less than twenty-four hours. When the sun rises on the new day, he moves on.

Maybe that is one of the reasons we are so fond of the parable. The good Samaritan story is in some ways a quintessentially American story, by which I mean it is a story of the road. It suits a people who have always imagined themselves in transit, who are fond of saying,

"It's time to put this behind us and move forward." Westward, ho. Whatever the parable illustrates about the universality of human neighborhood, it also typifies what Joan Didion once called "wagon train morality," which she defined as not allowing your dead to be eaten by coyotes. Surely even the priest and the Levite would not object to that code. The question remaining is how well it suffices for those of us who do not travel so lightly as the Samaritan or the Son of Man. In other words, how adequate is wagon train morality for those of us who live some distance from anything resembling the Oregon Trail?

Perhaps the first place to seek the story's larger application is in the specific coordinates of its own geography. The hapless traveler is assaulted on the road between Jericho and Jerusalem—that is, between one of the world's oldest cities (possibly one of the first places where cultivated wheat was grown) and the city that has come to symbolize our highest hopes. He is our neighbor because he is and has always been our fellow traveler. Along with the rest of the human race, he thinks of himself as going somewhere. Joseph Conrad wrote, "The true place of God begins at any spot a thousand miles from the nearest land"; perhaps our true place is any spot on the road between Jericho and Jerusalem, wherever human progress is more or less trudging along.

If you happened to notice that the traveler is moving away from Jerusalem rather than toward it, you are close to raising the question that many a would-be good Samaritan has muttered to herself: "Why was he going *that* way?" Answer: for his own reasons. The waylaid traveler is just that, waylaid in his own pursuit of happiness. If his predicament happens to waylay the Samaritan, that certainly wasn't part of his original plan. Our sense of someone's claim on our assistance grows stronger and more poignant exactly at the moment when we remember that he wasn't looking for our help to begin with—just as it can begin to grow resentful and unwholesome when either party starts to believe otherwise. When she was first diagnosed with cancer and first becoming aware of the help she was going to need from her children, my mother-in-law kept saying, "It wasn't supposed to be this way." If the half-dead man ever became conscious of the Samaritan, he might have said the same thing.

There is another way to locate the traveler. We could say that he has fallen through the crack between lawlessness and propriety. He is a victim of brutal and predatory violence. We can take the robbers who attack him as symbols for any power that behaves as a law unto itself. Whenever people speak of market forces or the global economy as if those things were acts of God instead of human constructions—or to put it another way, as though lawlessness itself were *the Law*—then we know that robbers are not far away. We know that it will not be long before we find a person, a country, or a landscape stripped, beaten, and left for dead.

I spoke not long ago with the Reverend Brian Cole, a young clergyman who works with a congregation of the homeless at the Church of the Advocate in Asheville, North Carolina. With reference to his parishioners in general and to the disabled veterans among them in particular, he said, "We are a society that goes through people." In other words, we are a society that can behave like the robbers.

The priest and the Levite who pass the wounded man on the other side of the road represent the false opposite of lawlessness, what we might call "propriety." They are not necessarily the coldhearted individuals we sometimes take them for. If their destination is Jerusalem, they are quite likely on their way to work, where most respectable people are headed on most days of the week. In the case of these two, that means work in and around the Temple precincts, work for which contact with a dead body would render them ritually defiled. So their seeming indifference needs to be balanced against the presence of other virtues, piety and conscientiousness being only two. Might another be that "basic trust" that social scientists never tire of telling us is the foundation of all mental health? In other words, the priest and the Levite may assume that the man, whom they probably take for dead, will not lie there for long. They operate on the very civilized assumption that not every perceived need is their responsibility. They assume, in a way most of us find unsettlingly familiar, that somebody else must have this covered. Somebody must know about this problem and be working on it.

As it turns out, their assumption, or what I'm assuming to be their assumption, is roughly correct. Someone will soon be working on it, though he is not part of any benevolent organization, and he is certainly not the sort of person either they or most of Jesus's audience would have imagined in the role. In some ways, he too is a man who has fallen through the cracks. In my experience, the person who helps frequently is.

It is easy to forget that the word *Samaritan* did not originally mean "philanthropist" or "do-gooder" but referred instead to a minority sect within post-Exilic Judaism. The origins of the Samaritans are obscure, but by Jesus's day they were well entrenched in their refusal to acknowledge the authority of the Jerusalem priesthood or the canonical status of any books in the Hebrew Bible besides the first five. The Prophets of Israel, who took social justice from prescription to passion, were very literally not in their book. Their outlook was conservative; their focus, narrow—or perhaps it would be fairer to say, local. They thought God was best worshiped on Mount Gerizim, in their own province of Samaria, rather than south in the City of David. From the point of view of Jesus's listeners, Samaritans were of the wrong religion. If John's account of the meeting between Jesus and the Samaritan woman at the well is to be believed, Jesus shared the judgment of his coreligionists. "You worship what you do not know; we worship what we know," he tells the woman. Lest she have any illusions about who *we* are, he adds, "for salvation is of the Jews."

That apparently smug dismissal, far from contradicting the universalism of the parable, actually brings it into sharper relief. Jesus's intention in making a hated Samaritan the hero of his parable may in fact be more radical than we suppose. It is usually taken as a token of tolerance—akin to that of a Hollywood director who casts a minority woman as the detective who solves the case (though from what I've seen, she is more likely to be cast as the jiving sidekick of the white detective who solves the case). Jesus is doing something else, I think. It is one thing to celebrate diversity in terms of race and gender; it is quite another to recognize the potential for goodness in someone whose basic belief system is, in your view, completely off the mark. Different is one thing; misguided is quite another.

I may seem to be forcing the point, since Samaritans had many more similarities with Jews than differences, but in matters of religious or political controversy, rancor usually *increases* with the amount of common ground. A fundamentalist evangelical is more offended by a liberal Protestant, and vice versa, than either would be by an orthodox Hindu; Trotsky had more good to say about the Jesuits than he did about fellow communists of rival wings.

What Jesus seems to be saying is that "correct beliefs" are not nearly so important as compassionate actions and, furthermore, that correct beliefs are no guarantee of compassionate actions. We repeatedly read of his telling some person, "Your faith has saved you," but we never once hear him say, "The soundness of your belief system has enabled you to save someone else."

In his memoir, *The Pillar of Fire*, Karl Stern describes how, with the rise of the Nazis to power, he came to a realization not unlike that which informs the parable of the good Samaritan:

> It was in connection with Doctor Schulz [a physician who subverted the Nazi program of forced sterilization] that it first dawned on me that the Great Dividing Line in Europe, in fact, in the entire world, is not the line between Right and Left. . . . In this respect the Nazi years taught us a lesson. It happened not infrequently that you met a friend whom you had known for years as a "staunch liberal," and he turned out to be eagerly ready for any compromise to save his skin. On the other hand, we saw people whom we had disdained as "reactionaries" go to concentration camps and to the gallows. In the beginning it seemed confusing. But gradually the issue became clearer, and it was obvious that the only thing that counts in this world is the strength of moral convictions.

And maybe not even that. Himmler had moral convictions too. He forbade members of the SS to steal. What counts even more than moral convictions, according to philosopher Jonathan Glover, are "human responses," without which "morality is useless or worse."

And yet we should be careful not to reduce the idea of a human response to an emotional category, with the aim of declaring emotion superior to ethics. If Himmler had moral convictions, Hitler had human feelings. He wouldn't eat meat; his heart bled for the humiliations of his countrymen after the First World War. Saddam Hussein is known to have shed tears for the people he liquidated, and there are observers who feel this was more than show. "The devil never sleeps"—but he weeps.

The response of the good Samaritan derives from something deeper and more primal than sentiment or creed. Luke says that he is moved by pity, but we find ourselves impatient with the word; we know of too many cases where people are moved to pity but not to action. We want a better mover. In their landmark study titled *The Altruistic Personality: Rescuers of Jews in Nazi Europe*, Pearl and Samuel Oliner characterize the response of the rescuers in this way: "Unable to comprehend or tolerate brutality as anything but destructive of the very fabric that gives their lives order and meaning, they react in much the same way as if caught in a flood—holding back the tide through whatever means possible."

Instinctively, in other words. One can imagine someone caught in a flood, numbed beyond all pity or fear and cut loose from all conviction, who continues to pile up the sandbags anyway. "The Way is empty," says Lao-tzu, "yet use will not drain it. . . . Deep, it is like the ancestor of the myriad creatures"—and perhaps for that reason, it is loath to discriminate between them.

Elsewhere in the Tao te ching—in a passage that calls to mind the admonition of Jesus to imitate the God who sends "rain and sun on the just and the unjust"—Lao-tzu also says, "Highest good is like water. Because water excels in benefiting the myriad creatures without contending with them and settles where none would like to be, it comes closest to the Way."

A quality like water that causes a human being to act as if caught in a flood—is that our best depiction of what makes the good Samaritan good? It is not a very satisfying depiction, though it suits the nearly universal detachment with which many rescuers seem to regard their own acts. "I only did my duty," says one of the Righteous Gentiles who sheltered Jews from the Nazis. "It all happened so naturally, we can't understand the fuss," says another. "I am not a hero," says Luba Tryszynska-Frederick, the "Angel of Bergen-Belsen," a Jewish woman who performed the almost unbelievable feat of rescuing, hiding, and nurturing fifty-four children intended for death *within a concentration camp*. John Stuart Mill described a truly benevolent personality as one who "comes, as though instinctively, to be conscious of himself as a being who *of course* pays regard to others." Sometimes the verbal expression of this "of courseness" can sound almost like obtuseness, as when an American couple who adopt five Romanian orphans "are adamant in their feelings that they haven't done anything special." Well, come on.

The robbers who leave the man for dead by the side of the road would probably say the same thing. What they did wasn't anything special either. *Of course* they took advantage of the man's vulnerability. *Of course* they beat him up. This stuff has been going on for a long time; it's only natural. The competing claims of rescuer and robber leave us with something of a conundrum. If we dismiss the claim of the rescuers as mere modesty and insist on regarding them as extraordinary human beings, then we have in effect reduced our own obligations. We cannot be expected to rise to their level. The filmmaker Pierre Sauvage makes this point with regard to his documentary *Weapons of the Spirit*, which pays homage to the village where Sauvage himself was sheltered from the Holocaust as a child: "If we pass along a legacy that does not include the righteous . . . we're giving humanity an alibi. One doesn't even have to aspire to do better, because it isn't possible."

But if we choose to take the rescuers at their humble word and regard their acts as "merely human," then we are left with the dismal possibility that most of humanity is dysfunctional—not only unwilling to help but past help itself.

In the end we may have nothing more illuminating to say about the nature of human helpfulness than what Jesus says at the close of his parable: "Go and do likewise." Or don't. The central question is not whether the Samaritan's actions are simply what anyone else would do. The central question is always what you will do.

Just as the Samaritan is wrong for the part in the eyes of Jesus's audience, he may be wrong in our eyes too. Our best guess is that he is some kind of itinerant merchant. He has his own ride, and he has cash. Of the latter, he can shell out the equivalent of two days' wages and presumably have enough left over to continue his journey. He stays in inns; he doesn't sleep under the stars. We guess that he is a regular on this route. He is known at the inn (unless of course the innkeeper is so informed with "basic trust" that he takes the word of every traveling Samaritan who promises to pay him on the way back). In short, the Samaritan belongs to that class of individuals who, in a modern retelling of the parable, would likely be among the persons who pass by on the other side of the road. "And then this businessman in a three-piece suit came driving by in his nice new car, and he didn't stop either." Probably on his way to have a drink with the lawyer who questioned Jesus.

We would have liked someone more romantic or at least closer to the soil. The people who first heard the parable were probably anticipating someone along those lines when they came to the third punch of the story: first the priest, then the Levite—the holier-than-thou types—then the ordinary child of Abraham. The salt of the earth, albeit kosher salt. But if, like Blanche DuBois, we have had more than one occasion to depend upon the kindness of strangers, we know there are no reliable demographics for the prediction of helpfulness. We know that the only salt of the earth is tears, that populism is just another form of prejudice—and one dangerously close to Nazi ideas of the *Volk*. What we may not know is that among those listed in the Gestapo files at Düsseldorf as *Judenfreunde* ("friends of Jews"), males, older Germans, small businessmen, and white-collar workers were especially prominent. Had the Gestapo files been as complete as ours, they would have shown more women and peasants, but after all the evidence is in, the sociology of compassion remains something of a crapshoot.

Psychology is more instructive—and philosophy more instructive still. One of the characteristics of Holocaust rescuers identified by the Oliners, and perhaps the one most relevant to the parable of the good Samaritan, is a tendency to believe in one's own ability to affect events. The Oliners found that rescuers were less inclined than bystanders to see themselves as victims of circumstance. As a rule they were "more accustomed to feeling personally potent." Apparently "Shit happens" would not have been their bumper sticker of choice. This helps to explain not only their altruistic acts during the Second World War but also their tendency to exhibit "occupational advantage" in the years thereafter; taken as a group, their accomplishments outstrip those of bystanders. (In matters of health, they did not seem to be doing so well, but one imagines that the extra stresses of Samaritanism in Hitler's Europe took their toll. At the very least, we would not be surprised to learn that some of the rescuers took up smoking or upped their daily intake from one black-market pack to two.)

We can easily intuit the same lack of fatalism in the Samaritan. As much as by the way he acts, he is distinguished by the way he sees. Jesus (or Luke) is careful to let us know that all of those who pass by the man on the road see him; the verb *saw* is repeated every time a new person comes upon the scene. But the Samaritan is the only one who *looks*—we read that he "drew near"—and the reason is that in addition to seeing a wounded man, he is able to see the possibility that the man might still be alive. In the Samaritan's eyes, the universe is not a closed or predetermined system. It is not enough to say that he sees "providence in the fall of a sparrow"; sometime in his childhood he nursed a fallen sparrow back to health.

The best of human benefactors probably see in the same way. Mother Jones also had Samaritan eyes:

> I would look out of the plate glass windows and see the poor, shivering wretches, jobless and hungry, walking along the frozen lake front. The contrast of their condition with that of the tropical comfort of the people for whom I sewed was painful to me.

Certainly many others besides the Mother saw them—even her comfortable employers may have spared a tear for them—but not everyone saw the makings of a militant union in the sight of poor, huddled masses. "I'm not a humanitarian," Jones once said. "I'm a hell-raiser." She most certainly was, but what hell-raisers of the Mother Jones type have in common with all humanitarians is the ability to imagine something better than what is, to *raise* hell closer to heaven.

Brian Cole, the young priest who told me about the society that "goes through people," had this to say about the role of imagination in trying to help them:

Most of the people we encounter [that is, street people] want to see their lives transformed. It's often amazing to sit with them as they experience their pain—but if you just stay there that becomes abusive, and you wind up mining them for sermon illustrations or for some insight about yourself. I need to be able to say, "I can imagine this person not being homeless, I can dream this person not being addicted, and maybe some of that happening will involve some resources or gifts I bring to this." Thoreau said that the condition of life is joy, or something like that. Often it's all too easy for me to be emotional, dramatic, and tragic, but I'm convinced that God put us on this earth to be able to enjoy each other and the creation instead of being satisfied with the tragic. We need to acknowledge the tragic but hopefully heal the tragic.

Presumably healing the tragic begins with abolishing the tragic fatalism in our own heads. Seen in that light, the parable of the good Samaritan cuts two ways; that is, it incorporates two lines of vision: at the same time as the Samaritan opens his eyes to the wounded traveler, we open our eyes to the Samaritan. His willingness to believe that the man might not be dead is matched by our parallel willingness to believe that good Samaritans might not be extinct.

Not long ago I was at lunch with an editor friend of mine and told her I was writing a book on help. People are not very prone to that, she said. I did not take exception to her remark, nor did either of us feel the need to cite examples to support it. We were sitting too close to a Manhattan sidewalk for sentimentality. I had recently done an article on noise, in which I cited a study showing that people are less prone to altruism in the presence of unpleasant sounds. Researchers posed someone in a situation of simulated difficulty—say, trying to pick up an armful of fallen parcels with one arm in a sling—in two contexts, one quiet and the other disturbed by a loud piece of machinery. Passersby were less prone to help someone in the latter instance. I had used the study to underscore the power of noise, but I might just as easily have used it, in a different article, to underscore the fragility of altruism. Or I might have cited a remark by Edward Hoagland, a writer both she and I admire, who in an early essay titled "The Problem of the Golden Rule" noted:

When I was a child I remember how my astonishment evolved as I realized that people often would not do the smallest thing to convenience another person or make him feel easier for the moment. Of course I'd known that *kids* wouldn't, but I had thought that was because they were kids. It was my first comprehension of the deadness of life.

But no sooner had the observation left her mouth than my friend felt a need to qualify what she had said. She recalled a day when she had lost one of her contact lenses in Penn Station. This was in the days before Rudolf Giuliani performed the dubious miracle of making the homeless disappear from the stations and terminals of Manhattan. As she began her all but hopeless search, she became aware—presumably through the corrected vision of a single eye—that various vagrants were searching alongside her. In another moment an entire posse of the dispossessed was engaged in the search for the missing lens. It was comic and pathetic at once; why should people lacking a clean change of clothes care about a professional woman's corrective eyewear? Apparently, they cared quite a bit. After a few minutes of frantic searching, she looked up and saw her lens held out to her on the end of a man's chapped, grimy finger.

"Now make sure you wash this," he said.

When our lunch is over, after she has returned to her office, I am on the street again, where in the space of a New York minute I may come upon someone in desperate straits or become that person myself. An ambulance goes by, sirens wailing, and I realize how infrequently I hear this sound in the rural place where I live. Only certain pieces of music can move me more. If noise shuts down compassion, this must be the wrong noise.

I think of it as one of my peculiarities—though I wonder if it is all that peculiar—the way tears come to my eyes at the sight and sound of a rescue vehicle. This is pre–September 11 for me, and I imagine its roots are preambulance as well. It is something very primal. I want to wail with the siren, and although I have never been an ambulance chaser or entertained even for a moment volunteering for the local rescue squad, I understand the impulse that sends certain people charging madly after police cars and fire engines, to the great detriment of those at the scene. To say that I identify strongly with the people in trouble or with those coming to their aid falls short of what I feel. This is about something else.

What I think I am sensing, and responding to so powerfully, is the frantic reunion of two human beings. Mortality and chance are pulling them apart, threatening to place an unbridgeable chasm between them. The siren is the voice of their mutual distress at this impending separation and of their absolute desire to prevent it. If there is dignity in resignation, then an ambulance admits to no dignity. Speed limits and stop signs, tuxedos and tank tops, even skin and bone will be torn and thrust aside before the lovers will allow themselves to be wrenched apart. This is passion at its highest pitch, eros drained of all languor—nothing left but the drive to maintain the union of life with life that is our common humanity. Or, as Dante put it, this is "the love that moves the sun and other stars." It is against death and what Hoagland calls "the deadness of life," but its only word for death is *separation*.

In his book *A Fortunate Man: The Story of a Country Doctor,* John Berger points out the ways in which illness acts to separate human beings from each other and the role a doctor plays in social healing.

> In illness many connexions are severed. Illness separates and encourages a distorted, fragmented form of self-consciousness. The doctor, through his relationship with the invalid and by means of the special intimacy he is allowed, has to compensate for these broken connexions and reaffirm the social content of the invalid's aggravated self-consciousness.

Obviously in the case of violence and oppression, the separation is felt more acutely; it is not the subjective by-product of a "condition" but a deliberate policy of those in power.

> Things changed that horrible day when I saw Marianne and her brother Leo with a star on their clothes. That was a *horrible* experience. . . . We had heard of it by then, of course. But then you saw, suddenly, the dividing of people; how malicious it was. Yes, I can still feel that now—the fury that such things are possible.

Is it too much of a stretch to say that the Samaritan registers his own version of that same fury, that behind his labored breathing, as he cleans the man's wounds, a siren wails in protest? First, that such things are possible as have been done to this poor man, separating him from his goods, his clothing, and perhaps his life itself. And second, that such things are possible as have separated the traveler from the Samaritan, making them outcasts to each other and to such an extent that one of them has to be beaten half to death in order for their hands to touch. In *Heart of Darkness*, Kurtz is heard to whisper, "the horror, the horror"; in a heart that has begun to admit the light, maybe all we hear is the fury.

After disinfecting the man's wounds with oil and wine, the Samaritan puts him on his animal. If you're big on defining moments, this is the moment you've been waiting for. It certainly is for me, at least as far as this book is concerned, because with that action the Samaritan walks, quite literally, into one of the central paradoxes of helping those in need. If the paradox should strike us as a no-brainer, that only means that we have not given it much thought. Let us think about it now, taking only as much time as it would have taken the Samaritan to adjust the man's body on his beast.

According to Dr. Rony Brauman, former president of the French section of Médecins Sans Frontières (Doctors Without Borders), humanitarianism poses the question "What is a human being?" and answers, "One who is not made to suffer." The journalist David Rieff rightly speaks of this as "deep radicalism," which is another way of saying that Dr. Brauman is making a statement of faith. In fact, his is a classic example. What makes it such a beauty is that, like a statement of belief in an all-powerful and benevolent God, it would strike and has struck millions of people as self-evident, even though it is contradicted by some fairly weighty empirical evidence. "Human beings were not made to suffer"—you might as well say that they were not made to die or, as Dorothy Day asserts in her autobiography, that they were "meant for happiness." I happen to believe every one of those statements, but only because I am willing to take them on faith. Were I more of an empiricist, I might be inclined to say to Dr. Brauman, "You don't get out much, Rony, do you?"

But Brauman's humanitarian faith points to the paradox of the parable's defining moment. For to *act* as if one truly believed that human beings were not made to suffer—and I am told that the Hebrew word for "faith" as found in some of the biblical prophets translates literally as "*doing* the truth"—we are often compelled to suffer ourselves. That is, we are compelled to behave as if denying our statement of faith were the only way to fulfill it. To help a person in distress is to give yourself over to the same universal entropy that creates distress. To help another person toward greater self-determination is sooner or later to give that person power over your self-determination. Of course, this is not the case when help is given in a mutually satisfying enterprise—helping your sister make a pizza, for instance, or helping your brother-in-law reduce his overstock of beer. But dare to chop down a cross, and sooner or later you will find yourself nailed to one.

Whether we were "made to suffer" or not, it would seem that we have but three basic choices with regard to deciding whether someone else was made to suffer. The first is to say that yes, he was. Either he was or I was, and the choice is in my hands. Therefore I choose to inflict suffering in the hopes that those afflicted will be rendered powerless to afflict me. This is the rationale of all oppression.

The second choice is to pretend that others do not suffer or else secretly wish to suffer or for some unknown reason must suffer—in short, to make one's peace with suffering on the best terms available. This was certainly the choice of the woman who wrote a letter of complaint to the Nazis who were massacring prisoners near her domicile: "I request that it be arranged that such inhuman deeds be discontinued or else be done where one does not see it." Or, as we might say, put that stuff on the eleven o'clock news because a lot of us are eating at six.

The third choice is that of the Samaritan, who by this time has finished the difficult task of getting a wounded man, who is either dead weight or groaning whenever the Samaritan shifts his weight, onto the donkey or camel. It is possible that the Samaritan has injured his own back in the process. It is also possible that he has had to abandon some of his baggage so that the animal can bear the new load. It is certainly probable that he has delayed his journey, perhaps at the cost of some hardship to those he serves or those he provides for. It is only a little less probable that the robbers are still in the vicinity and that if they decide to try for an encore, the Samaritan has reduced his means for getting away from four legs to two. In other words, he may soon become part of the catastrophe.

None of this will deter the good Samaritan because he is, after all, the *good Sam*aritan, which in this case may come down to little more than being good at the math. Whatever the Samaritan's risks or inconveniences, they add up to much less than those of the wounded man. We can imagine others who did the same computations. I may go into a concentration camp if I hide the person at my door, but he will definitely go if I don't, so his hundred percent overrules my fifty. But in situations less dire, the math can become more complicated. The equations involve more factors. Life given for life may actually be an easier sacrifice to make than an afternoon—and let's make it a sunny afternoon—wasted on a loser.

Yet even a so-called loser can contain multitudes. At least that will have to be our working hypothesis if we take to heart the formula inscribed on the ring given to Oscar Schindler by the Jews he had managed to save. I do not know if they were mindful of the outrageous parody involved in making it from the gold of their own dental work, but no parody could be so defiant of evil as the inscription itself.

Whoever saves a single soul saves the world entire.

Like the assertion that human beings were not made to suffer, this would strike many people as obvious and unimpeachable, though it remains a statement of faith.

The good Samaritan is not a hero. Perhaps that will seem obvious, perhaps not. According to the definition that has gained currency since the terrorist attacks of September 11, the man lying in the road is a hero, especially if it can be proven that his attackers were of Arabic descent. By that standard, the Samaritan is nothing less than a swashbuckler on a white horse. Of course, we could argue that in an era given to exaggeration, anyone so modest and sensible as the Samaritan deserves his own statue in the park. For he strikes us as a study in humanitarian sanity. He does his deed of kindness, and then, when his business calls him again, he delegates the deed to another. He is not above paying someone else to continue his care. Even at the scene of the crime, his ministrations consist of what he has at hand. Various commentators have noted that pouring oil and wine into the traveler's wounds may not have been best medical practice; the point is that they were the best disinfectants he had, and he made use of them.

Perhaps the most noteworthy thing about him is that he does not hang around long enough to be thanked. If the man he helped is married, the Samaritan never gets to meet the wife. We shall return to this theme in a moment, but for now let us simply note his apparent lack of vanity. I mean that in both senses of *vain*. He does not wait for something that he might not get—as a notoriously crusty physician in my area once told a younger colleague, "If you want gratitude, get a dog"—and he makes off before anyone's gratitude has a chance to "get" him. In short, he slips out of the trap of becoming "The Good Samaritan." One thinks of that episode in the Gospels where Jesus withdraws from the multitudes when he perceives that they are about to "take him by force to make him king" or the resurrection story where he says "Touch me not"—or as it is alternately rendered, "Do not cling to me"—when Mary Magdalene goes to embrace him in the garden. In some ways, we can also imagine the Samaritan as "risen"— both from "the deadness of life" that Hoagland saw in the callousness of his elders and from the deadness that comes of allowing oneself to become the graven image of anyone's sentimental admiration. "Go and do likewise," Jesus says to the lawyer—but the Samaritan has already said "Giddyap" to his ass. I find—don't you find too?—that there is no place in the tale where I am rooting for him more than when he finally gets away.

For a contrasting portrait of a good man who cannot get away from his own benevolence and whose narcissistic need for gratitude nearly destroys him, we can turn to Richard Price's recent novel *Samaritan*. There we meet Ray Mitchell, former husband, former screenwriter, and former coke addict. At a crossroads in his life, Ray returns to his old neighborhood, now in the advanced stages of urban blight, in order to do good there. For starters, he decides to run a writer's workshop at his old high school. Mostly, though, he doles out money to virtually every ne'er-do-well—along with some might-do-wells—who come his way. In the process he nearly gets himself beaten to death in his apartment by an assailant he knows, though he refuses to disclose his or her identity.

Ray's deliverer and foil is an African American police officer named Nerese Ammons, who grew up in the same neighborhood and knew Ray when they were kids. She has a twofold piece of detective work: she must discover who almost killed Ray, and as part of that investigation, she has to explore what drives him to do what he does. She solves the last mystery first.

> Nerese got it, was starting to get it. The guy fell apart because the moment was about gratitude. . . . He could act out his selfish selflessness over and over . . . until . . . he got the obituary that would vindicate him, bring tears to his eyes; key word, "beloved," if only he could figure out some way to come back from the dead long enough to read it.

Ray's ex-wife draws the same conclusion when she tells Nerese, "Ray says he wants to make a 'dent'—what he wants to make is a 'splash.' Ray likes to sweep people off their feet." Nerese's reply allows Ray his claim to decency even as it confirms her own: "Yeah, well, that character flaw most likely eluded the family he helped."

One can read the novel for a while—at least it took me a while—before realizing that the *Samaritan* in the title refers as much to Nerese as it does to Ray. After all, it is she who comes to the rescue of a man left for dead. But she is a Samaritan of a very different kind. While Ray is for the most part a freelancer, Nerese does her helping largely through her job. And while his altruism is an attempt to compensate for his failures as a father and husband, Nerese does her job partly to take care of her teenage son and her aging father. One could argue that Ray's philanthropy is purer because more gratuitous, but it is Nerese who emerges as the truly good Samaritan. She has promises to keep, and they're part of why we trust her. The luxury of sweeping strangers off their feet is overruled by the necessity of staying on her own, which she has to do because other people are depending on her.

Both Ray and Nerese can be called dubious Samaritans but in different senses of *dubious*. Nerese is dubious in the sense of skeptical; Ray, on the other hand, is a questionable Samaritan—precisely because he doesn't give enough weight to his doubts. Even when he knows "with absolute certainty" that the life of his chief beneficiary will never amount to anything more than "one long unbroken cavalcade of elaborate excuses and self-defeating con jobs," with an occasional armed robbery thrown in, he continues to dole out assistance.

But the largest difference between the two characters has to do with gratitude. It is a difference simply stated. Whereas Ray helps because he lusts for gratitude, Nerese operates *from* gratitude. Ray had stood by her during a painful episode in her childhood, and though she can see the grown man's flaws quite clearly, she never forgets the goodness he had as a boy and still has as a man. Nietzsche said that the essence of all great art is gratitude, and Nerese's help is something like a work of art. That is to say, it achieves a beauty that Ray's never does.

A parable does not show us its characters' motivations in the way that a novel does. We cannot know the good Samaritan's heart. Perhaps it is enough to say that he is a character after Jesus's heart. Both of them are itinerants. Both of them do their work and move on, Jesus often issuing the warning to someone he has helped to "tell no one of it." There is an implicit corrective here for people like Ray Mitchell, whose caring can become confused with their neuroses, and for those so tormented by their own sense of obligation that they can soon be tormented by everyone who figures that out.

I knew a woman who in her prehippie days worked as a volunteer in the Civil Rights movement. One of the pickup lines she got was, "If you're really for us, you would go down for us." For all I know this might have been intended as a test of her sincerity, for if this young white woman was truly "for" her black comrades, she would have met their ludicrous proposition by telling them to go screw themselves. Whatever the proposition's intent, she was lucky to hear it in such a crude form. It is likely to come to our ears in subtler language. If you really cared . . . If you really believed . . . If you are the Son of God . . .

Like the Samaritan, Jesus doesn't go down. He may "go up to Jerusalem" to be crucified, but he never goes down. In fact, it comes as something of a jolt to realize that Jesus is hardly ever seen doing the three helpful things we are most often called upon to do. He never donates money, gives advice (in the specific sense of "Here's what you ought to do"), or offers support (in the uncritical sense of "Everything you're doing is perfectly fine"). We see him reaching out to those at the margins of society to remind them that they too have a place in the kingdom of God, but we never see him sacrificing his time or his agenda on the altar of another person's loneliness. Nor do we see him investing much energy in helping people to get along, as that is generally understood. "Master, speak to my brother that he will divide the inheritance with me." To which Jesus replies, "Man, who made me a judge or a divider over you?" adding a few disparaging words on covetousness for good measure. Surely the most underrated answer to the currently popular question "What would Jesus do?" is "Nothing."

So it is possible, then, to see the parable of the good Samaritan as both admonition and liberation. "Wishing to justify himself," the lawyer finds that he is justified indeed. Loving your neighbor as yourself turns out to be easier than he supposed. And yet, one can feel that it was a little too easy. If the good Samaritan is intended as the exemplar of human helpfulness, he turns out not to be that helpful. In fairness, we need to remember which question the parable addresses: "Who is my neighbor?" not "How do I love my neighbor?" If the story has been loaded with more freight than it can bear, that is not the fault of the narrator.

Still, I can find myself losing patience with it. I find that I want to tell it again in different versions. I want the Samaritan to be traveling along on the most beautiful morning imaginable; I want him to hear the breezes blowing and the birds singing—and his donkey ringing. I want him to take the phone from the saddlebag and hear the voice of his wife, his sister-in-law, the police telling him that someone he dearly loves is "at it again." I want the man by the side of the road to be his father, his little brother, or his only begotten son, and I want him to be drunk as a skunk *and* stripped, beaten, and left for dead. I want this to be the third time in as many months that this has happened.

Or I want the traveler to be a woman, and I want her to cry through her swollen lips and loosened teeth that although she knows this is a terrible thing to do to another person, she'll never be able to leave the man who did it to her because she loves him more than life itself and if he goes out of her life she would just as soon be dead. For good measure, I want her to say that she still thinks she can help him. I want the good Samaritan, also a woman, to cry out, "Are you nuts?" followed by a question more sober but no less pertinent to the situation: "Am I?"

I want the Samaritan—very much I want this—to get into a big argument over putting the victim on his animal. I want to see him stand in the middle of the road in the pose of someone daring God to strike him dead on the spot, and I want to hear him scream, "Just get on the fucking donkey." I want the man on the road to say that if it's all the same to the Samaritan, he'd just as soon not because right before the robbers arrived he managed to slide his entire colored glass bong collection into the bushes, in which he has invested, like, pretty much his whole life savings and which, thank God, the robbers never found, being hugely distracted with kicking the crap out of him, and because a donkey's never going to be able to take all that weight, okay? So, like, could we put the pipes on the donkey and maybe I could ride on you?

I want the Samaritan, on his return visit to the inn, to learn that the wounded man has recovered enough to trash his room, harass several other guests, and molest the innkeeper's nine-year-old son. I want the Samaritan to have an epiphany akin to that of the young aid worker in Rwanda who said, "I've been busting my butt for a bunch of ax murderers!" I want the innkeeper to tell the Samaritan that his money is not good there anymore, in the one place on his circuit that he really enjoyed, with that nice bread and the little bar out under the olive trees. Actually, he had almost decided against taking the wounded man there on a hunch that this very sort of thing might happen, but then he rebuked himself for being so mistrustful and paranoid and not loving his neighbor as himself.

Or—just one more, and I'm done—I want him to find the wounded man still at the inn because his wounds are in fact much worse than he initially thought and the innkeeper hasn't called a doctor for fear that he'll get stuck with the bill and also because he felt he ought to wait for the Samaritan to return to see what he wants to do since the whole thing was sort of his baby from the get-go. Right?

In short, I want to see it get complicated. And along with that, I want to see it take time, all kinds of time. That is part of my impatience with this story, and on bad and sacrilegious days, it can become an impatience with the Gospel story itself—I mean the quick turnover of the whole thing. The average duration of rescue in the Oliners' study of the Holocaust was two to five years. The usual estimate of the entire career of Jesus is three. That's two to five years of having a stranger in your house, to say nothing of being that stranger, at the daily mercy of strangers—of constant peril, constant stress, where in at least one case I read about, two of the hidden adults were in the maddening habit of sticking their heads out during house searches by the Vichy police and asking if the coast was clear. (Anyone who's ever taught school or served as a supervisor will believe that story without batting an eye.) Your children huddled against the wall and other breathless children huddled in hiding elsewhere in the house, and from the cracked cellar door comes a still, small voice: "Is it okay to come out now?" The only reason it hasn't been heard is that the gendarme is barking into your face: "Are there any members of your household not present at this time?" And the only thing you can think to say is, "The good Samaritan." He left before any of this happened.

Most of us will drive somebody to the hospital—even a stranger, even someone who, in better circumstances, we would not necessarily ask to lunch. Most of us have the decency to forgo Humphrey Bogart's great line (though I've had occasion to *think* it once or twice): "I don't want him bleedin' all over my cushions." Most of us are willing to sacrifice our cushions. Most of us are good Samaritans in the limited sense that the term has come to have and that the parable in no way contradicts. But the lawyer wanted to know something else, namely, what he had to do to be a good Jew, which is something considerably more difficult because it involves keeping the Law, not on the open road so much as in close quarters—that is to say, with neighbors he has been commanded to love as he loves himself. And since most of us have been known to maintain ties of solipsistic affection even when we're a far cry from lovable, it is of little use to say that the neighbor no longer ought to be loved when he no longer deserves it. Had I ever thought to love myself solely on the basis of my deserts, I would have blown out my brains years ago.

The obligation of loving our neighbors as ourselves becomes more problematic as we become more accomplished at loving ourselves—or as we become more preoccupied with it. We have a pretty good ear for the music of compassion when the notes are life and death, but it's another thing to play it on the three-stringed instrument of life, liberty, and the pursuit of happiness. We know any number of people whose lives are not in danger, whose blood is not pooling up around their fallen bodies, who have more liberty than most, but who are to all appearances miserable beyond belief. We can trivialize their misery because of its relatively privileged circumstances, but I am not sure we want to do that, mainly because I'm not sure we have such a good handle on what constitutes privilege.

I never expect to see it done, but I can imagine a study comparing the lives of adults born in concentration camps in times of war with the lives of adults raised in neglectful households during times of peace. In both cases, of course, we would be looking at only the survivors, and I would not expect anyone to declare that life in a concentration camp was the preferable fate. Still, I wonder: on an index of comparison that included such factors as health, income, satisfaction in work, ability to form relationships, criminality, sense of accomplishment, how easily could we distinguish—no peeking allowed—the child who first saw the world through the slats of a cattle car from the one who saw it on television in the trailer down the road? Am I not allowed to wonder that?

It is not all a person might wonder. For even after we have gone so far as to include our neighbors' happiness under the obligation of loving them as ourselves, we can begin to wonder if everyone even wants to be happy. Certain Buddhists say they do, and Socrates would not have disagreed. In Tibetan Buddhist meditation, one cultivates compassion by "realizing that everyone wants happiness and does not want suffering." According to Jeffrey Hopkins, Buddhist scholar and former interpreter for the Dalai Lama, the beauty of such an approach lies in its self-evident foundation.

The appeal of the practice of equanimity . . . is to feeling—heart—not abstract principles. Nor is there an appeal to "Buddha said so." The ground to work from is natural feelings. It's merely our nature that we want pleasure and do not want pain; no other validation is needed. It may seem like an abstract principle, but we live from within aspirations to happiness and avoidance of suffering all day long.

The same point is made more succinctly in the title of a popular book on the subject, *Buddhism Without Beliefs*. But though the Buddha may have shown us a way out of suffering, it would take a better Buddha than we have so far seen to show us a way out of belief—especially when it comes to believing that all people want to be happy. Which idea calls for a greater leap of faith, when you really think about it: believing that a handful of people among the billions who have walked the earth were capable of walking on water, or that *all* people—not who have ever walked the earth, let's just say who have ever walked into your house for dinner—wanted to be happy? Even a generous allowance for mistaken notions of happiness doesn't fully account for the human propensity to be miserable. If such a thing as hell exists, and if angels were to descend to deliver the damned from their torment, I am convinced that the latter would be less interested in rising up on the wings of mercy than in seeing all that fine white plumage catch fire and burn.

But were we to take the Buddhist proposition on faith, which I am more than willing to do—especially seeing as no one has a better idea—we would still be left with the question of how far a good Samaritan ought to go in acting upon it.

Harriet Tubman is supposed to have carried a pistol, which she pointed at the heads of runaway slaves who started to have second thoughts on the way north. Presumably this had much to do with ensuring the safety of others in the group, but at least a part of her action may have been motivated by compassion for the faint of heart. I don't necessarily see her compassion as ironic. There are far less desperate situations where the only helpfulness that seems to make much sense involves putting a gun to someone's head and marching him away from his bondage of choice. But did Tubman ever wonder at the contradiction of forcing someone to be free? Did she ever ask herself if it was worth risking her life and liberty on behalf of people who apparently desired their liberty less than she did? If she asked, we know her answer. She would have said, along with Albert Schweitzer, that her life was her argument. But are we willing to call her a good Samaritan too? Are we willing—and this is how we test the sincerity of our answer—to conclude an account of her life by saying, "Go and do likewise," including the part about the gun?

Or, leave out the gun. I spoke not long ago with a nurse-midwife who told me about one of her most difficult cases. The obstetrical part was not what made it difficult. The first factor was the age of the mother. "Our view is that there is no such thing as consent at thirteen." The second factor had to do with the use of coercion to deliver the mother from a coercive situation.

The midwife came to suspect that the girl had been given to the man who impregnated her as part of a drug deal involving her family. The girl's mother would later tell the investigator from social welfare that although she knew the man was sleeping in her daughter's bed, she didn't think they were having sex. No harm done, though, because the mother was ecstatic at the thought of becoming a grandmother.

The girl herself showed no emotions. "She was so shut down that she was practically nonverbal." During her first physical exam, the girl's pubic hair was found to be infested with lice, yet she seemed unaware of them. "She was so disconnected from the sensations of her own body that she felt no itching. We'd never seen anything like that before."

Largely owing to the testimony of the midwife and the agencies whose help she had enlisted, the courts ruled that the state—for the first time in its two-hundred-year history—would take custody of a baby at the moment of birth. In keeping with the ineffable mysteries of family law, the pregnant teenager was permitted to remain with her family. "But our hope," said the midwife, "was that the mother would follow the newborn."

At first it seemed doubtful that she would, or could. But at the very last second, with the social workers about to take the baby to a foster home, the girl said, "I'm going too." Her family was enraged, so much so that the midwife was worried for her own safety (and for that reason, among others, remains anonymous here). "This is a family that rides on the edge of violence." But the girl has begun to show signs of revival. "She has more animation now. Her truancy has ceased. She's still slogging through. We don't know how the story will end. But for me, that was also a form of midwifery."

I used to work with a teacher who had posted on her office door a favorite quotation she attributed to Rita Mae Brown: "When help ain't asked for, it ain't help." The midwife's story adds a corollary: When help is most urgently needed, it usually ain't asked for. Often it can't be asked for. The man the Samaritan found half dead by the side of the road wasn't doing much asking either. In that case, of course, it was easy to deduce the request from the predicament; in the case of the pregnant teenager, maybe a little less so. We gather that Harriet Tubman wouldn't have felt any qualms about acting in either instance. But what she would have said—or for that matter, what Rita Mae Brown would say—in response to hearing Billie Holiday sing these lines, I am not sure.

Well, I'd rather my man would hit me
Than for him to jump up and quit me.
T'ain't nobody's bizness if I do.

Perhaps no more than to note that, while the lady may have sung the blues, it was a pair of gentlemen who wrote the song.

One could say that the pursuit of happiness is exactly that—something we pursue, on our own, without anyone else's help. It is the fruit of life and liberty, which once those basics are secured is up to the free and lively individual to determine for herself. Runaway slaves and victims of statutory rape may present special cases, but as a general rule one should take the laissez-faire approach to another person's bliss. Otherwise we inevitably fall into the presumption of claiming to know what will make others happy or how happy they have a right to be. So a good Samaritan, in whatever guise, is someone who helps in the preservation of life and the achievement of liberty and then steps back. And maybe that is what Jesus was saying in his parable. Ensure the basics, then be on your way.

But a schoolteacher, wishing to justify himself, said to him, "What is liberty? And when are we entitled to call another person free, which is to say, when does he graduate from our care? And did St. Augustine know what he was talking about when he said, 'He who says he has done enough has already perished'?"

A former student of mine called me up a few hours ago. Were I to tell his story, and someday I may, I would probably be accused of trying to parody the more lugubrious passages of Charles Dickens. Abuse, neglect, abandonment, indentured servitude, sadism, prison, the dashing of nearly every hope—and perhaps the most poignant firsthand story I know about the struggle to be human in spite of every degradation. He tells me again what he has been telling me lately, that his "whole body is shot," his back, his elbows, hands, and knees. He's smoking weed now as much for the pain as for the high, though he's been trying hard to cut back on weed, attends his substance abuse support group faithfully, tries to stay clear of the dopers in the apartment across the hall. He would quit his part-time job at the junkyard but for fear that he would go nuts with so much time on his hands, plus he would hate to give up his salvage privileges. His boss says that if he quits he will no longer be able to volunteer there, as he now does many hours beyond his paid time, which means no more free junk. He tries to stay in the office and avoid as much lifting as possible, but he finds it hard to resist helping the boss's sister, who also works there and whose body "is more shot than mine." If the pain continues, it's likely that he won't be able to supplement this winter's income by shoveling snow from his elderly neighbors' sidewalks and roofs, and "that's a bummer too," because their small gifts and thank-yous are among the rare affirmations of his life.

But what's really bothering him right now is that he keeps picturing himself in his coffin. His is not a morbid fantasy, for it is utterly lacking in fascination. He says it "scares the shit" out of him.

When he was in my classroom he was nineteen years old; I was in my late twenties. I am fifty this year, which means he's older now than I was when he first began to call me "Mr. Keizer." He still does, in spite of repeated invitations to use my first name. It's a form of address that still conjures up the image of a raised hand, the sense of a need requiring my help. Mr. Keizer, my pen just ran out of ink. Mr.

Keizer, I need to go to the nurse. Mr. Keizer, I keep seeing myself in my coffin.

Should I propose that we swap visions? Should I tell him that I grew up in a time of Studebakers and the *Betty Crocker Cookbook*, along with the repeated reminder that there were millions of hungry little children in Africa who would be only too glad to eat my cooling portion of casserole and all my asparagus as well? And in time my shoulders broadened and whiskers darkened my chin, disco came and went, a space probe shot beyond Mars, and then my middle broadened and my beard turned gray—but those little children in Africa are still there, still watching me eat my dinner. Should I tell him that seeing yourself in your coffin is not nearly so bad as seeing yourself in hell?

I have been musing lately over a quotation by Bruno Bettelheim, one that grows out of the year he spent at Dachau and Buchenwald during the dark historical period from which I have taken so many of my examples. In fact, you may feel that there are too many from that time. You may already be sick of them. In that case, the quotation will have an extra resonance for you.

I repeat it here mainly to qualify the notion that any angst or misgiving we might feel with regard to helping others belongs to pampered times and privileged circumstances but that in a real crisis, when life and liberty are on the line, everything becomes clear, including our heart. Maybe I also cite it as a warning against the danger of inferring that God is trying to tell you something when it is merely your human limitations talking, and what they're saying is that you have human limitations. Maybe all I mean to say is that I'm getting a little tired. Like my poor friend's body, my heart is shot. In any case, here is what Bruno Bettelheim says: "A few screams evoke in us deep anxiety and a desire to help. Hours of screaming without end lead us only to wish that the screamer would shut up."

I don't mean to suggest that I wish anyone in pain would shut up, not the children in Africa and least of all my friend, whose stoicism can put me to shame and whose faithful solicitude has more than once helped me deal with the day. Rather, I mean to suggest that the parable of the good Samaritan is only about how we respond to those first few screams. It cannot pretend and it does not intend to give us an example for dealing with the rest, for knowing the line between compassion and coercion or how much suffering is demanded of us in order to eliminate suffering for others or how dubious we ought to be in regard to the complaints of others or how much the happiness of others ought to be our concern or when the desire for gratitude has become too much our concern.

"Go and do likewise," Jesus says to the lawyer, not "Go and do this" or "This is all you need to do," and the lawyer would have been sharp enough to know the difference. He would have been able to see that the simple imperatives of *go* and *do* cannot overshadow the necessity of interpreting the more ambiguous *likewise*, especially over the long haul. That remains the necessity of all good Samaritans still on the road at this hour of the night.

THE DREAM WE
NO LONGER ADMIT

If we felt like playing games with words, we could say that the good Samaritan doesn't actually help the wounded traveler because the latter is in fact helpless. He has been left for dead. The Samaritan cannot *help* the man get onto his beast; he must put him on it, much as he would hoist a sack of grain or a bolt of cloth over its back—unless, of course, the traveler is not so helpless as we picture him.

That is a curious word, *helpless*. We think we know what it means: basically, helpless people are unable to do anything on their own behalf. If they are not already suffering, they are likely to be. They are vulnerable, like infants. But the implications of the word are much more interesting than its simple definition. They tell us something important about the nature of help, and if that were not enough, they tell us something about our nature as well.

For if we denote a weak or vulnerable person as someone lacking assistance—someone *less* help—then the word *helpless* amounts to shorthand for "No man is an island." It implies that none of us can exist happily for very long without help. This has its irony because in the very act of disparaging someone as helpless, we imply that we owe our own strength and seeming self-sufficiency to the help of other people. We have managed to get by with a little help from our friends. Otherwise we would be helpless too.

And yet, even after the good Samaritan arrives, we continue to call the half-dead traveler helpless. In so doing, we acknowledge something else the word implies: that help, by its very nature, is a shared act. Unlike love, it needs to be requited to exist. Those unable to co-operate with their benefactors can only be saved or otherwise advantaged, not helped; thus we refer to them as helpless.

Our everyday speech confirms that meaning. If I say that I helped my father up the stairs, you will assume that I did not carry him up. If a mother says that she helped her daughter with her algebra homework, we infer that the girl did at least some of it. If the mother worked out the problems and supplied the answers, then she may (or may not) have done her child a favor, but she certainly didn't help her with the math. In that respect the girl was—or acted or was treated as if she were—helpless. Seen in this light, the old saying "God helps those who help themselves" turns out to be a circumlocution. It is enough to say, "God helps"; human participation is already implicit in the verb. "Jesus saves" is a different matter.

In the midst of a situation like the one presented in the parable of the good Samaritan, these kinds of semantic distinctions will seem tiresome and irrelevant. Who cares what we call the traveler's plight or the Samaritan's intervention? The need is clear, and the obligation is no less clear. The clarity is part of Jesus's point. What is more, we could say that no human being is ever completely helpless because even in the worst extremity of need, one's body labors for life—as the wounded traveler's body surely did—and is therefore able to cooperate with another's assistance. As long as we have a heartbeat, we're susceptible to help.

But in situations less dire and more obviously cooperative, we leave the narrow road where the good Samaritan finds the wounded traveler and enter a sprawling marketplace where the goods and the costs of our actions are all subject to negotiation. That is to say, we enter the place of desire. It is here that a blind man cries out to Jesus, "Son of David, have mercy on me!" and Jesus replies, with an admirable lack of presumption, "What do you want me to do for you?" That is, what do you desire?

Aside from cases of almost total helplessness, help is usually about your desire and my desire and which of them will take precedence for the time being. Perhaps our desires can be fulfilled mutually, perhaps not. In the parable of the good Samaritan, the traveler's need and the Samaritan's duty are both so absolute that the element of desire is virtually absent. The traveler has no desire beyond his primal will to live, and the Samaritan no desire beyond an equally primal compulsion to save. But as soon as the traveler is conscious enough to talk, then the question of help becomes complex enough to argue. And the argument has been going on since Eden.

If we were to define a human being as a creature who helps—*homo adiutor* is how a classics professor rendered it for me—we could also define large areas of cultural history as an ongoing conversation about how much help a human being needs, wants, and is inclined or obligated to give. In the case of those excluded from the conversation, the question often devolves to how much help "they" deserve from us. Or how much we can coerce from them. All matters of definition, in any case. To define literally means "to set limits to"—and when do we find our limits so sharply defined as when we try to give help or when we are crying out for it?

In his *General Introduction to Psycho-Analysis*, Sigmund Freud is careful to define both the help and the helplessness of his profession. After noting that "hereditary disposition," "childhood experiences," and "frustration in reality" are all beyond the means of therapy to affect, he states that psychoanalysis can only make patients consciously aware of their unconscious conflicts: "We do nothing for our patients but enable this one mental change to take place in them." What is more, "so far as possible we refrain from playing the part of mentor; we want nothing better than that the patient should find his own solutions for himself." Lest his colleagues be tempted to imagine themselves as more helpful than they are (or their patients as more helpless), he adds this humbling observation: "People who can be so easily influenced by physicians would have found their own way to that solution [that is, to resolving the repressed conflict] without this influence."

Freud is talking about psychology, of course, but no less is he talking about anthropology. He is offering a partial, tentative answer to the question posed by both Sophocles and the Psalms: "What is man?" If humanistic discussions are often about defining help, then what we have to say about help often reveals—in some cases, we might say, it betrays—what we think of human beings.

Of course, much of what I have just said is grossly simplistic. You cannot reduce everything important to a question of help. But I would put my reductive little rooster into the pit with all the others and expect it to do fairly well. The *thing* we're often talking about—whether our language belongs to psychology, politics, religion, or everyday gossip—is help. And, to play with words once again, it *helps* to know that. It helps because, as anyone who has ever tried to be helpful can attest, the slide toward helplessness is always accompanied by a sense of futile isolation. That is true for the patient, and it is also true for the doctor. *I'm all by myself here.* So it helps to know that in our own Samaritan perplexities we are part of a much larger conversation, perhaps the largest there is or has ever been.

You can hear it going on in any number of places, but one good place to listen is in the history of Buddhism. As his teachings have come down to us, the Buddha taught a religion of radical self-reliance. In fact, some have argued that this aspect of his teaching is so radical that it precludes the use of the word *religion*. Gods or goddesses might or might not exist, according to the Buddha, but they cannot enable an individual to break free of the cycle of birth and rebirth in which men and women are doomed to suffer. This they have to accomplish by themselves.

> Self is the lord of self, who else could be the lord?
> With self well subdued, a man finds a lord difficult to find.

> Let no one forget his own good for the sake of another's, however great.

> Make thyself an island, exert thyself, and that promptly, be wise!

Nearing death, the Buddha speaks of "relying on myself alone" and exhorts his disciples to be resolute in imitating his example.

> Therefore, O Ananda, be ye lamps unto yourselves. Rely on yourselves, and do not rely on external help.
> Hold fast to the truth as a lamp. Seek salvation alone in the truth. Look not for assistance to anyone besides yourselves.

The poet Rilke gave similar advice to his protégé in his *Letters to a Young Poet:* "Nobody can counsel and help you, nobody"—though it could be argued that this itself is counsel. The mentor who tells us we are beyond his help is also helping.

The Theravada branch of Buddhism claims to have maintained the original emphasis of its founder. Its ideal is the arhat, the individual who wins nirvana through his or her own exertions on the Noble Eightfold Path. But the school of Mahayana (meaning "big vehicle," as in room for everybody) emphasizes universal salvation and the ideal of the bodhisattva, who resolves: "From all terrors I must rescue all beings." The reversal was radical enough that certain Mahayana thinkers felt the need for some explanation. The crux of their argument was that the Buddha himself showed a Mahayana bias by turning to teach others. Had he entered nirvana straightaway without turning to guide us toward enlightenment, he would not have been the Buddha. So those who would follow in his footsteps are called to help "all sentient beings."

Perhaps the Mahayana approach is no more a contradiction of the Buddha's original teaching than when the apostle Paul says, in the same epistle, "Bear one another's burdens," and then later, "Everyone shall bear his own burden." It is possible, is it not, to be self-reliant and still help one's neighbor. (What's a little harder to imagine is how anyone could manage to do either if everyone insisted on doing both.)

Still, it is obvious that Buddhism underwent a significant shift as its message traveled across a continent and through successive centuries. Enlightenment seemed either too hard to attain without some help from others or too shallow a goal in the absence of any benefit to others. Perhaps both were evident from the start.

The emphasis appears to have continued shifting. The Ch'an, or Zen, branch, which grew out of the Mahayana tradition and is regarded by some scholars as its fullest flowering, lays great stress on self-reliance. Every serious practitioner of Zen strives to achieve satori, an awakening no different from what the Buddha himself achieved under the bo tree. True, the disciple receives intensive help from the master and presumably from the example of the Buddha himself. Nevertheless, the disciple is urged not to be overly reliant on that or any other example. It is from Zen that we get the saying, "If you meet the Buddha on the road, kill him"—which makes you wonder what you're supposed to do if you meet the good Samaritan.

We find the same tension at work in Christianity. How helpless is humanity in relation to God? Is grace the all-sufficient source of salvation, as per St. Augustine? Or does grace amount to divine help for a not-so-helpless soul, as per Augustine's archrival Pelagius, who taught that human beings were capable of doing some good on their own? As in Buddhism, it seems hard for the tradition to make up its collective mind.

The debate has political parallels, no less in America than in imperial Rome. Who was more generous in his esteem for humanity, Franklin Roosevelt or Ronald Reagan? To answer either way is to invite a dope slap from the Zen master. Liberals say that conservatives downplay the importance of compassion and the necessity of help. Liberals also point out that conservative espousals of self-reliance are frequently a sham. Inheritance is not the same as initiative. Those who have been helped from the beginning by the accidents of class and the privilege of color have an obligation to help those whose social karma has not been so favorable. Liberals believe in bodhisattvas. Eleanor, Martin, and Bobby.

For their part, conservatives argue that the liberal view paints the picture of a helpless humanity, subject to every whim of economic and social determinism, with no credit or blame given respectively for industriousness and sloth. If you can in fact manage to keep a good man down, is it even possible to lift him up? Conservatives believe in the arhat, the self-motivated saint whose diligence is disdainful of any big-vehicle government programs.

The Christian debate over help and helplessness continued, with variations, through the Reformation. Are we predestined to salvation, as Calvin said, and thus helpless to determine our ultimate destiny, or can we manage some cooperation with divine grace, as the Dutch reformer Arminius insisted that we can? Are we interwoven in a great community of saints who, whether on heaven or in the visible Church, assist us, or do we stand alone in existential nakedness before God?

The one question we do not hear—though the Synod of Dort and the Council of Trent would have been infinitely more interesting had someone thought to ask it—is which would we prefer? If God were to say, "*You* tell me," what would we answer? If we find ourselves tongue-tied, not to worry; history is fully prepared to speak on our behalf: *We're stumped.* We would like to have the comforting assistance of a Catholic universe with the radical individuality of the Protestant. It would be nice to light an efficacious candle in front of a statue of the Virgin without being tied to the apron strings of a hierarchic church. Or, to put it in Buddhist language, we would like to have the bodhisattvas on our side but out of our way. We'd like to kill the Buddha, just not fatally.

The image of a toddler squirming in a mother's arms—what we might call "The Philosopher's Madonna"—is a perfect symbol of the dilemma: the child wants to be held but also wants to get down. And the child can grow increasingly restive and irritable with the discovery that, while it may be possible to have both, it is impossible to have both at the same time.

The peculiar Christian form of the question of self-reliance carries over to another theological argument: the one over the Holy Trinity. The conundrum—how do you get Three and One to coinhere, how do you avoid denigrating the identity of the persons, on the one hand, without destroying the unity demanded by a monotheistic religion, on the other—is the theological counterpart to a basic political problem. How do we pay the necessary deference to our human interdependence and still preserve our autonomy? How do we build a just and harmonious society and still leave room for Jack Kerouac to be a dharma bum? How do we provide for everyone to have a place at the table and still keep a plate warm for someone like Howard Hughes? And should we want to?

In a brilliant essay on Hughes written nearly forty years ago, Joan Didion made the claim that the reclusive billionaire represented aspirations deep in the American soul. After noting that "the secret point of money and power in America is neither the things that money can buy nor power for power's sake . . . but absolute personal freedom, mobility, and privacy," she went on to say:

There has always been [a] divergence between our official and our unofficial heroes. It is impossible to think of Howard Hughes without seeing the apparently bottomless gulf between what we say we want and what we do want, between what we officially admire and secretly desire, between, in the largest sense, the people we marry and the people we love. In a nation which increasingly appears to prize social virtues, Howard Hughes remains not merely antisocial but grandly, brilliantly, surpassingly, asocial. He is the last private man, the dream we no longer admit.

Perhaps we have grown better at admitting that dream since Didion published her essay. She was writing almost a decade before the remnants of the counterculture would retreat to the hinterlands—well before we would acquire the technology for watching movies in our laps or the predilection for bowling alone. It can seem as though we have not merely admitted the dream but determined to dream it with a vengeance. But who am I kidding with this high-horse rhetoric? It is my dream too.

That came to my attention rather forcefully with the reading of a parable of heaven and hell, which is also a parable of helplessness and help, and which I first encountered in Barbara Kingsolver's novel *The Bean Trees.* Supposedly, in hell the damned sit around a great pot, all hungry, because the spoons they hold are too long to bring the food to their mouths. In heaven people are sitting around the same pot with the same long spoons, but everyone is full. And why should that be? Because in heaven people use their long spoons to feed one another.

Though I was never in the habit of preaching on hell, I couldn't wait to use the story in one of my sermons. I reveled in the congregation's visible "aha" at the punch line. Beware of preachers bearing epiphanies. The more I reflected on the story, the more its epiphany seemed like another version of hell. I don't want anybody feeding me my dinner with a long spoon. That's heaven? If it is a vision of anything at all, it is a vision of what often passes for charity on this absurd earth. Where I make a sandwich for someone because the economy of which I am a willing and swilling participant has deprived her of the means for making a decent wage. So my long spoon reaches her mouth with a few morsels of compassion, and her spoon reaches mine with a little tidbit of righteousness. Something in me wants to cry out: Why can't we just have our own spoons and be done with it?—though that is apparently the sentiment that keeps the damned so helpless and hungry in hell.

To call Howard Hughes the embodiment of "the dream we no longer admit" is to imply that we were once better at speaking our asocial minds. If that is true, we may have reached the height of our powers with the American Transcendentalists. Here is Ralph Waldo Emerson in an essay called "Self-Reliance" (and in an accent uncannily like that of one E. Scrooge):

> Do not tell me, as a good man did to-day, of my obligation to put all poor men in good situations. Are they *my* poor? I tell thee, thou foolish philanthropist, that I grudge the dollar, the dime, the cent I give such men as do not belong to me and to whom I do not belong. There is a class of persons to whom by all spiritual affinity I am bought and sold; for them I will go to prison if need be; but your miscellaneous popular charities; the education at college of fools; the building of meeting-houses to the vain end to which many now stand; alms to sots, and the thousand-fold Relief Societies;—though I confess with shame I sometimes succumb and give the dollar, it is a wicked dollar, which by and by I shall have the manhood to withhold.

In a statement that sounds a good deal like social Darwinism (though *Origin of the Species* is still some twenty years away), he says in the same essay, "Nature suffers nothing to remain in her kingdoms which cannot help itself." In other words, the helpless are and ought to be doomed to extinction.

Emerson's friend Thoreau, whose experiment at Walden Pond amounts to a low-rent version of the dream we no longer admit, is only a little less strident. While allowing for "the praise that is due to philanthropy," he is more interested in those persons "who by their lives and works are a blessing to mankind." If I read that correctly, he is saying that talent trumps compassion. (Yes and no; he also says, "You must have a genius for charity as well as for anything else.") Qualities like benevolence he compares to "stems and leaves" that are used to brew herbal teas "and are most employed by quacks." "I want the flower and fruit of a man," he says. What he doesn't want is any kind of gratuitous assistance.

> If I knew for a certainty that a man was coming to my house with the conscious design of doing me good, I should run for my life, as from that dry and parching wind of the African deserts called the simoon, which fills the mouth and nose and ears and eyes with dust till you are suffocated.

I never read that passage without recalling some of the more insufferable idealists of nineteenth-century literature, characters like Angel Clare in Thomas Hardy's *Tess of the d'Urbervilles* or Gregers Werle in Ibsen's *The Wild Duck* (1900)—or without inwardly shouting "Wait for me!" as Thoreau heads for the deeper woods. Nor do I fail to realize that in some ways I would be running away from myself, from my own tendencies toward suffocating helpfulness.

Part of what we're seeing in Emerson and Thoreau is the heady independence of a new nation coming into its own. A nation of opportunity. Alms and pensions—do they not belong to that former world of liege oaths and monastic vows, our parents' world? There is something adolescent about the Transcendentalists, including an enviable adolescent brashness. They put me in mind of that song by The Who, "Baba O'Riley," the one with the refrain of "teenage wasteland" and the Promethean cry: "I don't need to be forgiven." We don't need anybody's help, say the boys, especially if it comes with any overbearing instructions from on high. To hell with "on high."

We find the same attitude in our national myths, our tall tales. In older mythologies, assistance was mainly from above; Odysseus is helped by a goddess, Sinbad by a genie, and the fairy-tale princess by her fairy godmother, but Paul Bunyan has a blue ox and Huck an escaped slave, and the Pilgrims and the Lone Ranger have Indians for their acolytes—all representative of creatures and peoples subdued to our heroic purposes. In the American imagination, help tends to go up the chain of being, not down; it is evolutionary. Help that condescends is either humiliating or wasteful, depending on whether you are the recipient or the giver. "Ask not what your country can do for you"—only people on welfare ask that—"but what you can do for your country." Kennedy said it, but Nixon couldn't have agreed more. Yes, we do have God, and we do trust him—mainly not to interfere. It is our hard-earned Pelagian money that we trust to save us in the end.

What we may also be seeing in the Transcendentalists, though I have to say that I fail to see it, is an existential awareness of our human solitude. In Emerson and Thoreau we have what amounts to a "manly" insistence on the right to be left alone. Turn to Elizabeth Cady Stanton, and you find something more sober and in its own way more courageous: a recognition that we are at Walden whether we like it or not. No need to say why you went to the woods; we've all been there. How astounding that after decades of working in solidarity with other women in the suffrage movement and of occupying the center of a bustling household, Stanton titled her last public address "The Solitude of the Self." Her argument: that helplessness ought never to be instilled as a defining mark of womanhood because solitude is one of the inescapable conditions of a human being.

And where are we going with all of this? First, as I noted before, to the recognition that the doubts we have about help and helplessness are not unprecedented. We have always been haggling over help—that is, over our sense of what it means to be fully human. The altruistic misgivings we may feel at the middle of life or the start of a century are nothing new. In a manner of speaking, Dante's dark wood is an old-growth forest. So too are the woods into which Thoreau is ready to fly at the first sign of unsolicited benevolence. To wish that you could just be left alone is, at least in historical terms, to place yourself in a rather large crowd.

If this is true, then help *helps* us to read our times. A period of history can be described not only by its relative degrees of innovation and stability, prudery and license, poverty and wealth, but also by how it values and expresses helpfulness. Jack Kerouac put his dowser's thumb out along the highway, and when he found that people were less likely to pick him up than they had been before, he pronounced that the times they were a-changing. The days of his "rucksack revolution" had come to an end. This may have been a more profound observation than he realized—that the life of a bohemian free spirit always depends on the willingness of at least a few squares to provide the free rides—but as mere prognostication, it left something to be desired. The heyday of the vagabond was actually about to dawn, but by the time it did, poor Jack was too far gone with drink and despair to see how much of a bodhisattva he had been.

In her 1999 book, *Ordinary Grace: Lessons from Those Who Help Others in Extraordinary Ways*, clinical psychologist Barbara Brehony offers her own reading of the times. According to her, we are on the verge of "a new consciousness," "a harkening back to the old days where neighbors took care of neighbors." She says,

> As we cross over into a new millennium, we find ourselves in the midst of a paradigm shift, a change of heart—a metanoia—and the evidence for it is all around. More and more people are experiencing a call to awaken, to bring spirit into their lives, to feel the presence of the divine.

Perhaps she is right, and we can hope that she is, though I am not sure that "the evidence all around us" is as conclusive as she finds it—and of course, some new evidence has been flown in since she wrote her book. At least some of the evidence I see suggests that what people are experiencing is a call to cut their losses in the face of impending mortality and overwhelming odds. Rhetoric alone will not tell us the score. The actual value we place on benevolence cannot be determined simply by our readiness to celebrate benevolent behaviors. There is perhaps little practical difference between beatifying Mother Teresa and debunking her; each can be a ruse for maintaining a respectably safe distance from a leper colony.

At the very least, I think we might say that the strains of skepticism we find in Emerson and Thoreau—who presumably were alive in "the old days when neighbors took care of neighbors" (and ran away from them too)—are still with us. And that may be a good thing, particularly in a culture where so much creative energy goes into counterfeiting. If we can make cheese that is not cheese and convince ourselves that it is, then we can also practice charity that is not charity.

We have already seen how the theme of bogus charity is developed in Richard Price's *Samaritan*, where the compulsive good works of Ray Mitchell are thrown into sharp relief by those of the policewoman Nerese as she tries to help him. In Nick Hornby's novel *How to Be Good* we are given an equally illuminating, albeit comic, pairing of Samaritans. Katie Carr is a doctor who serves down-and-out patients in a North London clinic; her husband, David, is the curmudgeonly writer of a column called "The Angriest Man in Holloway," in which he attacks social evils such as old people who take too much time making change on the bus.

At the start of the novel, Katie has just had a brief, unprecedented, and apparently not very satisfying extramarital affair. She breaks it off almost immediately but not before telling her husband that she wants a divorce. The couple remains together, though, and before long David begins a dalliance of his own, not with a lover, but with a faith healer named Good News who relieves David's back pain and then convinces him to take a walk on the altruistic side. Soon David is giving away his children's computers and inviting unsavory characters to stay at the house. He has not had a religious conversion per se. "I don't believe in Heaven, or anything," he tells his wife. "But I want to be the kind of person that qualifies for entry anyway."

As in the case of Ray Mitchell in *Samaritan*, we suspect that David's conversion is as much a reversion as anything else. Just as philanthropy is a new drug for Ray, it amounts to a new form of aggression for David. Take a mistress, even in retaliation for an infidelity, and your wife can call you a philanderer or a fool; take on the misery of the whole world, and whatever she says will only reflect badly on her. If Katie doesn't exactly know this, the author surely must. He also seems to know how the people most in need of serious help are often the ones doling it out—a truth familiar to anyone with an extensive experience of social agencies.

But the novel is about Katie more than David; she is its narrator and the author's main concern. The urge to do good is nothing new with her. "All my life I have wanted to help people. That's why I wanted to be a doctor. And because of that I work ten-hour days and I get threatened by junkies and I constantly let people down." But something has happened to her along the way:

I suspect that I closed myself down, that something in me just got infarcted, or dried up, or sclerotic, and I let it happen because it suited me. . . . Oh, I'm not talking about romantic love, the mad hunger for someone you don't know very well. . . . I'm talking about that love which used to feel something like optimism, benignity. . . . Where did that go? I just seemed to run out of steam somewhere along the line. I ended up disappointed with my work, and my marriage, and myself, and I turned into someone who didn't know what to hope for.

So in David and Katie we have two moral journeys: one from idealism to emotional sclerosis, and the other from virtual misanthropy to over-the-top benevolence. As presented, they look like two different roads to nowhere—and yet, as in *Samaritan*, skeptical compassion performed in the context of a day job proves to be more sincere and durable than big-splash philanthropy.

Neither character's dilemma is ever fully resolved, but Katie does make a resolution, which is to live a life with greater pleasure and privacy than she has previously known. She is inspired by the artists of the Bloomsbury Group, Virginia Woolf and the rest, who seem to have lived life on the level of art. "Maybe I can't live a rich and beautiful life," Katie says, "but there are rich and beautiful things for sale all around me," and she aims to have some. She estimates her minimal requirements at the cost of three hundred pounds for some books and music and a Discman. Even then, she is willing to cut down the costs, borrow the books and CDs,

> but I need the Discman. I don't want anyone else to hear what I'm hearing, and I want to be able to block out every last trace of the world I inhabit, even if it's just for half an hour a day. And yes, yes: just think how many cataract operations or bags of rice could be bought for three hundred pounds. And just think how long it would take a twelve-year-old Asian girl to earn that in her sweatshop. Can I be a good person and spend that much money on overpriced consumer goods? I don't know. But I do know this: I'd be no good without them.

Katie's admission strikes the perfectly ambivalent note that a good novelist aims for. On the one hand, her argument seems paltry. If we take it for the author's argument, it seems like pandering. Can't you just see all those middle-class commuters saying a hearty and sanctimonious amen to Katie's vital "need" for the Discman? And if you could throw in a hot tub, so much the better. You want to say to her, Okay, take the three hundred, buy the Discman, and the CDs—in fact, take five hundred and get yourself a very nice cabinet for the lot. Now, what about the kids in the sweatshops? Her Scarlett O'Hara pose—*I'll never go without a Discman again!*—is absurd. But on the other hand, it rings so true. How can you not say amen? I wanted to applaud. What is she talking about, after all, what is she really straining to hear on her little music box, but the dream we no longer admit?

In the case of Samaritans like Ray Mitchell and David Carr, we suspect the helpful impulse because we suspect its motive. That was at the root of Emerson's suspicions of philanthropy. "The virtues are penances," he wrote in "Self-Reliance," and he for one was not interested in doing any penance. "I do not wish to expiate, but to live. My life is for itself and not for a spectacle." Albert Schweitzer as much as admitted that his humanitarianism was an attempt to expiate—not for his bad deeds but for his good fortune. In his 1933 autobiography, *Out of My Life and Thought*, he wrote of his youth: "It struck me as incomprehensible that I should be allowed to lead such a happy life, while I saw so many people around me wrestling with care and suffering." As a child he had refused to eat his soup because other children did not have it, and he took to wearing the wooden shoes of the common people. Years later he told an American surgeon who came to visit him in Africa, "Those who receive beauty in life must return it. Those spared of pain must help share that pain with those who have it." This is not necessarily the same thing as guilt, nor was Schweitzer being self-righteous. He candidly told the same surgeon, "Rarely could I ever get out from under this obsession of responsibility and be master of my life." He also told him that he could not recall a single day in his life when he had been completely happy.

On the one hand, we can imagine Nerese saying that this is a character flaw likely to be missed among those the doctor helped. If this is an obsession, more people ought to have it. On the other hand, we tend to share Emerson's instinctive mistrust of help that comes by way of expiation, especially when we discover that motive at work in ourselves. Aside from the attendant unhappiness, it carries at least two dangers.

The lesser of these is that those we help will locate the source of our benevolence and learn to manipulate it—to our detriment and probably to theirs as well. This is certainly what happens to Ray Mitchell.

An even greater danger is that we will begin to project the voices of our guilty conscience onto those we help, imagining manipulation when all we're actually seeing is pain. Then the hungry will begin to appear demonic. We will wish that the screamers would shut up.

The paradox here is that a desire to atone for privilege can coexist with a desperate desire to preserve it. On the most superstitious level, this involves helping others in the hope of insuring oneself against loss. If I serve a turkey dinner to the homeless on Thanksgiving, my house won't catch fire on Christmas. On a more sophisticated level, expiation can amount to seeking situations in which one will always be regarded as a god. One goes to the poor to make amends but also to shine in the absence of competition. St. Francis is said to have kissed lepers, presumably as a sign of his love for them. We trust he was sincere, we know he was young, and maybe the lepers knew nothing besides the joy of being kissed. And yet, what other act could set you so far above a leper as that of kissing him?—for it is precisely the leper's inability to indulge in gratuitous acts of affection that sets him apart from other people. Kissing a leper for his edification is a bit like riding a unicycle in front of a quadriplegic for his amusement. You had better be a saint to try a stunt like that.

Ideally, help is an attempt to lessen the differences in fortune between the person assisting and the one assisted. It is an attempt to bring two levels of well-being into greater proximity and two persons into something like a reciprocal relationship. Very probably that is what Francis wanted to do. Dorothy Day spoke of the "reciprocity of giver and receiver . . . the help the helpless offers to the helpers."

We reach out to help others as a statement of our own need for help. We are all beggars and sinners. We are all in more jeopardy that we dare acknowledge. When I offer bread to the hungry, I am feeding my own soul's hunger. . . . When I offer someone a place to stay, I am reminding myself how homeless we all are—unsure on many mornings or evenings, of where we belong in God's eyes!

That is one thing; wanting to be God in someone else's eyes is quite another. "I believe he is a god," says one of the patients among whom Dr. Paul Farmer, a modern-day Schweitzer, does his work. Given Farmer's astounding combination of dedication and accomplishment, it is not hard to imagine how such an accolade would come about. It is harder to imagine that Farmer is the type to seek it; he spends too much time haranguing and haggling with people unlikely to regard him as divine. But we can readily comprehend how an act of help can be a bid for worship. Ray Mitchell's consuming desire for gratitude is at bottom the need to hear words most fervently spoken in a church: "How Great Thou Art."

For this reason, I am never all that surprised when a medical doctor is found on the staff of an interrogation squad or a concentration camp. Though an infinity of moral distance lies between the healer and the sadist, there is perhaps this much psychological similarity: the thrill of meeting someone at the most primal extremity of need, the look of helpless dependence in his (and especially her) eyes that says, "In this moment, you are my world." *Thou alone.*

We do not all aspire to divinity. We may help simply because we want to feel good about ourselves. When I asked a young man why he had signed up for a two-year stint in the Peace Corps, he included among his several reasons: "I wanted to prove that my mother had been right about me." This is hardly the confession of a flaw. To disparage an act of altruism because "it made *you* feel good" is like disparaging the birth of a child because the parents enjoyed conceiving it.

In his brief introduction to ethics, *Being Good,* Simon Blackburn writes, "We need stories of our own value in the eyes of each other, the eyes of the world." Speaking not only of the motives of Holocaust rescuers but also of their feelings years after the war, Samuel and Pearl Oliner concluded, "Rescue allowed them to preserve their sense of integrity and identity. Their image of who they were and what they represented has remained intact." That old sixties slogan, "If it feels good, do it," is not so morally feckless as it sounds. Nevertheless, anyone who survived the sixties, or simply her early twenties, knows that feeling good about what you are doing is no guarantee that you are doing any good. You can feel great about your part in an antiwar demonstration that did nothing but strengthen support for the war.

Quite often, however, helping others is not even a matter of feeling good about yourself or your actions. It is a matter of feeling good within the moment: a sensation of exhilarating clarity.

Once during a summer cookout at the home of some friends, my host and I were accosted by a distraught neighbor who said that she feared her two small boys were lost and perhaps injured in the woods. The kids had taken their dog for a walk, but the dog had returned without them. We immediately formed a small posse and joined in the search. Though I have never been what passes for a runner, I preserve a vivid recollection of running through those woods like a deer. I recall a palpable sense of clarity. This was not adrenaline; I know about that. This was about the dilemma of using time—experienced as the absence of any such dilemma. Even at a cookout, you can start wondering when you ought to be getting home. The lawn needs cutting, and it's the first dry day in a week. But in the moment of searching for those boys, I had nothing more important to do and nothing in that moment that I wanted to do more. That happens at other times, of course, usually those marked by intense pleasure—but minus the booster of a purpose.

My ecstatic dash through the woods (which took me well out of earshot of the mother's cries of relief when her boys ambled into the yard several minutes later) came to mind recently when a small boy became lost in the New Hampshire White Mountains. He had somehow become separated from his brother during a hike, but he was not the type to run off, his parents said. He was in fact afraid of the woods. That added to the general alarm when his absence exceeded a day. Searchers began combing the area. Here in northeastern Vermont, a man who owns a roofing business gave his entire crew a day off with pay to join him in searching for the boy. He had grandchildren. He "liked kids." Exchanging places with his grown son, he left him in the office where the older man usually sat answering the phone and headed for the horizon. East, where the sun rises. I think I know how those men felt on that morning. I think there was never a day when any of them felt better about going to work. I can hear their voices, read their minds. We're going to find this kid. We're roofers, for Christ's sake; if we have to, we'll climb the trees and spot him that way. Hang tight, little fella. The hope that he was still alive was engorged with the sense they had of being more alive themselves. They will remember that ride as long as they live. If only it had not had such a tragic outcome. The boy was found facedown in the leaves where he had lain or fallen and died of exposure even as the mountains filled with people calling his name. The solitude of the self.

The clarity that comes with an opportunity to help can amount to a dangerous distraction, sometimes from the very responsibilities that want our help most. In other words, it isn't clarity at all. It's fog. Our children wander off into the woods because we are so absorbed in providing free therapy to a pesky neighbor that we never see them go. We park our mother on a blind curve in order to help a stranger change a flat tire. Or we leave our family parked at home while we go off to listen to a friend or a client complain how drinking has kept him from being a good father, only to return, hours after our kids are in bed, drunk and stinking from the wine of our own benevolence. How bitterly one can come to regret those binges.

Do you remember, when you were in school, the yearning that always followed a teacher's request for help, especially if it meant being sent out of the room? Up went all the hands. Of course the thrill was only superficially one of service. Unless you felt especially indebted or attracted to the teacher, most of the thrill had to do with the benefits of authorized truancy. Meandering to the main office, checking your reflection in the display case windows, making faces at your friends in other classes, you were for the meantime exempt from the grind, the discipline, the moment-by-moment judgment of sitting in a classroom. The act of helping or seeming to help another person can bring on the same rush. The phone call in the night, the sound of sobbing in the office cubicle next to ours, is like the teacher's welcome request: "I need someone . . ." and our hands are up before she even tells us what she needs. Anything to get us out of here. If, as Marx told us, religion is the opiate of the people, acts of charity can become their crack co-caine—readily available, relatively cheap, and highly addictive.

With the help of this drug, David Carr can avoid coming to terms with his precarious marriage and Ray Mitchell with his life's vocation, which might entail becoming an inner-city teacher instead of a drive-by writer-in-residence. Both men are using charity as an excuse to go truant. Katie Carr understands the syndrome only too well: "Who are these people, that they want to save the world and yet they are inca-pable of forming proper relationships with anybody? Staying civil to someone with whom you've ever shared Christmas turkey—now, there's a miracle."

Or voting for a society civil enough to share its Christmas turkey as a matter of course—there's another. I know people who would stand in line for an hour to donate their blood, their bone marrow, and even one of their kidneys but wouldn't see their property taxes raised by fifty bucks per annum to hire a school nurse. Universal health care? Forget it. No buzz in that. Just business. They'd rather give blood, like Christ.

If I can describe the territory, it is because I am no stranger to it. The distraction of being helpful can occur even when we *are* tending to business. When I taught high school, I was known for giving extra help to students. Early in the morning, after school, during my lunch break, I was always available. At the same time, I was often behind in correcting my assignments, and though I managed to develop some creative lesson plans, I never spent as much time on revising them from year to year as I would have liked—or as I claimed I would have liked. I have wondered if I didn't work out a little deal with myself: set a standard so high it requires your help, make that help available in large doses, and thereby give yourself time away from the harder, more solitary, and less heroic work of enabling your students to learn on their own. I'm not interested in striking poses of self-deprecation. I did my job—better than some, as good as most. All I'm trying to say is that being helpful is not the all-purpose amnesty we sometimes take it for.

I once tried to list all the reasons besides compassion that we can have for helping people. I came up with around twenty-five. Some of them, like helping in the hope of receiving help in return, seemed perfectly reasonable, if not very altruistic. Others were simply venial or vain. For instance, we can help people because we want to share in the limelight of their need. We show up bedside like celebrities at a championship fight. Was that Liza Minnelli? Yes, she brought the cookies. But where's the harm?

Anna Freud spoke of those who helped in order to identify with the unfortunate and thereby place themselves beyond reproach. I'm not sure I could call that vain or venial either. If you give your life trying to free slaves, maybe you are beyond reproach. It is not an exclusive privilege in any case. Anna could have had it too.

The distinction that counts most, it seems to me, is between helping from mixed motives and pretending to help from cynical ones. As an example of the latter, we can "help" someone who doesn't even need our help in order to share in the glory of his achievements. When Dr. Johnson was about to complete his monumental *Dictionary of the English Language*, he discovered that the work was being promoted by a nobleman whose early promise of support, in Johnson's view, had fallen short. Johnson's famous "Letter to Lord Chesterfield" is the most eloquent description of spurious help that I know. (Chesterfield himself was so taken with the letter that he is said to have displayed it prominently on his table.)

> Is not a patron, my Lord, one who looks with unconcern on a man struggling for life in the water, and, when he has reached ground, encumbers him with help? The notice which you have been pleased to take of my labors, had it been early, had been kind; but it has been delayed till I am indifferent and cannot enjoy it, till I am solitary and cannot impart it, till I am known and do not want it. I hope it is no very cynical asperity not to confess obligations where no benefit has been received, or to be unwilling that the public should consider me as owing that to a patron, which Providence has enabled me to do for myself.

Perhaps artists are especially susceptible to this kind of presumptuous encumbrance. After one of Chopin's more brilliant performances, his friend and rival, Franz Liszt, rushed to the piano and tried to "help" the frail composer by taking him up in his arms and carrying him off. (The press saw his grandstanding for what it was and satirized it.) Elsewhere in the history of music, we find an example of yet another subgenre of spurious assistance: "helping" someone to do things our way. In film footage of the Beatles recording one of their albums, we overhear an earnest Paul telling a sullen George, "I'm trying to help you, but you're getting annoyed"—apparently too young or too full of himself to realize that he could hardly have chosen words more annoying. The Beatles were a love-and-peace band; one shudders to imagine Paul offering his help to Johnny Rotten.

Finally, one of my favorites: hypocritical help can take the form of "empowering" people—students, workers, patients, consumers—by removing their "dependence" on advocates—parents, unions, doctors, watchdog agencies—so that they will be an easier mark for the authors of their empowerment—school officials, bosses, HMOs, crooks. As a precedent we have the serpent who "empowered" Adam and Eve. Empowerment as it's often practiced is nothing more than fleecing sheep with the help of a motivational speaker. You might as well say that the Monroe Doctrine was about empowering the peoples of Latin America.

We don't have to be suspicious of motive to be suspicious of help. Common wisdom alliterates the word with *hindrance*, even in the face of good intentions—perhaps especially then, because that is a harder face to turn away. On Johnson and Boswell's celebrated tour of the Scottish Hebrides, a fierce storm blew up as they were traveling between the islands at night. Johnson was asleep in the hold, but Boswell was up on deck, impetuous as ever and eager to pitch in. When he asked how he might help, the young Highland chief in charge of the boat handed him a rope and told him not to let it go. Only later did Boswell realize that it was fastened to a place having no nautical value whatsoever. Of course, his assigned task was not so bogus as it first appeared, and Boswell seems to have grasped that as readily as he did the rope. The chief had not only saved himself the trouble of tripping over Boswell; he had possibly saved Boswell from washing into the drink.

Just as we can rebel against duplicitous or suffocating assistance, we can also rebel against the obsessive deconstruction of our every effort to help. The historian John Lukacs calls the attribution of motive "the most pestilential intellectual habit of the twentieth century." Simon Blackburn strikes a similar note in attacking "the dispiriting view that everybody always acts out of their own self-interest":

> The move is not only boring but a nuisance . . . this is not the language of mankind. It would have us saying that if I stand back in order for the women and children to get in the lifeboat, then my self-interest lay in their being in the lifeboat rather than me. And this is just not the way we describe such an action. It appears to add a cynical reinterpretation of the agent, but in fact it adds nothing.

In a nutshell, we might say that "the pestilential habit" of attributing motives is about hiding the dream we no longer admit by suggesting that anyone more helpful than we are has something to hide.

Our analysis of helpful people often says more about us than about them. When Robert Coles interviewed a young activist who had turned his back on his privileged background to work among black sharecroppers in the South, he was issued this challenge: "Have you thrown [your question] at yourself, and people who work nine to five in banks and insurance offices and law firms? Have you ever asked them to think about their lives and 'conclude' something?" As Coles readily conceded, the young man had a point. Confronted with the biography of a J. P. Morgan or a Donald Trump, we tend to ask not why he did what he did but how. It is only with a Dorothy Day or a Paul Farmer that we demand explanations. This is probably because we don't feel accused by the financier in the way that we do by the saint, but it may also be because we regard amassing a fortune as more natural than trying to house the homeless or cure resistant strains of TB. As I said before, arguments over philanthropy are also discussions of anthropology—of what we really think we *anthropoi* are. The arguments tend to fall into either of two major categories: (a) these people who give so much help may not be so nice after all, and (b) these people who need so much help may not be so nice after all. Guess what?

In general, the knowledge that mixed motives exist seems to me a great liberation—especially if one has the good sense to apply the knowledge in moderation and to oneself. It is like going to a magic show knowing a thing or two about the art of illusionists; you don't need or want the secret of how every trick is done, just the assurance that miracles remain appropriately rare. In other words, it's good to know that your good deeds are not altogether wondrous. It makes forgetting them so much easier.

Not long ago a friend and I were discussing the question of motives. We had started out talking about Christopher Hitchens's scathing indictment of Mother Teresa, *The Missionary Position*. My friend had read it when it first came out in 1995 and found it vicious; I had read it just that week and found it rather persuasive. He told me that at one time he had read every book he could get his hands on by or about Albert Schweitzer. "Now you want to talk about someone with psychological issues. All very complicated stuff. But at least these people are there," he said, meaning where they can help.

Then he added: "In the end, the only real answer to the question of why we feel motivated to serve others is *Fuck you*."

If we wanted a metaphor with which to embody all the historic dilemmas of help, we could hardly find a better one than the missionary. Many of the conflicts we have identified thus far—between interdependence and self-reliance, between the aims we profess and the motives we conceal—are found in the story of those who left their familiar world behind in an effort to make the rest of the world more familiar. We believe there were places on earth that might have remained close to paradise without their interference, yet there are documented instances of their having been recalled or censured for trying to build paradise on earth. From the broadest perspective, "the missionary position" turns out to be everything in the Kama Sutra.

David Rieff has said that as recently as the 1930s only communists and Christian missionaries acted "on the basis of an ethos of universal solidarity." The comparison is instructive, for good and for ill. Both groups believed they knew the truth, that it was irrefutable and destined to conquer history. Both believed in a world better than the one they saw. Both believed that the primary way of bringing that world about was to bring people to their point of view. Finally, both were willing to travel. In some ways the young Americans who went to fight for the Loyalists in the Spanish Civil War were missionaries; at least they could sound like them. Salaria Kea, the only African American woman to serve in Spain with the Abraham Lincoln Brigade (as a nurse), might be a guest preacher "lately returned from the mission fields":

> I'm very proud that I went to Spain because I feel like I have done something in this world to help people. And that's what I'm here for. *That's what we all are here for.* [my emphasis]

The story of the missionary is the story of every benefactor and bodhisattva who comes unbidden into our lives. Somewhere between the exclamation "Truly this was the Son of God" and that of "Pale Galilean, you have conquered," we make our equivocal peace with influence.

Actually, I wanted to be a missionary when I was a boy. Another dream I no longer admit. My motives were probably as complex as those of Livingston or T. E. Lawrence (a definite missionary type, if not exactly a missionary): a combination of adventurism and callow piety, a Gauguinesque confusion of exoticism and the first stirrings of lust. I decided early on that I would go to New Guinea, supposedly the wildest place on earth, where remote tribesmen made trophies out of human heads. I was hoping the practice would last at least long enough for me to stamp it out. With no effort I can still conjure the *National Geographic* photos of a Papuan warrior crouching near the thick wooden corner post of his hut, his spears and bow clutched in his fist, a sallow skull hanging from his belt, looking not at all fierce but as steady as a young man could ever hope to look (and would need to look in a your-head-or-mine world); and on another page, a lavishly masked figure recognizable as a woman only by the large conical breasts swelling under an immense bib of colored beads. I was not sophisticated enough to recognize that I was enticed by the very aspects of Papuan culture that it might be my mission to dilute or erase.

However much it may have been shaped by the values of a conservative, evangelical church, my desire to enter the mission field may

have represented an early attraction to liberalism. I do not recall anyone in my childhood making the association, but missionaries were in
some ways the embodiment of what liberals of my era were purported
to be. Missionaries were idealistic and impractical, tireless in the solic-
itation of handouts; they dressed casually, ate exotic foods, and were
known to consort with Negroes. As bland and proper as they might
have seemed passing the plate back in the sponsoring church, there
was something almost bohemian in the image of a married couple eating barbecue under a thatched roof with a lot of half-naked black people, even if they did all sing "Rock of Ages" come Sunday. Years later,
when I began to read the poetry of the locally notorious Allen Ginsberg, of holy madmen "dragging themselves through the Negro streets
at dawn, looking for an angry fix," it might have seemed to my elders
that I had abandoned the enthusiasms of my childhood, but I am not
so sure that I had.

It turns out that one of my distant relatives was a missionary. My father came upon her book and sent it to me, *Pioneering for Christ in the
Sudan*, by Johanna Veenstra (1926). Cousin Johanna, as I like to call
her, worked at Lupwe "in the foothills of the Cameroon" among a
tribe called the Dzompere, which she tells us translates as "man
eaters." Apparently, they had modified their diet prior to her arrival,
though the white man's smallpox and influenza had already eaten many
of them.

It is difficult to see Cousin Johanna as a tool of colonialism or of
much else. If she is a tool, no one seems all that interested in using her.
The missionary school she attends is straight out of Dickens. It is
barely supported even by its parent church, much less by any state.
Four of her classmates contract TB there and die. The eagerly awaited
leftovers from a local church's turkey supper turn out to be a tureen of
bones and skin, left standing at room temperature from Friday to
Monday, out of which the aspiring missionaries are expected to make
soup. I began to like Johanna as soon as she told that story, which she
could not have delivered with greater scorn had she used the phrase
"sanctimonious cheap bastards." I liked her even more when she refused to eat the soup.

Her story follows a pattern as old as John Bunyan, whose *Pilgrim's*

Progress probably stood in her home next to the family Bible and whose autobiography, *Grace Abounding to the Chief of Sinners*, strikes notes similar to her own: early "waywardness" of the most innocuous kind (she had a dancing lesson!), a sense of unmistakable conversion, a decision to do the Lord's work. But waywardness will have out, and one senses Johanna's need for a deeper breath of air. When she finally gets on that steamship, she is bidding stenography good-bye. Eventually, she will train to be a midwife. She rides down narrow jungle paths on her bicycle, trusting in Providence to keep her tires inflated. Teasingly, she warns her readers not to brave her accounts of wild beasts too close to bedtime, so fearsome are these leopards and pythons. But in the village, the peaceful village, my cousin sleeps tonight. And I think that Elizabeth Cady Stanton might have been able to divine some of her dreams.

More than once she must have awakened with a start. Speaking of her beleaguered converts, she writes, "On every side of them is polygamy, gross immorality, beer drinking, and immoral dances." She had never been an undergraduate. But she doesn't lack a historical perspective; she compares her village to Corinth in the first century, a strained comparison perhaps but not a disdainful one. She could certainly be obtuse. Noting that the natives have no words for *preach*, *repentance*, or *sin*, she invites us, apparently without any sense of irony, to "think what that means to the missionary." One wishes she would have thought harder.

Her inability to see past her own cultural bias is perhaps best illustrated by her contrasting observations of two babies receiving a bath. First, the traditional method:

A mother was sitting prepared to give her wee boy a bath. She greeted me and smiled pleasantly, and offered me her little stool to sit on. Beside her was a clay basin that contained about a cupful of water. She put some water in the palm of her hand, and then held her hand close to the little fellow's mouth. Her hand acted as a dipper to give the baby a drink. Then she laid him flat on her lap, and from the basin she took a mouthful of water herself. Then she spit this water on the body of her boy and began to rub with her hand. One mouthful gone, she took a second mouthful and continued this until the water was finished and until the whole body of the baby was wet. No soap, no wash-cloth, no towel.

Then she describes one of the converts giving her baby "such a lovely wash" in an enamel basin of warm water. "The baby splashed and en-joyed it."

> What made the difference? The first woman was a heathen. The second mother has been a Christian for some years, and the gospel is helping to influence every part of her life.

Leaving aside the question of how one of these women came to have an enamel basin and why the other had neglected to make one from the bark of the enamel tree, one is aghast at Johanna's failure to appreciate the intimate economy of the "heathen" bath. *Except you be-come as a little child*—with your belly full of your mother's warm milk and your skin anointed with a stream of water warmed in her smiling mouth. A man would gladly be born again if only to be bathed in that way. (You can see what kind of missionary I would have made, proba-bly the kind who is finally retrieved in disgrace, weeping inconsolably in the stern of the boat as his wives and children grow smaller and smaller on the shore.)

"They are a child race," Johanna says, and though she is arguing for a gentle approach to their culture, we are offended by her choice of words. We should be. We are more comfortable with someone like Dr. Farmer, who looks for the beam in the eye of Western medicine before removing any specks from the eyes of his Haitian patients.

Just recently a TB patient from a village called Morne Michael hadn't shown up for his monthly doctor's appointment. So—this was one of the rules—someone had to go and find him. The an-nals of international health contain many stories of adequately fi-nanced projects that failed because "noncompliant" patients didn't take all their medicines. Farmer said, "The only noncompliant people are physicians. If the patient doesn't get better, it's your own fault. Fix it."

We would applaud these sentiments—and again I would say, we should. Nevertheless, were I one of the physicians working with Farmer, I doubt I could resist asking how it can be an adult's fault when another adult doesn't take his medicine. It is only an adult's fault when a child doesn't take his medicine.

"My skin is different from yours, but my blood is just the same"; Johanna says that too. "We do not encourage them to change their names," she writes, "but sometimes a person has a slave name or a name connected with spirit worship and wishes to drop that for a Bible name." Considering the merits of opening a boarding school, she poses a question not unlike one I heard a Dartmouth student teacher ask about the rural kids he was encouraging to apply to college: "Dare we permit them to foster a growing dislike for their own village?" Flying in the face of a popular practice, both then and now, she refuses to allow the faithful back home to sponsor an individual child; if they wish to benefit the children, they should contribute to the common pot so that gifts of equal value can be bought for all. So she is a communist of sorts.

Probably not a feminist, and yet . . . when a villager tells her how some women accused of sorcery were recently put to death—branded with hot spears as they danced to exhaustion, then tied to trees and speared—Johanna asks if male sorcerers are punished in the same way. They are dispatched more quickly, she is told, and they are allowed to drink beer before they die. I am reminded of something a feminist scholar (Mary Daly?) said when it was suggested that to criticize the practice of female genital mutilation was to "impose our values on another culture." "It's the *same* culture," she quipped. Right down to the beer and the burp.

Missionaries are out of favor now, even among many of the religious. The bible of choice is the *Poisonwood*. Of course, the West never stopped exporting its religion; it merely changed its religion. It would be disingenuous to pretend that this has never been a change for the better: medical care, for example, is a religion we can all agree on. All peoples (except perhaps those whom religion has made sick) believe in being well. I am glad I did not become a missionary. Still, no sooner have I said so than I recall Cocteau's wonderful line about "those intellectuals who have clean hands but don't have any hands." The missionaries, at least, had hands. Johanna speaks about "the sadder part of life that a missionary must know by seeing and handling." My wife and I have a friendly debate; she can see no good in going abroad to seek conversions—in "the nerve" of it—while I suppose I still can, including when swamis and shamans come over the waters to convert us, and providing that the conversion sought is never coerced and always mutual. For me, going native is one of the prerequisites for going to the natives. Though my theology has changed greatly since childhood, I continue to be fascinated by the idea of going to a people in the totality of who you are and encountering them in their own totality, with enough faith to believe you have something to share and enough humility to believe you are in need of instruction. It goes without saying that each party will share what it regards as most important.

It also goes without saying that what I've just described is essentially the archetype of all teaching. It may also be the archetype of helping at its best.

Instances of mutual conversion are not entirely missing from the record, though they stand out as anomalies. The example that comes readily to mind is that of the Jesuits in China, where Catholic priests dressed in the robes of Confucian scholars and studied their classics. One can only imagine what China might have become, and Europe might have become, had the papal authorities not gotten nervous and called off the experiment. Given what may be described as an overly gastronomic imagination, I tend to think in terms of benefits like a yin-yang pizza (to be truly whole, you must eat the whole pie); a richer image may be found in the life of Schweitzer. Evenings he would play his pipe organ in the compound at Lambarene, and from out of the forest came the answering sound of drums. Perhaps that is "mission" in the fullest sense, to make music in a dark wood and to be answered by a different music, by a mating call that invites us—not to take liberties but to move a little closer.

•   •   •

I wanted to talk to a modern-day Johanna, preferably not religious but definitely young. I was looking for what a seventy-year-old American veteran of the Spanish Civil War referred to as "the kind of naïveté that the world needs and will always find somewhere, among the youth especially." I found the person I was looking for in a twenty-seven-year-old Peace Corps volunteer from a small Vermont town. Ben is committed, agnostic, and idealistic—though I would hesitate to call him naive. He had critical reservations from the beginning. So did some of his "progressive" friends.

> I caught a lot of flack. They're like, what are you doing? This is awful, it's just colonialism, these people don't even want your help. I shared some of those issues. But the way I justified it in my mind was, I knew I was going to a small town, I knew I was going to be all alone, and I felt like, when I'm there, *I'm* the Peace Corps.

The small town where Ben would "be" the Peace Corps was a remote village of about 350 Guarani-speaking farmers in Paraguay. The bus that brought him in took three hours to complete the last twenty miles of dirt track. He had asked for it, sort of.

> They'd asked me if there were any countries where I didn't want to go. I said, "Not eastern Europe." We're pretty isolated up here [in northern New England]. I wanted to go somewhere with some different colors. They called me and said, "You want to go to Paraguay?" "Sure." Then I got off the phone and had to look up on a map where Paraguay was.

His official designation was "environmental sanitation volunteer." One of his first projects was to build sanitary latrines (the main object of which is to trap the flies that spread disease). When he arrived, nearly all of the fifty-odd houses in the village had latrines consisting of two boards over an open hole in the ground; about half the households had TVs—"a really weird kind of priority thing." The teacher in the village had the special distinction of owning a car. His latrine was also two boards over a hole.

The Peace Corps had recommended that the volunteers hook up with teachers, the village intelligentsia as it were, but Ben found the local teachers unwilling to do much in the way of work. If not exactly the idle rich, they were in their context the upper crust. Instead, Ben took up with a farmer who lived next door. Together they built oxcarts while Ben learned Guarani. His Spanish was of minimal value. Though the villagers understood Spanish (the language of TV), they refused to speak it, convinced that their pronunciation, like their status overall, was inferior. The bulk of Ben's language education and of his community organizing later on took place while observing the local custom of gathering for several hours a day to imbibe an herbal concoction drunk from an ox horn.

The farmer next door was to become Ben's gateway to the community and his mainstay once he was in. He is of a type who often appears in stories of men and women with a mission. Whether his name is Sancho Panza, Simon Peter, or simply Sonny, we know him when we see him—the solid sidekick, the person whose altruism always cuts two ways, to the helpless and also to the helper, whom he rightly senses may have the greater vulnerability. Sometimes he plays the part of a disciple, though not in this case. The farmer had already gone through his own resurrection. He had worked as a logger for various ranchers earning a dollar a day doing slash and burn until a tree had fallen on his leg, pinning him for several hours and leaving him bedridden for the next two years and unable to work for the next four. He had spent much of that time trying to piece together the money and the connections that would enable him to have an operation. When Ben found him, he was at the center of the community's life, a local icon of help. He was the church coordinator in a place where everyone was a Catholic. ("Saints are huge down there.") He was "always working for his community." So it remains an open question who enlisted whom. "I know I was a successful volunteer," Ben told me, "and I think it's really from him that I learned how to be one."

With his new friend, he took on what was to be his most ambitious project: building bread ovens. The leading cause of death among women in rural Paraguay is respiratory illness, caused by smoldering open fires on the floors of their houses. There is no chimney or smoke hole per se; the smoke eventually leaves through the gables. An inch-thick ceiling of creosote hangs from the thatch. Small children are sometimes injured from falling into the fires.

Together Ben and his neighbor built the village's first oven, the neighbor buying the bricks and Ben the rest of the materials. The design they used was aimed at enclosing the fire, venting the smoke, and raising the whole business a safe distance off the floor. The villagers were impressed by what they saw. Soon Ben was helping to organize fund-raisers so that every interested household could have its own oven. Only when that was possible would they begin building. Not everyone participated, but when the first batch of ovens was up and running, most of the remaining households signed on for a second round.

The ovens amounted to a small revolution. Because they stayed warm for much of the day, people could cook whenever they wanted, and nutrition levels improved. Children were no longer getting burned. Still, there were complaints. People missed the pleasure of being able to squat near an open fire. Like the old doctor said, if you want gratitude, get a dog. A project to improve the school building followed, but the auspicious precedent of the ovens did not seem to make the task of community organizing any easier.

> One of the hardest things was getting people to work together. These people have been screwed over so many times, by the government, by different aid organizations. It's hard to get them to work in a group. But when's the last time [my hometown in Vermont] had a community-wide project?

One of Ben's difficulties lay in resolving the timeless animosity between the grasshopper and the ant. Cutting people who did not follow through on their commitments out of a project created hard feelings; cutting those people any slack whatsoever alienated the rest. A "solid family" in the village boycotted an important workday because Ben had failed to enforce a deadline with some of their less solid neighbors. He was dumbfounded.

> I can give up two years of my life to work here, and you can't give up one Saturday to work in *your* school for *your* kids—you can't do that? You can't give up your ego to do that? But . . . it is what

it is. You can't go down there for the thank-yous. Number one, you may not get them. And even if you do, it's not enough of a reason to go down there.

Other volunteers were less stoic. Perhaps some had gone down with not enough of a reason. Ben would hear their complaints during short leaves in the capital city when they met to drink and talk, and the more forlorn to drink and drink. He would sympathize with some of their frustrations—particularly those of a lone black volunteer who came up against what Ben described as widespread Paraguayan racism. But some of his co-workers could also frustrate him. "They would say these things."

"What things?"

"Oh, like 'frigging Paraguayans.'"

Here is what Ben said to me. If I quote him at some length it is to accommodate the subtle shifts of his discourse. He was allowing me to overhear an argument with himself that is also an ancient argument. All the important parties were there: the young socialist with heart and the old conservative with brains, the Buddha and the bodhisattva, Henry David Thoreau vowing to run like mad from the uninvited do-gooder—and Henry David Thoreau not running because he is too ill to move and thankful that someone cared enough to look in on him.

[The experience] made me realize that the world is much more complicated than I first thought. In college I was starting to get pretty left-wing. I was constantly thinking of things as this huge class struggle between the richest ten percent and all the poor people. And I was thinking that with poverty comes, like, a righteous dignity—that these people are living just lives because they're poor, like Franciscan almost. I thought, I need to be a part of that. I need to stop living my privileged life. And it's hard because I went down there, and I ended up realizing—and maybe I was naive—that one of the first things that go when you're poor is your dignity and any sense of righteousness. You can't even afford to be righteous. They'll wheel and deal and screw each other as much as anybody will, almost out of necessity. It was really an eye-opener for me. It was kind of tough because I think at the end of the day, I wanted to see these people as victims and to see myself as a kind of martyr-type going down there to help those victims. It ends up not being that way at all. When you show up, you don't know anything at all. They feed you. They take care of you when you're sick. They show *you* around . . . but, I always assumed they were going to be good, good people—and they *are*. But at the end of the day, they're just people.

So has this young man abandoned his politics or deepened them? Perhaps, as befits someone who has no religious beliefs, though he claims to envy those who do, what he has deepened is his agnosticism. Or rather he has broadened it, including earth along with heaven. "At the end of the day they're just people"—himself included. There is another way to put it. At the end of the day, these people who were "just people" managed somehow to help each other.

But it was never easy. The dilemma of how to help persisted throughout Ben's experience. Often it fell disproportionately on Ben, just as poverty had fallen so disproportionately on his hosts. Going over the transcript of our interview, I find him repeatedly using the word *huge*. In his case it may be more than a twenty-something idiom. A young woman in the village contracted AIDS. Her father brought her to the public hospital in the capital city, where thirty patients are housed together in a single room, where whole families live on the street in order to be near a hospitalized child, where the woman died leaving two young children behind. Where it is so huge. Inevitably people approached Ben for money. "Write to your parents," they would say. "And I could have," Ben told me, though his parents are hardly rich. Neither was he. His salary in the Peace Corps was half that of the village teacher, less than a hundred dollars a month. He had gone to the village to promote "sustainable" community-based projects, not to be a one-man relief agency. And still, he gave a young man in the village a hundred dollars when his pregnant wife was sick and told him not to pay it back. Then he stood him five for his share of the latrine project—a loan this time—and the man didn't pay that back either. The hundred Ben was happy to part with, but the five irked him—to a point. "Who am I to sit here complaining about five dollars?"

Late in the second year of his term Ben's father became very ill. The doctor told his mother, "You better send for Ben." He flew home bracing for the worst. His father rallied; I like to think he also rallied his son. Several weeks later Ben returned to Paraguay for yet another eye-opener: colored shards of his own reflection moving among the huts and houses. In his absence, some of the villagers had stolen his clothes.

They seemed in no hurry to return them. "We thought you weren't coming back," they said. Well, he was back now. I suppose that had he taken his cues from the Sermon on the Mount, he would have offered them his duffel bag also. I say that not to disparage him or the sermon, only to say that I think there are times when a person is most Christlike, and most genuinely helpful, when he has lost any wish he might ever have had to be a god. If it is important to be able to say, "I am the Peace Corps," then it is also important to know when and how to say, "I am not the Peace Corps." I am, in fact, the owner of that jacket, which was a gift from my girlfriend, and I want it back.

We get tired. Even the young get tired. But it is not usually the theft of your clothes that tires you. It is the staggering number of naked people. Perhaps more than that, it is the number of half-naked people willing to steal someone else's half an outfit. The sense of overwhelming futility. Of helplessness. Schweitzer had to build two compounds to house the sick because the members of one local tribe would not lie down in the same room with members of the other. What he liked to call "the brotherhood of all who bear the mark of pain" turned out to be a brotherhood in his head, a dream he could profess but only tentatively realize. Perhaps G. K. Chesterton was closer to the truth when he said that it was mistaken to believe that love is what unites people: "Love diversifies them, because love is directed towards individuality. The thing that really unites men and makes them like each other is hatred."

That may be one of the unstated themes of David Rieff's *A Bed for the Night: Humanitarianism in Crisis*, described by its author as "a book begun in despair and completed . . . in whatever state of mind lies beyond despair." The publisher has classified it as a work on current events, an accurate enough designation in the sense that the humanitarian disasters of Rwanda, Bosnia, and Kosovo that the author explores all happened within recent memory. On a much deeper level, though, the book is current only in its examples. The statements they support have to do with something much older: what Rieff refers to as "a world too sad, murderous, and wicked to transcend," where "we delude ourselves into thinking that the answer to the . . . horror lies within our grasp, when the fact is that it does not."

One may balk at hearing a self-described "vertebral nonbeliever" strike such somber Augustinian chords—or, coming from a different direction, one can marvel at the fact that vertebral nonbelievers are apparently the only people left with enough backbone to make the music. Were I a college professor, I would teach Rieff's book in the same course that I taught *Paradise Lost*. I would tell my students that it was essentially a theological thriller in which a man discovers the existence of original sin. Perhaps that would be an overly dramatic way of saying that he has laid bare some of the knottier problems of help.

Rieff insists that we look not only at the horror of the world but also at "the horror of the cost of a good deed." He shows us what can happen when "humanitarian crisis" is used as a euphemism for genocide or when humanitarian aid is used by timid or apathetic governments as an excuse not to act or when, in cases where those governments intervene with force, humanitarian agencies become the handmaids of military action. And he shows us what Ben also saw in much less drastic circumstances: how "the language of oppressor and oppressed" is not "of much use in describing the reality of a Rwanda or a Kosovo, where today's oppressor is all too commonly tomorrow's victim."

I do Rieff's book a disservice if I present it as a case for despair. He is always on the side of the angels, which in his case means the side of the aid workers themselves: "They have always been desperate to help. That determination to help is the relief worker's abiding glory and the reason why, for all my criticisms, I shall always admire them more than any other group of people I have ever met." He would like Ben, I think. And Ben would doubtless nod in assent to Rieff's formulation of a basic humanitarian dilemma: "Lose if you stay, lose more if you go."

After reading *A Bed for the Night* one remembers that the other side of the dream we no longer admit is sometimes the horror of the nightmare we can no longer face. Part of what Katie Carr longs to hear on her Discman is something *not* the news. Our reason for going to the woods may not be, as it was for Thoreau, "to front only the essential facts of life," but rather that we have already fronted those essentials and found them rotten. More often than not, the misanthrope is an unrequited lover of humankind. It is in the writings of Celine, a French physician who chose to practice among the poor, that we find humanity denigrated as a bunch of "vulgar shitbags."

Rieff's book is a reminder that the essential humanitarian question is not how we defeat hunger or cure disease or curb the tide of genocidal nationalism. Rieff himself would seem to be pessimistic that those goals can even be achieved. Rather, it is how we wrestle with our sense of futility in the face of those disasters. How we find the courage to go on helping others "in an era that," as Rieff puts it, "no longer can distinguish between cynicism and pessimism." All our means for helping are necessarily material. But the fundamental problem "at the end of the day," as Ben would put it—the thing that's really huge—remains spiritual.

Are you getting a tad restless, and are the concerns of missionaries and global humanitarianism too remote from the knockabout dilemmas of your day-to-day life? Because if so, my mother-in-law is on the phone, which means we both may get a little break here. That is to say, we may get a chance to explore some of these topics out in the field, albeit the very quotidian mission field that I now inhabit. David Rieff and Ben, I trust, are reading something better suited to the worlds they move in.

A couple of months ago, we moved my wife's mother from New Jersey to an apartment about two miles up our dirt road. We did this so we could be of more help to her at a time of failing health. We made arrangements with neighbors and home health nurses so they could help us. And now, less than sixty days after she took up residence on top of a remote hill, it seems that someone has come asking help from her.

"There's a man by the back door with blood all over his face. I think he fell off the roof next door" (that is, at the landlord's vacant seasonal home).

"Is he there now?" I shout into the phone. My mother-in-law is hard of hearing; I can only imagine how she's been getting on with him of the bloody face.

"No, he's outside moving a tractor."

That means he's one of the people who work for the landlord, probably the caretaker, a man from whom we buy fresh vegetables in the summer and to whom we owe the tip about the vacant apartment. A good guy. I picture him riding off on the tractor, dizzy and exasperated, unable to make any headway with Mom. I start to remind her about the 911 button I set up on her memory telephone—"the one that's painted red, remember?"—but then figure it will be easier if I make the call myself. I get the ambulance, give the directions, and tell them to keep their eyes out for an injured man on a tractor. Then I grab a fistful of dishtowels and washcloths and speed up the road.

I find the man storming about the dooryard and wiping at a deep gash in his brow. I leap from the car and tell him to sit tight—an ambulance is on its way. That's the last straw for him.

"I don't want an ambulance!" he cries. "Oh, for the love of . . . All I wanted was for her to take a look at my face. I fell off the roof. She wouldn't even open the door for me. This ain't New Jersey, for God's sake."

The criticism of my mother-in-law coupled with the slighting reference to our ancestral home doesn't do anything to bring down the already high levels of my adrenaline.

"She's an eighty-two-year-old woman who's hard of hearing and has lived here for all of a month. She's doesn't know you from Adam—and you expected her to open the door for you?" (I admit, I'm a little surprised that she didn't.)

"Call it off!" he shouts back at me. "I just wanted her to look at my face. I don't have health insurance. I'm not paying for any ambulance."

I go inside my mother-in-law's apartment—she's been watching us from the window—and try to abort the rescue, but I'm told that once the ambulance sets out there's no turning back. My five-foot mother-in-law looks dazed and helpless in her big glasses and her head scarf. Through her description, I get a picture of how the man looked at her door; in fact, I see him as if for the first time. He hasn't had a haircut in a while; he's wearing old clothes and a greasy cap. "He showed up at the door covered with leaves and dirt, all bloody. I thought he was a drunk who'd come out of the woods. I thought he was some tramp."

Only after he'd thrown up his arms and left the door did she see him
go to the tractor parked behind the other house and deduce he was the
handyman. At that point she also deduced, correctly, that he was in no
mortal danger. Even so, she took the precaution of calling me.

I go back out to tell him that the ambulance is coming anyway, at
which he starts in again about "her in there." I tell him that given his
unreasonableness I shall tell my mother-in-law *never* to open the door
for him under *any* circumstances, which he says will be fine by him. It
amounts to a classic little argument: he reproaches her for lack of sympathy with him; I reproach him for lack of empathy with her. Canni-
bals and missionaries. Frigging Paraguayans.

The ambulance arrives, and the medics want him to go with them.
They all but beg him to do so. His gash will require stitches, and his
pupils appear enlarged. He'll have none of it. I'm still angry at him,
but I feel a grudging admiration too: this is one tough hombre. You
can throw him off a roof, and he gets up feistier than he was before.
Lucky for me that our words didn't come to blows.

At the point when he's ready to sign the papers absolving the ambulance of responsibility, I prevail upon him to ride to the hospital with
me. He refuses at first. Of course, the actual terms of the argument are
all subtext. If I get him to go with me, I score a goal for the New Jersey
devils; if he refuses and falls down and dies, he can have it engraved on
his stone that he came mortally wounded to the door of a neighbor
from down country . . .

Finally, he agrees to let me take him, though he insists on driving
home first to change his clothes and deposit his dog. I follow in case he
passes out. Several hours later, well after dark, I drive him home with a
bandage around his head and a bottle of painkillers. He looks like
someone from a Revolutionary War battlefield. We chat like old bud-
dies, which means we have the sense to stay off subjects that won't get
us anywhere, such as "her" behind the door. It also means that I have
achieved one of my ulterior motives, that of remaining on good terms
with the man who may be the first line of defense in an emergency involving the aforementioned her.

The next day she is still talking about what happened. She hopes the
man is all right. He's fine, I tell her. Today it's her turn to drive with

me to the hospital, though there is no emergency other than the slowly emerging crisis of her health. "I thought he was a tramp from the woods," she says. I tell her yet again that I am glad she didn't open the door. And I find that yet again I am gripped with a desire to retell the story of the good Samaritan, not as a man encountering an unconscious stranger on the road, but as an old woman faced with a bloody stranger at her door. Go and do likewise? Do what?

She speaks of her refusal to open the door as a learned habit. She grew up "over the store" as the daughter of an Italian grocer in a neighborhood where doors were never locked and neighbors seldom stood on ceremony about going in and out. "Is Angelo home?" But after the war she got married and moved to an apartment in a different neighborhood, a place of strangers and random crime. Her husband would come home from work and "throw a fit" to find that she had neglected to lock the doors. "Finally, I got into the habit." (More or less.) It occurs to me that my father-in-law's ghost may have stood at her ear as she beheld "the tramp from the woods." It occurs to me how often the decision to help or not to help has less to do with the disposition of our hearts than with the controversy of voices in our heads. "Behold, I stand at the door and knock," says the Lord—and the Boston Strangler too.

Then she gives what strikes me, for the moment at least, as a satisfactory conclusion to the whole business. "I guess we all did what we thought was right." And we did, which is to say, we did what came to us instinctively. Still, I am much less certain about the soundness of my instincts than I am about hers. I feel she acted prudently. I am not so sure about myself. In a way I pushed my help on someone who did not want it (a bit of the missionary there?) and in so doing supported his stubbornness and advanced a largely specious claim for my own compassion. Yes, I was worried about my neighbor. But I was no less worried about losing his potential usefulness to my family, and I was also worried about the potential guilt I would feel if, through his own fault, he had put himself in jeopardy. But am I my brother's keeper, and is that an invalid question simply because it was first posed by a murderer?

I also had to wonder how much of my benevolence was due to a lack of self-discipline. There are days when almost anything seems easier and thus more enticing than sitting at my desk. And here was a neighbor in need. Can't walk away from a neighbor in need. "Class, I need a student to drive Mr. O. to the hospital. You don't need to jump up like that, Garret, just raise your hand." Had I a boss and a time card—for that matter, had I my own health insurance plan—would I have been so quick, and so able, to turn from my job and play at being the good Samaritan?

Actually, I do have health insurance, through my wife's plan, and therein lies what I decide is the crux of this whole incident. More than anything else, I felt guilt over what my neighbor lacked and what I was able to take for granted. I felt guilty that with blood running from a deep gash in his face, and with all doors barred to him, as it were, he would still have to take into account the cost of a ride in an ambulance. In other words, I felt what most "helping people" feel at one time or another—not only the guilt that compels them to act, but deep resentment at the ridiculousness of the larger circumstances inspiring their guilt. Depending on your mood at the moment, you want to become either a revolutionary or a recluse.

This would be a better book if my neighbor had health insurance. It would be a better book, first of all, because I would have had another half a day to work on it, and in my occupation an extra half a day can prove invaluable. My neighbor would have either accepted the ride in the ambulance or rejected it with no debt accruing to my conscience. "Fine," I could have said and gone back to my desk. His choice.

This would be a better book also because in a society where my neighbor had health insurance, I could have devoted more space to writing about help on a higher level, as a celebration of what we all had rather than an expiation for what only some of us had. As things stand with us now, a person's immediate need for help is frequently the result of a larger refusal to help him. He cannot afford an ambulance so we give him a ride to the hospital. We give him a small sip from a long spoon. You could say that help is a social act often necessitated by our failure to be authentically social.

What you could not say, however, is that help is always the result of such a failing and that in a perfect world there would be no need for assistance. To say that is tantamount to saying that in a perfect world there would be no human beings. It is to define perfection as a state of perpetually self-sufficient helplessness.

In some of my sermons for Thanksgiving Day I have said that the most durable kind of prayer is thanksgiving because we will always be saying it. If the Christian hope is well founded, then there will come a time when the Lord's Prayer itself will be obsolete—why pray "thy kingdom come" once it comes?—but thanksgiving can never be obsolete. At the point of consummation, it can only be more real. I believe the same is true for help, and not for help only; I think it is true of work and art and sexual love. When the prophet Isaiah talks about people one day beating their swords into plowshares, he is not only prophesying a time of peace, he is suggesting that although we can envision a paradise without weapons, we would be hard-pressed to endure a paradise without tools. We will always want plowshares, and we will always want someone to share in the plowing. We will always want help.

We see this as soon as people have leisure. Among men in my neck of the woods there is a Saturday morning custom of going around to friends' houses to assist them in various projects—one week someone's garage roof, the next week someone else's woodpile. They launch their pickups like a fleet of little tugboats; they rumble past our windows in the morning fog. In this world every man is an island, but no man is alone. In certain cases, I suspect, less work gets shared than beer, but every case (and six-pack) involves conversation, the telling of new jokes and old stories. A good weekend for these men is to labor and wander and commune at will, both breaking the Sabbath and fulfilling it on a fairly high level. For me, these cycles of visitation are as much a vision of heaven as anything in a liturgy. But part of what makes the vision so beatific is the reciprocal and gratuitous nature of the help. These men are not ministering to the helpless, an activity in which the solitary Samaritan is also helpless—that is, beyond the mutuality implied by the word *help*—they are helping. And when they've had enough, they go home.

And with that we come back to Emerson and Thoreau and that secret yearning for privacy and autonomy that Didion called the dream we no longer admit. Side by side with that dream is a dream we no longer *believe*, though we admit it to the point of protest: the dream of a just society, where all enjoy the fruits of their own labor, and—to use the imagery of another Hebrew prophet—sit in the shade of their own fig trees. Where people eat soup with their own spoons, from a common pot, perhaps, but always with their own spoons. In this dream everyone has enough, including enough help, which means that in place of giving charity, people are living it.

Ironically, it is the domesticated, retiring part of me that is most strongly drawn to that sociable vision. "To be happy at home," Samuel Johnson said, "is the ultimate result of all ambition." Howard Hughes would probably have agreed; Thoreau, without a doubt. If I did needlepoint, I'd stitch it on a pillow and sit on it. But no one can be happy at home who hasn't a home. And no one can be happy at home when there are homeless huddling outside the door. Only when my neighbor is housed and clothed and otherwise cared for can I have any real hope of a truly private life. Only when no one has been left out in the cold can I be left alone in peace. That may be a cold way to put it but perhaps the only way to put it that doesn't leave me cold.

Might it be, then, that the way to realize a more sociable and helpful society is in fact *through* the dream we no longer admit? At least for those of us who still harbor the dream. That is to suggest, not that we become small-scale imitators of Howard Hughes, but rather that we understand the cause-and-effect relationship between justice and a decent solitude.

A part of that understanding means that we embrace not only the suffering necessary to erase suffering, but pleasure as well. That too is a dream that wants admitting. Katie Carr *does* need the Discman, and though she seems to have taken her cue from the aestheticism of the Bloomsbury Group, she might just as easily have taken it from the saints and bodhisattvas and from the missionaries too, from Dr. Schweitzer and his pipe organ in the jungle, from Dr. Paul Farmer and his love of a good hotel—even from the provident orders of Florence Nightingale that the hospital orderlies in the Crimean War be allotted "a pint of porter a day," God bless her. Otherwise, how shall we find the unflagging gratitude that motivates a person like Nerese and that Nietzsche said was the foundation of all great art? We think of ourselves as a hedonistic society; would that we were. Hypocrisy is not hedonism. Our hypocrisy is to hoard our private pleasures and feel guilty about them at the same time, instead of relishing them in such a way that we wish—and work—for all to have their share. We suck on bitter figs when we might be planting fig trees.

Perhaps this is the meaning of that peculiar story in which Mary of Bethany anoints the head of Jesus with an expensive perfume while Judas criticizes her for wasting what might have been sold to benefit the poor. Judas has a point, we think, and we're surprised and even offended that Jesus doesn't think so too. "The poor you have with you always," he says, noting that he will not always be around to receive such favors. In its context, the story works best as a riddle, and its solution might go something like this: Until you can accept the favor of a particular kindness (as Nerese did), until you can profess your own sense of honest entitlement (*that jacket was a gift from my girlfriend*) without guilt and without caving in to anyone else's moralistic carping, you will always have poverty staring you in the face. "The poor will always be with you." Only when you have embraced the dream you no longer admit will you be able to love—and help—your neighbor as yourself.

THOSE WHO
HAVE HANDS

I have a simple explanation for why a book like *Samaritan* or *How to Be Good* or even *Walden* (also known as *Life in the Woods*) rises up now and then to cross-examine our benevolence. The reason is that, with the notable exception of a few titles mostly confined to best-seller lists, books tend to be written by writers.

Like many theories, mine may amount to a case of psychological projection. Since leaving my work as a teacher several years ago and my part-time position as a parish priest within this past year, I have been increasingly concerned with the meaning of help. Not that I wasn't concerned about it before. But then it was defining me, and now I feel a need to define it, which may include a need to justify a life of greater withdrawal from the needs of human beings.

I have sometimes imagined an accusation coming from some of my former colleagues—though this may be a projection also—"If everyone did what you did, chucking it all to stay home and write, what a miserable world this would be." Of course if everyone did what *anyone* did, the world would be miserable. If everyone did what Jesus did, the world would die out in a generation. Still, if that response satisfied me, I'm not sure I'd be writing on the subject of help. Dorothy Day was no ordinary writer—she probably didn't see herself primarily as a writer— but she strikes a familiar chord when she says in her autobiography, *The Long Loneliness,* "The sustained effort of writing . . . when there are human beings around who need me . . . is a harrowingly painful job."

But writing is not only a job but a metaphor. Many occupations are. Socrates spoke of himself as a midwife, meaning he was a teacher, though by trade he was a mason. I recently spoke with a man who compared himself to a mason though by trade he was a doctor. Part of the social value of a profession consists of its usefulness in analogy. The ultimate dismissal for a given line of work is not to say that there's no money in it but that there's no poetry in it.

Actually, there is little enough poetry in being a poet, but what there is can be instructive. On the one hand, it is hard to imagine a profession more solitary and self-contained than a writer's. "Don't you ever get lonely?" a friend will ask. The fact is, if I don't get lonely on a fairly regular basis, I don't get paid. That is true to some extent for all of us; we have to inhabit a certain solitude in order to mind the store, feed the chickens, fry the eggs. If we step too readily into human fellowship, or linger there too long, we cease to work at all. Even the counselor, the professional confidante, has to maintain a certain aloofness in order to be effective. Get too chatty, and your client may never get to the thing that happened when he was eight.

On the other hand, unless a writer began as a wunderkind whose rise to prominence was of such force and velocity as to leave him permanently stuck to the firmament, there are few professions where one is more dependent upon the willingness of others to give help. Ours is an economy of favors. Few writers can stand at a bar and say, "Nobody ever helped me"—except those who are at the bar for the most depressing reasons. Those with a new book to toast generally have a page for listing acknowledgments.

This means that every petitioner who comes to a writer, including every aspirant with a manuscript in hand, is both a threat to the work and a poignant reminder of one's basic working requirements.

In that regard, the writing life is a metaphor for the helping life, for the *life* life. He travels fastest who travels alone, but one who's always alone doesn't travel far. We all have to negotiate that paradox—and beyond that, we have to determine how the help we have or have not received is to inspire our own standards of helpfulness. That may be one of the more important either-or distinctions between one person and another, as when we say, "Basically, there are two types of people. . . ." Except for *cruel* and *kind*, I know of no types more basic than these: the people who say, "I had a hard time coming up, and I want to make it easier for someone else," and the people who say, "I had a hard time coming up, so why should I help someone else have it any easier?" Isolate the causes of that distinction, and you deserve a Nobel Prize.

The patron saint of helpful writers is Dr. Johnson, who left us such an unsparing definition of *patron*. He lived at a time when the profession of writing was relatively new and already precarious. A well-known painting shows him reading the manuscript of Oliver Goldsmith's *Vicar of Wakefield* while the author sits nearby in suspense and a bathrobe and his landlady stands just outside the door. One of their contemporaries, a poet, fell on such hard times that he pawned all his clothes; he would sit naked on his bed, covered by a sheet in which he had cut holes for his writing arm and his head. Johnson's fortunes never sank so low, but he knew what it meant to walk the streets for a whole night because he could not afford a place to sleep. He never forgot those watches. He never saw his own path to success as a pretext for recommending hardship. His generosity in the form of loans, endorsements, and editorial help extended to writers of all kinds—minor, mad, or female. And not to writers only. He was well known, and behind his back ridiculed, for maintaining a household "menagerie" of unfortunates, including a Doctor Levitt, who dispensed medicines among the London poor, often returning from his rounds inebriated by what his patients had offered in trade. Both late sleepers, the two men took their breakfast together every day around noon.

Walking the streets of the city at night, Johnson would press pennies into the hands of sleeping urchins, apparently not so convinced as Emerson that charity was a wicked coinage. Asked why he gave to beggars, he retorted, "so they might beg *on*." When a friend of mine asked why I was writing this book, I cited Johnson and said, "so a reader might find some reason to *help* on."

That friend is also a writer and one of the most generous people I know. As with Johnson, his willingness to help goes well beyond any sense of vocational solidarity, though he has plenty of that. He once searched for days for a local untouchable who went missing, continuing long after the state police had given up and until the man was found at last (dead in a ditch). "I have never felt disconsolate or forlorn

in the act of helping someone," he once told me. I know that he is
telling the truth. I also know that he is fond of a good story. The very
word *story* conjures his respect. I'm not about to suggest that he helps
in order to get someone else's story, but rather that someone else's
story always has a way of getting to him.

There is a strong connection, I think, between the love of stories
and the love of one's fellow human beings. Both demand patience and
the faith that a satisfying outcome is possible—a desire that is even
stronger than faith. Can you imagine a true misanthrope who liked to
read novels? Only a handful of that tribe ever wrote them. The parable
of the good Samaritan is a story. The wounded man encountered on
the road is indicative of a story too, with a familiar beginning, a mysterious middle, and a to-be-determined end. To help is to step into
someone's story, which can be of special solace for a writer, who is so
often stalled or sequestered within her own.

Most aspiring writers are people who have a story to tell; so too are
most panhandlers on the street. Anyone who's taken altruism off campus, so to speak, knows that life on the margins is made bearable by
two basic types of stimulant: chemical and narrative. The latter comes
in familiar genres: the told-off boss, the forfeited fortune, the filial
blessing. "Then my daddy sat me down and said, 'Son . . .'" A daddy
who may never have existed beyond the hypothesis of ejaculation.
Those with a trained ability to suspend disbelief, or a journalistic compulsion to probe the unbelievable, are easily hooked. Joseph Mitchell
wrote two wonderful accounts—"Professor Seagull" (1942) and "Joe
Gould's Secret" (1964)—about his attempts to help out, and figure out,
a freeloading bohemian who claimed to have written an immense
"Oral History of Our Time." Eventually Mitchell discovers Gould's
secret—but Gould had probably discovered Mitchell's long before. He
would have discovered mine over our first cup of coffee. I may never
be able to walk into Elaine's and be recognized as a writer, but I can
scarcely walk into a bus station without being recognized as someone
with a writer's weakness, that is, with the ability to take in large quanti-
ties of bullshit.

Maybe some of that capacity grows out of one's own fears. Reading
Mitchell's stories, I found that I identified with Gould no less than with
the author. "There but for the grace of God go I" has an especially omi-

nous resonance for those in artistic professions, an implicit *will* ghosting the *go*. I've yet to meet a mentally ill person who didn't have a literary bent. When someone dies lacking the proverbial pot to piss in, he leaves his heirs a journal. Debbie Sunn left me hers. When you're young, you think the best way to have literary conversations is to get a job in a bookstore; after a summer of selling cat books, you're cured of that. A few years older but hardly less naive, you might even go to graduate school. A wider experience of the world brings the knowledge that if you want to talk about Shakespeare and Dostoyevsky with people who've read them as if they really mattered, the place to go is the upper floor of a mental hospital or graveyard shift at a glue factory—in other words, to the very place you fear you may be headed yourself.

And let us not forget prison. For a relatively brief period in the last century, it seemed as if writers and prisoners were about to form some tragic new alliance. William F. Buckley, Norman Mailer, and William Styron all acted as patrons of paroled felons, each attempt ending in disaster. Of course, the alliance was nothing new. For one thing, writers and prisoners have frequently been the same people. No surprises there: the job of telling the truth can get you into jail; a life of solitary confinement can get you into literature. But the cases I mentioned all had to do with the searching nature of stories, the need to tell them, hear them, and follow them wherever they might go—most of all, with the need to be believed. Writers and convicts go together as naturally as a gigolo and an heiress, and for many of the same reasons.

The most interesting and infamous of these stories has to do with Norman Mailer and the convicted killer and author Jack Abbott. When Abbott died in 2002 at the age of fifty-eight, roughly twenty years after the controversy surrounding his name, he was already a footnote. Norman Mailer and Jack Abbott—it was all so eighties, so *then*. Just that reaction is illuminating. Our hesitance to revisit is not unrelated to our hesitance to help. We don't mind giving to others; it's just that the thing we most like to give them is closure. But even the good Samaritan revisits. "When I come back," he tells the innkeeper, "I will repay you whatever more you spend."

The Abbott story is simply told, though nothing about it is simple. When Jack Abbott learned that Norman Mailer was at work on *The*

Executioner's Song, based on the life of death row inmate Gary
Gilmore, he wrote to the author from prison offering to provide him
with background material on the violent culture of penal institutions.
Abbott had spent most of his life incarcerated—he described himself as
a "state-reared" convict—and was currently serving a twenty-year sentence for the stabbing death of another inmate. He and Mailer corre-
sponded for four years, from 1978 to 1981, before Abbott was released
on parole. During that time Mailer had shown some of Abbott's letters
to an editor at the *New York Review of Books,* which eventually published a selection. This led to a contract with Random House that
would result in Abbott's first book, *In the Belly of the Beast.* It appeared
just weeks after his release.

In spite of popular perceptions, Mailer's part in getting Abbott
paroled was minimal. He had written a letter of support to the parole
board. He had also promised Abbott a job as a research assistant after
he got out. Mailer actually seems to have been surprised when the parole board, acting in spite of evidence suggesting that Abbott was "a
potentially dangerous man," released him from his Utah prison in June
of 1981. Mailer picked him up at the airport; he was temporarily settled in a halfway house on the Lower East Side.

After some initial reluctance on the part of Mailer's wife, the Mailers entertained Abbott at their home in Brooklyn. They also had him
stay with them in Provincetown. There was even talk of building him a
small retreat on the Cape or in Maine once he was permitted to leave
the halfway house. These are important details, I think—the ones I
was doubting I would find when I first read about this affair. I wanted
to know: Did Abbott have fellowship, and did he have something to
look forward to? It seems he had both. There are other questions,
though. How much of both would he have required to make it? And
would any amount have made a difference?

He hated where he was living, and I find nothing in my sources to
explain the wisdom of confining him there. (Perhaps I should consult
my own degree of receptivity should someone suggest building a
halfway house on my idyllic road.) The neighborhood was full of dere-
licts. Abbott saw a stabbing and the firebombing of a car. The expensive suit he had purchased on his release ("a three-piece navy

pinstripe" that "resembled one of Mailer's") was stolen. He began carrying a knife.

Just six weeks after Abbott's release from prison, and at an hour well past his curfew, he got into a disagreement with Richard Adan, a twenty-two-year-old Cuban American waiter at the restaurant where Abbott was keeping company with two women. The details remain unclear, but apparently Adan invited Abbott to step outside. Abbott's original impression was that Adan was "coming on" in an aggressive way and that he had grabbed a weapon of some kind on his way out. Another waiter later claimed that Adan had invited Abbott outside to urinate, since customers were forbidden to pass through the kitchen to the restroom. Abbott would accept that explanation, and he revised his recollections in its light. An investigating detective was more dubious; he suspected that Adan had asked Abbott outside to calm him down.

Believing or claiming to have believed that Adan was going to attack him in the alley, Abbott stabbed him in the heart. Adan was unarmed. He died almost instantly—smiling. He was a husband, an actor, a budding playwright. According to the chief investigating detective, he "never carried a weapon, never drank heavily, didn't use narcotics, not even marijuana. He was the type of person who always interceded when other people were having problems." On the same day as the stabbing, the *New York Times* review of Abbott's book appeared: "out of nowhere comes an exceptional man with an exceptional literary gift." No one, it seems, had fully fathomed the depths of *nowhere*.

Abbott was eventually captured in New Orleans and tried. Acting contrary to the pleas of family and friends, Mailer offered to testify for the defense. He did not want Abbott released, at least for a while, but he was also not ready to write him off. He stated publicly that he hoped Abbott would not receive the maximum sentence. At an explosive press conference Mailer made several inflammatory statements, including a remark that "culture is worth a little risk." A reporter told him he was full of shit.

Abbott was convicted of manslaughter and sentenced to fifteen years to life. He would eventually come to the conclusion that Mailer and he were "class enemies." Had Richard Adan survived, he might have come to the conclusion that he and Mailer were fraternal twins.

Among the legion of ironies that attended the case, that may have been the most pronounced and the least noted. Everyone saw the identification between Abbott and Mailer—and in this they were simply following Mailer's own lead. The greater similarity may have been between Mailer and Adan. Both had been minding their own business when Abbott appeared in their lives. Both had tried to help in a situation that turned out to be more than they could handle.

The distinction of having written the great American novel is up for grabs, but the great American story of freelance philanthropy turned sour may belong to Norman Mailer. All the classic elements are there. Anyone who was ever burned in a transaction of this kind can easily draw up the list.

The appeal to the power that is in our hands. We talk about help as empowerment—of "the other"—but its motivating thrill often has to do with the enhanced sense of our own potency. Recently a physician said to me, "You really *can* help people," as though he were delivering a revelation. I required no gloss on his emphasis. I have never succeeded in helping anyone, especially someone in dire need, without a sense that I was defying gravity. I have never gone hang gliding, but I know exactly how it feels: the heady sensation that the given limits are more permeable than they seem.

Abbott had been sent to reform school as a child. He had spent a total of six weeks of his adult life in the outside world. His fate seemed sealed from the beginning. Yet he had more than a spark of talent. And the talent was of a kind that Mailer was perfectly placed to champion. He could move a mountain with a phone call. If you want to understand more about the psychology of help, stop by someone's lakeside bungalow and announce that you're on a desperate mission that requires a boat. It is not only your appeal to the cottage owner's humanity that lights up his eyes, but your appeal to his equipment. You have offered to bless possession with purpose.

What works with a boat works even more powerfully with a talent. People who disparaged Mailer as though he had practiced a kind of incestuous altruism—"Of *course,* he would help another *writer*"—were missing the point. Who was he better able to help? Not only that, he was also trying to be more than a writer. He was trying to reach beyond the debased usury of making money out of words. No less than a doctor or a nurse, Mailer wanted to help another person *through his skill.* This is not to say that Mailer wasn't missing something; it is only to appreciate the poignant solipsism in what he was missing. He himself would see it in the end:

I was so egocentric about it. I saw it as a test for myself rather than a test for strangers. Part of the shock of it afterwards was to have looked at it so narrowly.

The appeal to conscience. We recall Schweitzer's unbearable sense of having what others lacked. That can include the privilege of a second chance. At a 1960 party to announce his candidacy for the mayorality of New York, a drunk Mailer stabbed his second wife, Adele. She was hospitalized but recovered. What if she had died? Jack Abbott was Mailer's version of "There but for the grace of God . . ." Of course there wasn't an amateur psychologist at the time of Abbott's trial who missed that connection, though it gets missed in other places all the time. "He who is without sin let him cast the first stone" is interpreted by a certain kind of guilty conscience as an obligation to pass out stones. So the teacher who cheated as a student wonders if he ought to grant an amnesty to his students who cheat. ("I saw it as a test for myself rather than a test for strangers.")

The conflict with family. Mailer's wife, Barbara Norris, was adamant at first about not wanting Abbott in their house or around the children. "You wrote the book about Gilmore," she told her husband. "Didn't you learn anything? It's not gonna work, these guys don't change." We can call it natural or we can call it strange that the altruistic impulse, which is not unlike the urge to procreate—both are about the desire for "others"—is so often at variance with it. We bring a homeless person into our house, and we bring children into the world, but either the house is too small or the world is too nuts. Trying to combine parenthood with philanthropy often feels like speaking a sentence with double negatives (though you are trying to juggle two positive values): you always wind up saying the opposite of what you meant.

Ironically, Norris seems to have invested at least as much time in helping Abbott adjust to his new life as Mailer did. Abbott found it easier to talk to her than to Mailer. He called her almost every day. After the stabbing, Norris wanted nothing more to do with him and wanted Mailer to sever his connection as well. But for a time she had fallen under the spell—a rather cheesy way of saying that she had acted with humanity—cast partly by her vulnerable dinner guest and partly by her indomitable husband. And this too has its familiar ring, its special psychology. We can fall into the altruistic ambitions of the people we have fallen in love with, or, on the receiving end of help, we can fall in love with the people our benefactors have fallen in love with (though there is no evidence to suggest that Abbott was in love with Mailer's wife). Altruism makes the strangest bedfellows—often out of people who are already in the same bed.

The appeal of the little child. This was one of the first things Norris noticed when Abbott came to dinner. "He was very sweet, very touching, because he was nervous and almost like a little boy." Abbott himself had said in a letter to Mailer, "At thirty-seven I am barely a precocious child." I have been told by someone who works extensively with traumatic brain injuries (TBI) that the person who sustains such an injury in childhood is often arrested at that level of emotional development. If other kinds of childhood trauma influence the development of criminality, we perhaps should not be too surprised—or too easily disarmed—by the childlike qualities of a killer. But if the killer has the heart of a child, what does it mean to have the heart of an adult? Is it not to respond to the plight of children? This may hold some clue to the mysterious symbiosis of abusive relationships: the violent partner is also "the child," and what mother will desert her child?

We are predisposed culturally no less than biologically to respond to "the child." Our souls have genes. "Whoever does not receive the kingdom of God as a little child will never enter it." The Baal Shem Tov is supposed to have had a dream in which he saw an evil heart. He pummeled it with his fist, and out came the sob of a little child. A powerful insight, but the Besht lived in the age before sequels. In *Evil Heart II* he sets the child free. The child then stabs the Baal Shem Tov.

The susceptibility to manipulation. Jack Abbott "was playing [Norman] like a violin," according to Jere Herzenberg, one of Mailer's assistants, who perhaps was unable to realize how beautiful it is to be a violin in a business where one is forever blowing his own horn. The impression that someone we love or respect is being manipulated—which by no means requires the presence of a paroled felon, merely an irritable child and two different levels of parental tolerance—creates its own alienation. The person who suspects the manipulation thinks, "Can't he see that he's being used?" while the person being manipulated thinks, "Can't she see that it doesn't matter? That it's better to be used than to feel useless?" As for the alleged user, he is thinking, "If they really loved me, would I need to pluck so many strings for just a little music?" This is the shadow side of charity, as of procreation: we come together in order to discover how much we are alone.

The appeal of narrative—inevitably followed by the discovery of certain narrative flaws. Shortly after Abbott's release from Marion State Prison, another inmate from the same facility wrote a letter to the *New York Review of Books* claiming that Abbott had been a paid informant, "a snitch." Mailer confronted Abbott with this. Abbott claimed that he had only informed on the attorneys of certain inmates. Detective William Majeski, who investigated the Adan murder, made an interesting point in this regard: "I wouldn't say [Mailer] was naïve—that isn't the appropriate term. But I think what Norman failed to do was make a separation between the man's literary ability and his personality, his capabilities outside the literary realm." As for the product of that literary ability, Majeski had this assessment: "I had read Abbott's book a half dozen times, and that's one of the things I confronted him with. He asked me if I'd read it, and I said, 'Yes, and although I think it's well written, I must tell you I think it's bullshit.'"

One doesn't have to be a detective to have a nose for bullshit, but it takes a certain hard-boiled courage to call bullshit by its name. Norris offered one of the more telling reflections on the entire episode when she said, "[Abbott] also told me some wild stories. . . . But I never turned to him and said, 'I don't believe you,' because I just didn't feel like getting into an argument." If commiseration ever takes the form of absolution, then Barbara, my child, thou art absolved.

The discovery of the bottomless pit. I am convinced that those fables about peasant families who rescue some cub, kit, or baby giant who grows to eat them out of house and home originate in the folk experience of giving asylum. Remember that inscription on the ring that was given to Oscar Schindler: "Whoever saves a single soul saves the world entire"? This is the other side of the proverb: A whole world resides inside a single soul. In a person like Jack Abbott, it amounts to a world of need. William Blake said, "He who would do good to another must do it in Minute Particulars." The particulars in this case were staggering. Abbott didn't know where to buy toothpaste. He was laughed at for trying to purchase it in a hardware store. He didn't know how to order food in a restaurant. He was baffled by a subway turnstile. He had missed the creation of the world.

Nor did his needs consist entirely of particulars. He was aware of broader, less tangible needs. In one of his prison letters he would say to Mailer, "No one, not even you . . . has ever held out a hand to help me to be a better man. No one."

You could write a whole book based on that one sentence. You might say Abbott's complaint stands as the ultimate indictment of do-goodism in all its forms, both individual and institutional. All too often, we help in order to certify our own righteousness. I am not talking about Mailer; I am talking about me. You too? We want to establish that we are good people. That this is a great society. Peter Maurin, the founder of the Catholic Worker Movement and a mentor to Dorothy Day, was closer to the mark: "We need to build a society where it is easier for people to be good." In other words, it's not about us. The most authentic altruism desires not only the good of other people, but also their goodness—as true love is said to bring out the best in a lover—and it honestly believes that the potential for such goodness exists.

This is why kids respond to demanding teachers and despise those too ready to lower the bar. It is why people who benefit most from traditionally liberal programs can sometimes be the most openly contemptuous of liberals. They suspect, not without reason, that an abundance of compassion betrays a dearth of confidence.

And yet, in the context of all that followed, Abbott's charge was outrageous. I find myself wanting to stand in for Mailer to answer it. Of course the desire says more about me than about him.

Look, I never set about trying to make you a better man. Even a person with an ego as big as the one I'm reputed to have would pause at that. Helping you to be a better man would presuppose that I knew what a good man was and that I lived up to my own standards. But I never approached you in that guise. I'm not a missionary. I'm not a candidate for anyone's book of virtues. Should I have refused to help you for that reason?

But let's pretend that things were different. Let's say that I did think of myself as a good man capable of making other men good. How would I go about that? What would be the concrete steps? I assume the program might include, for starters, staking my reputation on the belief that you could be a better man, or at least could avoid becoming any worse.

I assume that the program would include helping you develop your talent, which in your case as in mine has to do with writing, and which in any case is the best way I know for doing good in the world.

And I assume that helping another man to be good would involve acquainting him with the nearest approximation to goodness that I have experienced. I don't know many swamis; I doubt I could have gotten you an audience with the pope. But I introduced you to my wife, and one of my children met you at the door of my home and took your hand. It was the best I had.

What else?

What else, because Mailer did all of the above. It is a good question, and the only thing in my imaginary monologue that comes close to an actual quotation. "One way or another," Mailer would say, "and I don't know how, I should have been doing more with Abbott."

According to the twelfth-century Jewish sage Rabbi Moses ben Maimon (Rambam, for short), there are eight levels of giving, an ethical hierarchy that is the subject of Julie Salamon's recent book, *Rambam's Ladder*. The lowest level is "to give begrudgingly." The highest is "to hand someone a gift or loan, or to enter into a partnership with him, or to find work for him, so that he will never have to beg again." According to that schema Mailer stood on the highest rung of generosity.

There is, however, another ladder corresponding to this one; let us say for the sake of symmetry that it also contains eight rungs, though I haven't actually made a count. Each rung represents a level of blame that accrues to the giver when someone the giver has helped falls or leaps off Rambam's Ladder. The order of the rungs is not the inverse of Rambam's order but exactly parallel—at least by popular reckoning. Had Mailer begrudgingly written a letter of recommendation to Abbott's parole board and left it at that, no one would have said he had blood on his hands. At most he would have been derided for some ill-advised offtrack betting—even though, under the circumstances, that would have been a far more reckless approach than the one he took.

Mailer's ladder goes higher than Rambam's. Blame reaches beyond benevolence. In a Jack-and-the-Beanstalk stretch of the popular imagination, Mailer soon became "the person who got Abbott out." In fact, Mailer had done no such thing. If the allegations that Abbott had worked as a snitch are true, then Mailer's influence may have been almost moot as a deciding factor.

What is most interesting for our purposes is the way in which *help*—a word that connotes the partial and provisional—gets interpreted as total agency in the case of any notable outcome. Thus Annie Sullivan made Helen Keller. Abraham Lincoln freed the slaves. Norman Mailer sprung Jack Abbot from jail. A writer who was almost unable to convince his own wife that Abbott was a safe bet for dinner was apparently able to hypnotize an entire parole board, not a one of whom, I would wager, had read two or perhaps even one of his books. If the priest and the Levite in the parable of the good Samaritan give an extra wide berth to the man wounded by robbers, it may be because they know exactly who's going to take the rap if the schmuck wakes up and turns out to be a robber too.

Mailer himself seems to have embraced this skewed interpretation of his own agency. More than once he would state publicly that he had blood on his hands. Putting things in their best light, we would say that he showed an admirable willingness to shoulder responsibility. And yet, we can take responsibility as thoughtlessly as we might take a killer home for lunch. Credit and blame are almost always exaggerations, and people who help others do their work within an inflationary economy. After a while, they may have trouble knowing the true weight of their own acts. Depending on the nature of the miscalculation, the result is either grandiosity or some form of despair (which can also take the form of grandiosity).

It is perhaps too obvious to mention, but let's mention it anyway: the fact that perceived sins of commission are less readily forgiven than those of omission. A thousand acts of calculated neglect and blind inattention go to make a Jack Abbott, but when the bill comes due, we are most likely to send it to the last person who befriended him. Had Zacchaeus the tax collector recovered from his spell of penitence and gone back to his life of petty extortion, it would have been *all* Jesus's fault for calling him down from the tree.

Without a doubt, Mailer invited some of the calumny that fell on him, especially through some of his provocative remarks during the time of the trial. When at his disaster of a press conference Mailer said, "I'm willing to gamble with a portion of society to save this man's talent," a reporter from the *New York Post* pointedly asked which portions he had in mind. Waiters? Cubans? Things did not go calmly after that.

I find that single exchange almost more telling and certainly more ironic than anything else that was reportedly said during the Abbott affair. It is ironic to hear Mailer, who so often assumed the stance of a rebel, speak the ethos of "the system," indeed of all systems, an ethos expressed so strikingly by those Aztec priests who cut out the living hearts of their victims as a sacrifice to the sun. In actuality they were making a sacrifice to the pyramids. They were re-presenting the way in which the grand projects of a privileged few always factor out a dispensable portion of the anonymous many. Show me a pyramid, and I'll show you a basket of hearts.

What was even more ironic, though, was the howl of indignation that arose in response to Mailer's statement. How *dare* he say it aloud, even though what he said amounted to little more than a simple statement of a ubiquitous policy? In fact, Mailer ventured a clumsy comparison between his actions on behalf of Abbott and the risks Americans were willing to take with nuclear weapons. He needn't have resorted to such hyperbole; he need only have pointed to the practice of parole itself. Is that not a matter of "gambling with a certain portion of the population"—preferably the portion that lives on the floodplain? Is it the children of lenient judges who usually wind up murdered or raped by repeat offenders? You might as well ask if the theater critic is in any danger of dying in the third act of the play he reviews. Two different dimensions, babe. Two different worlds. Mailer's remarks about risk were childish in the sense that he showed the poor taste of saying something we all knew and with which we had all made our uneasy peace, much like the kid who interrupts the family seder to remark on her boozy uncle's smell.

That is not to say that his remarks should not have been challenged, much less that they should not challenge us. Within their context, Mailer's inflammatory statements ("culture is worth a little risk") together with his more remorseful statements later on ("I saw it as a test for myself rather than a test for strangers") join the parable of the good Samaritan as glosses on that troublesome commandment: "Love your neighbor as yourself." They restate the question that the lawyer asked Jesus: "Who is my neighbor?" And they challenge our tendency to conceive of "neighbor" only in the singular. For there is always the danger that we will love the neighbor to the detriment of the neighborhood. There is always the danger, perhaps unavoidable given our fallibility and interconnectedness, that we will carry our charitable purchases to the topmost steps of Rambam's Escalator, only to discover that we have been shopping with someone else's credit card. In this case it happened to be Richard Adan's.

Aside from visiting one of my former students several times during his ninety days in a minimum-security lockup, I've had little experience with the felonious side of life. Only once was I offered a watered-down opportunity of "doing a Mailer." I immediately declined. Following our metaphors back the way we came, we might say that the difference between my reluctance and Mailer's willingness to go where angels fear to tread is analogous to the difference between a minor writer and a major one. Actually, it was not as a writer that I was approached but as a priest, which may mean that we need to double the accent on *minor*.

The request came from a deacon within my denomination. She was calling on behalf of an evangelical minister who was trying to help a recent parolee. The man had been falsely accused of killing his wife, she said, and now that he was out, his in-laws were hounding him wherever he went. While in prison, he had embraced the Christian faith. He had read the Bible from cover to cover. The deacon wanted to know if anyone in my parish might be willing to put him up for a while as part of an attempt to get the avenging relatives off his trail.

I said that unfortunately I would not be able to ask any of my

parishioners for the simple reason that I myself had serious reservations about bringing a convicted murderer, whom I had never met,
under the same roof with my wife and child. As a general rule, I told
her, I did not ask people in my parish to take risks that I was not willing to take myself.

This was all true enough, though I should probably confess that I
have a certain prejudice about prison conversions. It is not that I doubt
they take place or that I do not respect them when they do, only that I
assume an authentic religious conversion would result in someone
wanting to serve out his sentence rather than in asking to have it reduced—especially with conversion as the keynote of his argument.
Perhaps I have an overly Catholic sense of penitence. In this case, the
man's conversion may have had nothing to do with his parole, and anyway he was purportedly innocent. Still, my hunch was that if I was getting the Jesus pitch now, others had heard it before me. Some of that
bias might have come through in my voice.

The deacon was undaunted. She said that I needed to present the
situation to people in my parish and let them make up their own
minds. I couldn't decide for them. She could understand my reluctance
to involve a household with children, but perhaps there was "a single
person" who would agree to take this on.

At that point I began to get annoyed. For one thing, I resented the
insinuation that a single person might somehow be more expendable
than a member of a family. For another, the business about letting people make up their own minds was typical clergy cant.

"It's not like I'm the guy next door. I'm the person who preaches to
them every Sunday. In a few cases, I'm the person who's heard them
make confession of their sins. As much as I've urged them to put all of
that in perspective, it's likely that for certain overly scrupulous people—in other words, the very same people who always get hit up for
stuff like this—saying no to me is going to feel like saying no to God.
The request is loaded from the get-go."

I felt it was time to cut to the chase. "Look, I'm not willing to take
this guy in, I'm sorry, and for that reason I'm not willing to ask someone else to do it either. But this is what I will do. I'll pick him up wherever he is, I'll take him to a decent motel, and I'll get him settled. I'll
pay for one or two nights' stay out of my discretionary fund. I'll see he

gets something to eat. I'll be on call while he's there, and I'll get him safely to his next destination. How's that?" (Pretty darn good, I thought.)

She said I'd need to speak to the prison evangelist who had contacted her. So I called him and repeated my offer. To my surprise, the man said nothing to manipulate my conscience; in fact, I found him easier to deal with than the deacon. Thanking me for my concern, he said that he and his colleagues preferred to have the man stay at a household. It was important to provide him with the warmth of human company. I understood all that, of course, but there was the small matter of his alleged crime.

"He did not kill his wife," the minister reminded me. "He did confess to cutting up the body, that's true, but he is not a murderer."

"Excuse me?"

"When he found the body, he was afraid he would be the one blamed for the crime, so he panicked and did a very foolish thing. But he is a different man now."

Well, goodness, why hadn't someone explained this to me before? I wasn't being asked to share my roof with a man capable of murdering his wife. All I was being asked to do was to share a roof with a man whose initial reaction to the discovery that someone *else* has murdered his wife is to chop up the corpse into manageable pieces.

I called back the deacon. Did she by any chance know about the chopping-up part? No, actually, she didn't. In fact, she knew very little about the case. She hadn't asked many questions. The call had come to her when she was very busy, and she had not known what to do with it. "I thought that if anyone I knew would be willing to help with this, it would be you, Garret." I'm still not sure how to take that. I was pretty sure I knew how I was meant to take it. Nothing doing.

Guilt came later. I had been pretty short with her. Mostly I had been indignant at the thought that she had taken a whole bunch of my time in order to save some of her own. Still, somebody had called her with the same confidence she had felt in calling me—and with better reason, as it turned out—because she was a fearless old bird. I meant to tell her so the next time we met. That happened to be at some crowded church function, where she looked at me from across the room as if I didn't exist. Still put out with me, I thought. Later I learned she was suffering from the early stages of Alzheimer's. She probably had no idea who I was.

Let's tell another story, because this one is starting to make me depressed. The one that usually comes to mind in connection with this episode is from Zen. An increasingly common ingredient in typical clergy cant. But here goes.

An old woman had sponsored a monk for many years, sending him food and providing him with a small hermitage. In time she began to wonder if her investments were bearing fruit. "I'd like to see what that fellow is learning," she said. So she hired a beautiful young woman to try to seduce the monk. "Go up there and offer yourself to him. Then come and tell me what he did."

After a short time the young woman returned and told the old woman that she had nothing to worry about. She had literally thrown herself at the monk's feet, but he had remained unmoved. He had rebuffed her with these words: "Just as a tree cannot grow from a stone, neither can lust take root in the mind of one who has truly mastered himself."

"He told you that?" the old woman exclaimed. "I'm going to march up there right now and burn down his hut!"

"But wasn't he supposed to resist me?" the young woman asked.

"He didn't have to give in to you," said the old woman, "but he could have shown some sympathy for your need."

I didn't have to bring the parolee home. I didn't have to get out the Bible or hide the meat cleaver. But I could have shown more sympathy, even just told a joke, to a fellow minister at her wit's end who had turned to me because she was as clueless and alone in her work as I frequently was. Sometimes I wonder if that won't emerge as our final indictment, after death or immediately before: not that we failed to assist every paroled felon and addicted moocher who crossed our paths but that we looked on those who were willing to assist with too cold a regard. Or too pat a judgment. Not the unwashed but the scrubbed up, our peers, the ones formed in our own sociological image, just with slightly bigger hearts—those will be the ones we have most let down.

As a friend of the Mailers said after the Abbott thing had blown up in their faces, "There weren't that many people around town who were thinking of picking up the phone to say, 'Norman, can we help?'"

"One way or another, and I don't know how, I should have been doing more with Abbott." We return to that dilemma. Probably Mailer will return to it until he dies. It is hard to imagine that he will ever find a satisfying answer. But I think we know the answer. Don't we? If this were a lecture instead of a book, this is where I'd pause, step from behind the podium, and deliver the question to the audience, pretending for a moment that it was not rhetorical.

"What was the most important thing that Norman Mailer failed to do in the case of Jack Abbott—the one thing that would have made all the difference?"

This is not a matter of historical trivia, I would say. This is, in fact, the one thing we absolutely have to know if we want to help people—especially if we want to be acknowledged and appreciated as helpful individuals.

Pause. Pace. And turn again.

"The essential thing that Norman Mailer failed to do with Jack Abbott was succeed."

I am biased toward people who have blood on their hands, that is to say, who have hands. Of course I want that blood to come from dressing wounds on the road between Jericho and Jerusalem. There are, however, circumstances in which it is unclear, or can be made to seem unclear, whether the blood is the result of the original wound or of botched first aid. I have read that in certain Latin American countries an especially luckless person is referred to as a "poor christ"; in the land of litigation, the good Samaritan is our euphemism for a poor sap.

But aside from that bias, I find that my sympathies and interest lean increasingly toward those people who make help their profession rather than their project. This is true even as (and perhaps because) my own helping activities have recently taken the opposite course. I am necessarily an amateur now. I envy the pros. I don't disagree with what Schweitzer said: "The hidden forces of goodness are embodied in those persons who carry on as a secondary pursuit the immediate personal service which they cannot make their life work." But I also find something attractive in what the Bhagavad Gita says: "Perfect action is called that which is *obligatory*, free from attachment, performed without desire or loathing, by one who does not seek the fruits thereof."

I take *fruits* to mean those of merit, which are harder to claim in conjunction with the fruits of a regular paycheck. As we have seen, people who help in extraordinary circumstances often say, "I was just doing my duty." We may find it easier to trust the modesty of those who say, "I was just doing my job." Part of what makes us critical of Mailer is that he wasn't—though we can see him straining in that direction. To the extent that his profession allowed, he tried to combine altruism with his line of work.

For all of its temptations to arrogance, there is something humbling about a profession. The person who helps for a living has confessed to limitation, that is, to the need for help: for training, remuneration, guidance, even censure. If I had to bet on the various paths of righteousness, I'd sooner put my money on the paid professional who saw herself bound by a code of ethics than on the freelance humanitarian bound only by a sense of her own mission. This is to say no more than that I tend to favor safe bets over big winnings. I also tend to regard a bet as safe in proportion to its lack of glamour. I used to be a schoolteacher. No doubt some of my readers will add, with justice enough, "You still are."

Sometimes when I am asked to speak before an audience of teachers, I invite them to imagine several reputedly great (or grandiose) historical figures engaged in one or more of a teacher's daily tasks. For instance, I tell them, imagine Winston Churchill in charge of a study hall or Mahatma Gandhi as adviser to the cheering squad. Give Napoleon a remedial reading class, or assign Isadora Duncan the task of maintaining order on the bus. My purpose is to show how easily mystique or bravado can be deflated by the typical teaching experience—and, by implication, how great the courage and how admirable the hard-won dignity of teachers who embrace their task. It is interesting, though, how well certain historical figures resist deflation: I can actually imagine Gandhi coaching the cheerleaders (partly as a test of his chastity, no doubt) and doing a pretty decent job or Malcolm X teaching the repeaters of last year's algebra class, in which case X =

single-minded devotion. Brash Mailer might have made the perfect
rhetorical example but for Jack Abbott. With that misadventure he
earned a place in the teachers' lounge. And yet, returning to the point,
I wonder if the misadventure might have been less disastrous had he
been able to help Abbott *as* a teacher, fulfilling his job requirements
before trying to exceed them.

I could say more about teachers, but we had been talking about professions as metaphors for help, and it may be that medicine provides
better metaphors. For one thing, the desire for help is less equivocal
there. The scanner on my car radio bumps into Pink Floyd's "The
Wall" and its children-of-the-damned anthem: "We don't need no education." I never expect to hear a song that says we don't need no peni-
cillin. There may, after all, be atheists in the foxholes, but there are no
relativists in the emergency room. Everyone there believes in the absolute of being well.

But absolute desires demand absolute results. Had Jack Abbott
been Norman Mailer's patient, Mailer would have been sued. Because
medicine implies a compass on which all the cardinal points are
clearly marked, we assume—we insist—that a doctor never be lost at
sea. Our assumption amounts to an interesting twist on Conrad's
statement that "the true place of God begins at any spot a thousand
miles from the nearest land": our belief that anyone sailing those waters had better be God.

I take the highway north from my home for an interview with Dr.
Thomas "Mike" Moseley, a pediatrician who practices close to the
Canadian border, not far from a sign on the interstate marking the
midpoint between the equator and the North Pole. I know the way.
Moseley began caring for our daughter from her second day of life. I
have always liked him. As if to spare me the trouble of articulating my
reasons, he tells me he's not "the Mr. Rogers type" of pediatrician. I
know what he means, but he has more in common with Mr. Rogers
than he thinks. He knows how to talk to kids, for one thing, not as if
he were talking to their parents' imaginary friends. He is gentle in examination, deferential rather than demonstrative, and the gentleness
describes a certain formality. Mr. Rogers always hung up his sweater.

The conditions are optimal for the interview I want. I am getting

Moseley after a full day, a tough week, and more than twenty years of rural practice. I first met him several months before our daughter was born; I am taking her to college in another month. Characteristically—for him and maybe for the best helpers—his tiredness doesn't come out as unguarded cynicism. Instead he repeatedly chokes up—uncharacteristically, I'd have to say—as he begins to talk about the rewards and the challenges of his work, a tally that calls to mind what a Harlem priest once described for me as "a lot of little resurrections and a lot of big death." He apologizes for his show of emotion; he says I am asking him things that he seldom gets to talk about.

"Much of what we're dealing with is so pathetic, so sad, that it takes a lot out of you to keep doing it." Some of that has to do with sick children, much of it with a sick society. His practice includes the poor, "not the romantically poor, just plain goddamn poor." He is not damning them to say so. The phrase comes out in his criticism of another physician who marked his departure from rural practice by publishing a brief memoir in the *Times* in which he presented himself, says Moseley, "as an Albert Schweitzer doing his work among the benighted natives."

I make a mental note of his refusal to assume that sort of posture; still, I keep a running tally of the frustrations. They're partly what I came to hear. They include:

"Kids who come in with Pepsi in a baby bottle at the age of two when they shouldn't have a bottle to begin with."

"Nice guys who, when they become football coaches, call thirteen-year-old boys sissies if they don't hit each other hard enough. And these are the good ones."

Then the ones not so good. Custody battles that are more about punishing spouses than claiming kids. The "criminal" effect this has on children's mental and physical health. The abuse of women that "makes you embarrassed to wear the chromosome."

"Parents who want their kids *fixed*"—usually through pharmacology—even when nothing is wrong. "Three-year-olds are *supposed* to have attention deficit disorder!"

Often what's wrong is that the child has healthy reactions. A little boy is referred to the practice by his teachers; he is not paying attention in school. It turns out that within the same week his grandmother died on the living room couch, his dog got run over by a car, and a part of his house caught fire. In fact, he had been paying very close attention. Most kids do. Moseley provides a generic example:

> Do you read to the kid? "No. I don't read much." How does he spend his time? "He rides a four-wheeler." How do you speak to your wife at home? "Shut up, you fucking bitch." You add all these things together and what do you have? A kid with the attention span of a gnat and the mouth of a stevedore. And the kid's in trouble.

And the doctor is berated for not doing his job by an adult with the same attention span and the same mouth. "I sometimes think that I've offended more people than I've helped."

"If anything gets the best of me it will be the sense that one man's effort is severely compromised by things that he can't really control." I recall what John Berger said in his study of an English country doctor about the disillusionment of working in "a society which is incapable of knowing what a human life is worth." The last sentence of his book reads:

> All I do know is that our present society wastes and, by the slow draining process of enforced hypocrisy, empties most of the lives which it does not destroy: and that, within its own terms, a doctor who has surpassed the stage of selling cures, either directly to the patients or through the agency of a state service, is unassessable.

Yet Berger had called his doctor and entitled his book *A Fortunate Man*, and Moseley seems to think of himself as one. "Doctors don't have a lock on this," he says, "but there are very few jobs where you have both the technical aspect and the intimate human aspect." He speaks of the "day-to-day satisfaction in doing the job well . . . in the same way as if I were a mason, building straight walls, doing things right according to an internal standard." He points to a picture he keeps in his office of a former patient, a girl with a disabling condition, now a grown woman and self-supporting. "Obviously her parents raised her, but especially in that first year, I spent a lot of time helping with that." He says he has seen "lots of kids who seem like they're destined for hell" who manage to defy prediction. And though it was to him that a doctor once said, "If you want gratitude, get a dog," and though Moseley quotes it by way of saying, "You can't do this looking for gratitude," he adds, "Sometimes gratitude finds you in the end. But I also know that people's gratitude bears little relation to the size of the mitzvah. People can be exceedingly grateful for things that seem trivial to me."

I ask him what he does to keep the darkness at bay. I ask on behalf of my readers, with the pretense of disinterestedness that people sometimes use when asking advice from a physician. "You see, I have this friend . . ."

The first thing he says is, "I'm trying to be informed by the insight that people are doing the best that they can. There are a tiny number of sadists, but they are special types of pathology. Even people who hurt their children are usually not setting out to do that. If you keep that in the back of your mind and take a deep breath . . ."

It seems he has given me a rule of thumb as well as a credo, something like those home pregnancy tests you can buy at the drugstore. People in helping fields could use it to test the viability of their own occupations. If you can sustain the insight that people are doing the best they can—if you can maintain some faith that this *is* an insight— you're solid. If not, maybe you should pack it in. Either your perceptions have become hopelessly jaded or your clients have become hopeless; in either case, there's little point in carrying on.

Needless to say, his insight is not always reciprocated. He speaks of the common belief that "children shouldn't be sick and that all problems can be solved if you know what you're doing," of "men who respond to the sickness of children with anger. It's quite a difference between understanding that and liking to be yelled at and abused."

I ask if he can cite another guiding principle; this time he speaks from the technical side of his profession: "If you only have a choice to be one, it's better to be thorough than to be smart."

He mentions a physician he admires, someone who practiced near where I grew up, William Carlos Williams of Rutherford, New Jersey. From what I know of Williams, he would have been pleased to have

Moseley's assessment for his epitaph: "He lived with the people he cared for. He was a fairly earthy type of fellow. He could be profane, he probably had his failings, but he always showed up." Shortly after our talk, I obtain a copy of Williams's *Autobiography*, in which I find a passage that would undoubtedly resonate with Moseley:

> My own conception of the job has been to consider myself a man in the front line, in the trenches. It's the only way I can respect myself and go on treating what comes to me, men, women, and children. I don't know everything about medicine and surgery but I *must* know well what I do know, besides which I must be thoroughly aware of what I do not know. I can't handle everything but I must never miss anything. I must play the game to win every time, often by referring a case with the greatest possible speed to someone else, get for the patient the finest service I can find in my region.

I can be slow to process, as they say, and it isn't until I am home reading William Carlos Williams that I begin to reflect on how Dr. Moseley worked his own questions into our interview, much as he would during the small talk that accompanies a physical exam— "What did your little sister think of your snowman?" followed by "Can you show me the toe that has the 'picky feeling'?"—asking why I had chosen help for my subject and if it might be seen as the counterpart to misanthropy, about which I'd published an essay not long ago, and how I was going to feel about leaving my church and having no other work but my writing, so that in the process of talking about his own vocation he in fact was making a quiet diagnosis of mine. He had even written me a prescription, which is to say, he had told me that he took encouragement from the life of a doctor who "always showed up," and who was still showing up, even after his death and even this far from Rutherford, New Jersey, because he had also been a writer.

Moseley's chief mainstay is one of the office nurses, who also happens to be his wife. One of my reasons for talking to him, and for meeting with Christine Moseley several weeks later, is that I am especially interested in people who combine domestic partnership and outward service in such a way as to enrich both. The Moseleys met at Boston Children's Hospital where she was a pediatric nurse and he was a bilingual social worker, recently returned from a stint in Venezuela with the Peace Corps. "We met over the supine live body of a little Puerto Rican kid." It is clear to me from talking to him, and will become equally clear when I talk to her, that their relationship is characterized not only by deep regard—"I admire her"—but also by a mutual appreciation of their different strengths.

"She can turn a lot of wrath away with a soft answer."

"I have a smaller bucket of compassion than she does."

"When I ask how people are, I get 'fine.' She gets confession and gives absolution."

He hastens to add, "She is not Pollyanna. She has a pretty hard eye—for my bombastic side and for people who are not doing their best by their kids." In other words, her larger bucket of compassion allows her to qualify the same insight ("people are doing the best they can") that he depends on in order to maintain his "lesser" bucket of the same. Theirs is a fascinating symbiosis.

> I realize some days working with Mike that he has more confidence in me than I have in myself. He believes I could do anything. He was really the first person apart from my grandmother that I had that feeling from. . . . I think we're each other's most loyal supporter.

Christine calls her husband "the most interesting person I ever met"; a third party would say that the distinction was a toss-up between them. For a time she worked doing well-baby care at a Black Panther clinic in Roxbury, Connecticut, the only white person on-site, the only nurse who had applied. She was told in the bluntest terms that as soon as a black nurse could be found, she was gone. (She invites me to imagine how she must have stood out at staff meetings; looking at her ruddy complexion, I recall that Woody Allen line: "I don't tan, I stroke.") "It was my first experience of being marginalized."

After the clinic got shot up one night, the Panthers required all personnel to be armed. Christine refused to carry a gun and was summarily discharged. Her face and name appeared in the Panther newspaper as a persona non grata. As she would later learn when she applied to work for the U.S. Public Health Service in a Native American hospital, her face and name were also on file with the government as a subversive. We laugh together at the double jeopardy, but on reflection I think the Panthers and the Feds had her pretty well pegged. Gentle service is the only true subversion.

Moseley's biography is that of a person who cannot *not* help. As one of her inspirations, she names the renowned Dr. Judah Folkman, a man "who could not *not* teach." She retains a clear memory of him standing in a stairwell at Children's Hospital, drawing pictures in order to explain a certain surgical procedure to a maintenance man.

I ask her about the hard stuff, the things that her husband finds "so pathetic and so sad."

"There are people who hate themselves and who hate their children." She tells me about a young mother she knows, a woman with "a distinctive face, and her children all have her face." One day on the street that runs in front of her church, Moseley saw the woman's boyfriend seize her arm and burn it with a cigarette in front of her children. Christine was frozen with horror while the family moved on. At a subsequent appointment she apologized to the woman for having done nothing.

"Oh, Mrs. Moseley, he would have punched your lights out. He doesn't mind beating up on people."

"But even if he had . . . it would have made a difference. You're a good mom. You take good care of your kids. Do you know what they're learning from this man?"

The woman responded that she could never leave him.

So you do feel hopeless. And then you think that basically the best any of us can do is plant seeds—a seed that says I see you differently. I treat you with respect. I believe there is potential, something lovable and something valuable in you. And some seeds take a really long time to sprout.

Christine is no stranger to hardship. Her father was an "abusive alcoholic" who committed suicide when she was eight. She found the body. Her brother also took his own life. "I got to be a nurse because my mother was a total noncaretaker, so I always got the job." Actually, nursing was only one of three competing aspirations. She had also thought of being an astronaut or a priest. Bad eyesight took care of the first; ecclesiastical backwardness effectively ruled out the second, at least when she was growing up. Religious faith continues to play a significant part in her life.

> There are people I can't talk to without praying. Someone's on line two—I close my eyes and say "Help." I try, like the Quakers talk about, to hear God's voice in that person. Mike claims to have no faith at all. . . . I don't know how he does what he does without praying, because I depend on it. I pray a lot every day. I have a vision of weaving this net of prayer around the community. I always pray for people in the ambulances, and people in the police cars, and the border patrol. I think one of the real blessings of living in this small community is that so many of those people have names. It's not "a state cop." It's John Roberts.

Of course, her net of intercessions also contains a certain agnostic pediatrician, who has told me, "I aspire to but do not possess a theological faith. I say I aspire, because I see that people who have it, like my wife, are better people for it." Says his wife, "Sometimes I think I pray for the both of us."

We had been talking about occupations and metaphors; nursing provides us with a complex type of both. A good nurse is a helper's helper, in the way we once spoke of a man's man (back in the days when we thought a nurse could never be a man). She helps the doctor, and she helps the patient. Sometimes she helps the patient to be independent of the doctor. In churches of the Catholic tradition, the deacon dismisses the congregation after the mass. In that sense the role of nurse is also diaconal; she sends the patient back into the world. Christine says, "I always like the part of nursing that involves helping people have the skills to do it themselves the next time or manage the crisis better the next time."

The nurse is the metaphor of that partner we have mentioned before, the heir of Sancho Panza and Simon Peter, whose help always goes in two directions, toward the one being helped and toward the principal helper. In a sense, Dr. Watson is Sherlock Holmes's nurse. It would be a mistake to attach a certain personality type to the role. In its professional incarnations, it has probably been a mistake to attach a distinct hierarchic status to the role. As in a marriage, there will be instances in which one or another partner is better equipped to take charge. She, or he, will often be identified by the service that the choreographer George Balanchine performed in the life of his favorite and perhaps most gifted dancer, Suzanne Farrrell. "I trusted him," she said, "not to let me be a fool."

We can become entangled in our own analogies, and I'd like to avoid that. Mainly I'm talking about the way that partners support each other in service. Still, it amuses me to apply the nurse analogy to the Reverend Brian Cole's description of his deacon at the Church of the Advocate, which serves a homeless congregation in Asheville, North Carolina. Brian is a tall, well-spoken young clergyman; in a different costume, say with a saber and a bouquet, he's the suitor who comes to court our Lilly Mae. His deacon is a gray-bearded, chain-smoking Vietnam vet, about five-feet-four, a "sort of fireplug" who rolls his eyes whenever he believes Brian "has been played again."

Gary is a solid, honest, frank, in some ways profane but also very devout Christian who does the truly hard work every day of working in the shelter. . . . He's the bouncer if there's a fight. He's also the unofficial counselor, not in a let-me-hold-your-hand way, more in a let-me-kick-your-ass way. . . . I think if someone came in initially and spent time with Gary, they'd say he's cynical. What I've discovered is that Gary's not cynical. He's deeply committed to basic justice. . . . He's able to live with the failings and shortcomings of the people he works with because he also has to live in the church, where people we have higher expectations for often fail us in the very same ways. He's much more likely to bust the chops of the priest or bishop who's shortchanging the gospel than he is to be anything less than compassionate in a way that is calling that homeless person into wholeness. Asheville is loaded with a variety of New Age and spiritual seekers, deeply connected to the poor and the work we do—and constantly wanting to guide that work. If the person wants three dollars, give him the three dollars! It was Gary who first told me that two dollars was the cost of Brass Monkey or Night Train. Sure, you can give them two dollars and help them get liquored up, or you can get more deeply involved in their lives. Gary is constantly reminding me to ask the harder question, or to listen harder to the person, and not just get caught up in the initial story that makes them feel good or me feel good.

Imagining Gary in partnership with Brian Cole, one is tempted to imagine him in company with someone like Jack Abbott. His "constant reminder" seems to go to the very heart of Abbott's complaint that no one had ever tried to help him be a better man. That is, no one had ever challenged his narrative, his fiction, his bullshit.

I want to turn off this road for a bit, though I intend to drive back to medicine later on. I want to be sure that the professions and the metaphors we visit are not too obvious or too exclusive or too much of a kind. I also want to get a haircut.

It won't take long. I go for the squeeze-in appointment, the ten-minute buzz cut with the three-eighths clipper. "You're easy," says she of the salon. ("No, he's not," says she who knows me best.) I'm not much interested in my hair, in fact. But I have always been interested in people who cut hair.

Some of that reduces to personal history. My first childhood crush was on my mother's Polish American beautician, lovely blond Josephine. I am also very fond of a former student of mine, a hairdresser, who stepped adventurously from cosmetology school to the deck of a cruise ship, where she cut and set the hair of fabulous Olympian gluttons before falling in love with a Greek sailor and bringing him home to be her husband in the vineyard-deprived hills of Vermont—a kind of postmodern *Odyssey* that she sends to me in brief, epistolary installments in return for my having assigned her the original in ninth grade.

I like her version a great deal. She owns her own salon now and has three beautiful, swarthy kids. Odysseus is studying to be an engineer. I used to help her with sentence structure; now she helps her old teacher construct a more felicitous outlook on the world.

Mostly, though, I'm fascinated by the tonsorial arts as suggestive illustrations of help—ancient illustrations, in fact. Older than cave paintings. The other blond diva of my childhood imagination was a young anthropologist named Jane Goodall, who looked quite fetching in a pair of khaki shorts and spent a lot of her time lounging around with the great apes, which put a boy in mind of another golden Jane, though with Tarzan conveniently out of the picture. As she relayed to her *National Geographic* audience, Goodall was much interested in grooming and the role it played as social signifier and soother among chimpanzees. It was under her tutelage that I came to appreciate that going for a haircut was at least as primal as going fishing—more so, because we ate bugs from each other's hides millennia before we ever thought to use them for bait. Grooming may in fact be one of the earliest recognizable forms of help. As a symbol, it embodies what help is at its best: serviceable, consensual, mutual, pleasurable, and as matter-of-fact as "What will it be today?"

There is another way to get at this. Our need for help is signified anatomically by the fact that none of us can see and few of us can reach every place on our own bodies. A man can give himself an orgasm with less bother than he can give himself a haircut. Leonardo da Vinci's famous sketch of a naked man in a circle, feet apart and hands outstretched to the circumference of perfection—I want another drawing of that same man trying to scratch an itch at the exact midpoint of his shoulder blades. This too is an image of humanity's glory, that untouchable spot we must ask another human being to touch. Just a little ways down. To the left. Oh, yeah. That helps.

Hairdressers make ideal illustrations of service because their orientation is necessarily toward the other. They work facing a mirror in which they are very much visible but that never allows them to forget who's making who look good. Most of them try to look good themselves, but that is pretty much beside the point. I fear that many doctors, teachers, lawyers, and clergy, if instantly metamorphosed into barbers and hairdressers, would find themselves standing in front of mirrors primping their own hair. God, I'm gorgeous. The hairdresser's attitude is perforce more humble.

The work itself is humble—deceptively so. William Carlos Williams said that people "die miserably every day for lack of what is found" in poetry; are there people who live miserably every day for lack of what they might have found in a mirror? The hairdresser reminds us that the poetry of human life often consists of the seemingly superficial, of adornment, compliment, the cup of cold water offered to the disciple, the bowl of porridge that enables the Buddha to sit down and be enlightened at last. Dorothy Day recounts a great story from when she worked as a nurse. A ninety-four-year-old patient was fighting with the nurses who wished to bathe her, flailing and scratching anyone who tried to come near.

> "Let us help you," one of the other nurses said soothingly. "Can't you see that we want to take care of you because we love you?"
> "Love be damned," the little old lady cried. "I want my wig."

Would any competent hairdresser have needed to be told?

We congratulate ourselves, some of us, for giving the Divine a feminine pronoun; a more laudable act of the imagination would be to give the Divine a traditional feminine profession. More laudable because more instructive. No less than a shepherd, a hairdresser might depict God. If that seems like burlesque, no wonder: the shepherd metaphor must have seemed so too, at first. I doubt, though, that a God with scissors would seem ridiculous to the customer who looks forward to her hair appointment as to a sabbath. The Lord is my hairdresser—She asks what *I* want. She maketh me to sit down and do nothing for a whole hour and a half. She maketh me formidable in the presence of mine enemies. She restoreth my confidence. She prepareth a place for me where I can talk and be listened to; my heart runneth over.

"Do you find that most of the people you talk to are happy?" I ask Amy Mayo, the owner of Shear Sensations (don't you love it?), who bought the business twenty years ago when she was all of nineteen years old. Most of the people she talks to are women (and most of the men don't talk). "I would have to say no," she says. She notes that many of her customers seem to come as much for conversation as cosmetology—including one who schedules appointments faster than entropy can manage to undo her hair. She also notices a change in herself over the past two decades. "I notice as I'm getting older that I'm focused more on the conversations than I used to be. When I was younger I'd think, I'm never going to have these problems, but now I realize that these are problems all people have." Part of her role as interlocutor is to share that realization. "People want to be reassured about their life when they come here." Along the same lines, a midwife told me that one of her functions is to "normalize" pregnancy and labor—partly with reference to her own experiences as a mother and to the experiences of other women.

Perhaps the conversation itself is normalized by the working environment of the salon; perhaps this is one reason people traditionally tell their troubles to barbers and bartenders—not only because they're cheaper than psychologists, but also because their therapy is tied up with other kinds of work. They're helping in other, more palpable ways. Some of the most helpful talks I've had occurred when I and my adviser of the moment were doing something else—fishing, tinkering, running the roads. If I were a psychologist, I think I might keep a big bushel of garden produce in my office and ask my clients to help me shuck, shell, or husk it while we talked.

Our hair continues to grow after we're dead, and our imagination extends beyond the grave; so our requests for help can outlive us. A customer names Amy Mayo in her will, not to receive a legacy, but to give her one last perm. Mayo has had daunting assignments before. As a student in cosmetology school, she had given haircuts at a penitentiary. "All I could think of was what if one of them gets my scissors and stabs me," but the prisoners had been as shy and proper as abbots. "Thank you, ma'am." This time, though, there would be a conspicuous lack of conversation.

I spoke earlier of profession as implied confession, as a form of humility. The professional helper has confessed a need for tutelage, boundaries, pay. But another humility resides paradoxically within that one: namely, the recognition that all those limits are provisional. That compassion and circumstance make them provisional. I know elementary school teachers who launder the clothes of their neediest students, partly out of pity for them and partly in deference to their own gag reflex. Who appointed them to be laundresses—or counselors, bouncers, nurses, surrogate mothers, secular priests? No one did. It just came with the territory. I am a hairdresser, not a mortician, not a coroner; I do hair, nails, waxes, wraps—it's all out there on the sign in the window—but then the reading of a will becomes a new commencement speech, and I find I have an additional certification on my diploma. This too is a problem all people have and one that the great myths try to normalize. Odysseus, "master of land ways and sea ways," must eventually visit that place where he holds no mastery; he must go to the Underworld.

I had to have one of the other girls go with me because I didn't know if I could physically do it. It was very difficult for me. The smells of the funeral home, working on someone who was dead. It was definitely . . . really . . .

She pauses, as though back in that moment, then says, "It didn't freak me out. I didn't have nightmares. I kept in mind"—what she keeps in mind every working day, even with customers who insist on the no-frills haircut—"it's what she wanted."

Of all human professions, perhaps none provides a more useful metaphor of what it means to help than that of midwife. It was Socrates' chosen metaphor; he helped his students give birth to wisdom. In other words, Socrates could not be wise *for* his students. He could only help. There is no cheating in midwifery. There is such a thing as surrogate motherhood, but there is no such thing as surrogate labor. True, an obstetrician can co-opt a labor, for a woman's benefit or for convenience, with surgery. But a midwife cannot take over in that way without ceasing to be a midwife. The honor of her vocation is always to play the supporting role. (The dishonor of her vocation, in this country at least, has been that increasingly she is forced to play a supporting role to the obstetrical establishment.)

According to midwife Peggy Vincent, the role includes knowing "when to speak, when to be silent, when to laugh, when to hug, when to be pliant, and when to stand firm. How to be '*mit wife.*' With woman."

If midwifery has the status I am giving to it, then its lessons will apply to other helping situations, even though its own application is very specific and restricted to one subgroup of a single gender.

Vincent's book, *Baby Catcher*, provides several pieces of evidence to support my claim. She knows things that the best physicians, clergy, teachers, and counselors also know.

For example, she knows not only that her office is to be "with woman" but also when that office is not exclusive to her. "Sometimes birth is such an intimate affair that I feel like a voyeur. To speak feels like a violation of some sacred and private event. . . . I moved to the window and gave [the parents] space."

Of course, that is an impossible move to make if the space is already occupied by one's own ego. I found a similar lack of presumption in a hospice volunteer (also a woman) who told me, "I always go in [to the home of a dying person] feeling terribly awkward, a stranger, intruding on someone's life"—the precise reason, I am sure, that people do not regard her arrival as an intrusion. A male therapist I know who specializes in problems of human sexuality told me, "I realized from the start that my job was to help the partners become more intimate with each other, not to convince the female partner how much happier she'd have been with me."

Vincent also reports that it is not unusual for women to become so absorbed "in the process, the pain, and the exhaustion" of labor that at the moment of delivery "we frequently hear their gasp of surprised awe, 'Oh, a baby!'" Can that be possible? We know it is. Many of my own shortcomings as a teacher, minister, and father reduce to my having forgotten—or having allowed the people I served to forget—the goal of our labor. I wonder if Jack Abbott had forgotten that too. Of course, there may be occasions—and childbirth may be one of them—that require a degree of amnesia. But I have always swum with more measured strokes when my head was above water and I could see where I was going.

Midwifery is such an apt metaphor because childbirth is often so unpredictable. *Baby Catcher* not only chronicles a long career's worth of wondrous, exasperating, and incomparable deliveries, it also recounts how one case of litigation virtually destroyed that career. With so much at stake, the midwife wants to guess as little as possible.

When I asked Dartmouth nurse-midwife Barbara Filbes to list the essentials of her trade, the first thing she said, without a moment's hesitation, was "Know your stuff. You need to be so technically competent that you can do that stuff automatically so you can take care of the other dimensions of the person. You have to go in with confidence."

The very next thing she said was "You also have to be completely humble." She quoted an obstetrician who had once served as her mentor: "The uterus can humble any man." She concluded by acknowledging the paradox. "Confidence and humility may seem diametrically opposed, but the very best people have both, all the time."

Taking midwifery as my primary metaphor for help, I had thought I could also use it to define where help left off and helplessness began. Cesarean section would stand as the dividing line. With the mother no longer actively engaged in labor, the midwife punches out. Not so.

Though some midwives are out of the picture at that point, and others switch roles and serve as surgical assistants, Filbes and her colleagues prefer—her words are "we love"—to accompany the woman and her partner into the surgery.

> We sit with the couple behind the anesthesia screen. . . . They are strangers in a completely strange place. An operating room is, in every way—the lighting, the noise—very alien. And it should be. It is a world apart. At that point we take on the role of saying, "This is a strange world to you, but it is not so strange to us. This is part of our homeland. We're going to tell you about it. We're going to hang with you while you're here."

Her role becomes that of narrator and interpreter; one thinks of the chorus in Greek tragedy and its homely vestige in the Stage Manager for *Our Town*. This is still the art of being "with woman" but on another level. Even when her hands-on part is over, the midwife continues to help.

Likewise, the woman in labor is not so helpless as I might have thought, for she can work with the midwife's narration, imagining it for herself, interpreting the interpretation. She can also reject it; she can silence the midwife or withdraw her attention to her own place of silence. She can be indignant, inconsolable. *Willful.*

It is the midwife's presence that enhances this choice, her help that permits the woman to be something more than helpless and nothing less than human. For what is it, after all, that distinguishes human labor and human suffering but the laborer's or the sufferer's consciousness—not pushing or blowing, but knowing. This amounts to the same answer given by those Greek plays to the question raised by extreme helplessness: What can you do when the fickle gods and your own limitations combine in such a way that your fate is sealed? You can be self-aware. You can reflect. You can rage, or you can be still. You can choose.

It is not difficult to apply this insight to other situations of help and helplessness, including those that come with child rearing. Filbes likes to speak of the art of midwifery as that of "building mothers," one in which the experiences of pregnancy and labor teach the skills of motherhood. The woman learns to marshal her strength, wait out her pain, listen to her instincts. The experience of cesarean delivery can also be a part of that building, a demonstration by the midwife of what the mother is able to do when her baby enters the no less alien world of puberty, the no less sterile place of formal schooling, the no less disappointing impasse of failure: she can describe and interpret even when she is no longer able to "deliver." She may not be able to make heartbreak less painful, for her child or for herself, but she can narrate the passage in such a way that it remains part of a human story.

Talking to Filbes gave me a greater appreciation, not only for her profession, but also for my own. The role of a writer is something like that of a midwife after the laboring mother has entered the operating room. I can have no other function beyond that of illuminating events that are very much out of my hands. You can accept or reject my interpretations, but at least I have offered you a choice. Even where I have proved to be less than helpful, I have served to remind you that you are not helpless.

I forget which writer it was—someone medieval, I think—who said that from the cry of the newborn and the last gasp of the dying we can only deduce that the time between birth and death will be spent in sorrow.

We can make another deduction. From our bedside attendance on the woman in labor and on the woman who labors for her last breath (historically she has sometimes been the same woman in the same moment), we can also deduce that human life calls out for help. That the cry is not only of pain.

The logic in this case is not so cold as the medieval but not so clear either. For it is possible to be born without help—say in the backseat of a cab racing to the hospital—and we die whether we have help or not. Death may be the only human accomplishment for which help is never required. Yet few predicaments strike us as more pitiable than that of the person who "died all alone." I suppose that is a good thing to remember when we talk too glibly about those who "will be just fine without any help from us." We thereby ascribe to them the self-sufficiency of the dying, a sufficiency few of us want for ourselves.

"I think about my own death every day. Most rational people do."

I am talking with Dr. Lloyd Thompson, a physician who lives about as far south of me as the Moseleys live north and whose specialty stands in something like the same contrast to theirs. Thompson was instrumental in founding the longest-running hospice program in my state. For a man who thinks daily of his own death, and who has plenty of reminders should he perchance forget, he hardly seems depressed. Having spent some time with the dying, I am not surprised. Neither is he. "Most people who do my work feel that they are enriched by it. That they are *saved* by it." Also, most people who do his work are dealing with the relatively natural, albeit tough enough, fact of adult mortality. The presence of dying children might lessen one's sense of enrichment. It certainly would for me.

Thompson sees himself as a pioneer, with all that connotes of adventure and hardship and perilous innocence. He has every reason to. The territory he entered was vast and largely unexplored, medically and in some ways geographically as well. To take on the task of enabling people in a region of mountains and hollows to die at home is, quite literally, to relearn the map. Thompson lays it out for me in what sounds almost like a Homeric catalog; if you enjoy that sort of thing, listen to the names:

We made house calls in every nook of Caledonia County, which extends to Groton and to West Groton, to Victory, the edge of

Lunenburg, Sheffield, Wheelock, and actually all the way over to Greensboro and up behind Greensboro and almost into Glover. The house calls were as long as seventy-five miles round-trip.

The track record to date is even more impressive. Of roughly seven hundred patients since 1979 who indicated a desire to die at home, all but five were able to do so. Thompson does not minimize the magnitude or complexity of the challenge. "You are alone with tremendously difficult ethical and intellectual questions—and if you're really going to do well by them, and keep them at home, it really is heroic." He is talking about the efforts of a whole cadre of people; as our conversation continues, I realize that in some ways he is talking about the heroic tenor of a community. In the midst of a blizzard, a visiting nurse places the corpse of a patient into her four-wheel-drive car and drives it from the house down the hill to the waiting hearse, which is unable to make it up the long drive. A relatively small thing, perhaps, but one of those particulars that Blake said we must embrace if we would truly do good to another.

Thompson gives me other examples. A volunteer named Beryl Eddy entered a remote house where a man lay dying "and realized that the essential thing was that the wife couldn't drive." With her husband's death, she would be completely isolated. This was an "absolutely incisive, intelligent, grounded way of understanding what was going on." To ground it further, Eddy offered to give driving lessons. I was eventually able to hear the story in her own words.

> I'd go out with this *very* timid woman, and we'd slide around on the ice and snow. That was terrifying. I was sure we'd all get killed or wreck the car. About a week before her husband died, she got her license. It was so exciting. We went to McDonald's and had lunch. She hadn't had an easy life. [Learning to drive] freed her up. She was able to get a job. She was able to drive to the train station to go down to see her daughter.

As Thompson describes his program, it seems often to work in this way. Great importance attaches to discovering what people truly want—an approach we can readily identify as characteristic of help at its best. We can also identify it as a natural outgrowth of the basic hospice idea: once you have determined a person's last wish and committed yourself to it, you have assumed a truly altruistic orientation, for the other. No doubt this approach is also an outgrowth of meeting the patient in the patient's own place.

"You break down when you go into their homes. All your presumptions disappear." Not surprisingly for a practicing Buddhist, Thompson speaks of that process as a form of meditation.

> [Hospice] takes you to a place where you usually aren't as a doctor, and it has to do with your being quiet, and sitting still with patients, and listening, waiting, being at their home, and making decisions *with* them, trying to find out what *they* want. Time slows down for you. It gets rid of all that intensity of decision making that you have to do day by day when you're seeing patients eight to ten minutes at a time. You can hear the clock ticking. . . . You're asking questions that are intimate, that are kind of desperate questions that need answers. Are you frightened? Are you religious? Those moments are precious to me.

Of course, not everyone in his profession was willing to sit meditation in that place. At first he found it difficult getting other physicians in the area to make house calls. He settled for asking if they could at least come at the end to certify the death. Finding the best way to make that happen was a matter of finding the right language.

> We'd call and say, "Someone has died in Sheffield. It's thirty-five below zero and snowing. Do you want to come?" And the doctors said no. So we changed the question. We would say, "When may we expect you?" And the doctors came. All we had to do is identify the altruistic edge of their relationship with the patient, and they would drive to Sheffield in a winter storm at thirty-five below.

The nature and scale of the undertaking meant that other professionals needed to be involved as well, including clergy. "We had religion involved from the beginning." This need to involve so many others points to yet another paradox of help. We often speak of the pioneer as someone who forsakes the herd; in professional terms, the pioneer is the maverick who disdains collegiality. In fact—and I say this as someone who prefers to go it alone and who habitually distrusts innovation—we fear pioneers precisely because we see them, accurately, as a threat to our autonomous isolation. The frontier does not tolerate isolation; one can only be alone where things are sufficiently settled. So the dreamer, particularly the altruistic dreamer, is always chafing against the dream we no longer admit. That is, the dreamer threatens to nudge us from our solitude. I have always found it curious how we sometimes refer to such a person as a lone ranger; for that matter, I don't know how the Lone Ranger got to be called the Lone Ranger. He is not alone, kemo sabe. No surprise, then, that the anecdotes recounted by an innovator like Dr. Thompson often amount to the exploits of this or that Tonto.

> This guy had this huge sister from down in Connecticut who came up here to make sure he took last rites and went back to his Catholic faith. In the tradition of Vermont, he was fully agnostic, but he was so sick, and she just sat at the bottom of the bed and abused him. "You're going to go to hell if you don't fix this!" So what we did was, we called the priest and said, "Father C——, we've got a Catholic who's acting up. What can you do?" So we pulled him in and he said, "Sister, you are not doing God's work. You leave your poor brother alone. Go home and say this many hail Marys"—and he kicked her out. And I said, "Father C——, I've never kissed a Catholic before, but I may kiss you now."

Among the various lessons that Thompson has learned and been compelled to learn in his work with hospice, perhaps the most important has to do with the anticipation of his own death. His teachers in this have been the dying.

> To have people become themselves and to really be okay in the face of intolerable circumstances and to live well as they're dying is such a powerful thing. There's a kind of grace people teach us that has to do with the way they die. To see people doing it in the

way they lived reassures you that your own dying has . . . that you can do it.

Of all the many paradoxes of help, this may be the most profound: that people at the mortal extremity of helplessness are able to help us in a way that no one else can.

Much of the challenge of hospice care has to do with relieving pain. The first thing that Thompson did as a doctor was to give a shot of morphine to a homebound man who was dying, in agony, with cancer of the penis. The gesture is simple, the relief almost immediate, but the clarity can be deceptive. For one thing, the doctor has taken an oath to do no harm. Conventional medicine insists that a doctor never act to shorten life as a means for reducing pain. The problem, of course, is that the distinction is sharper on paper than it sometimes is in a human body. Large shots of morphine are administered to relieve pain, not to shorten life—though of course large doses of morphine will, over time, do both.

The problem of treating pain is complicated further by the distinction between responding to pain and preventing it. According to Dr. Thompson,

The [best] idea of pain control is that you anticipate the pain. You figure out how to give the medications in a reasonable amount, and you don't ever let people get back to the pain level they were at before. [But] there's something in us doctors that wants to say, "We are responding to pain." We never want to be seen as somebody who's tipped somebody over and they die. So we have to wait for them to have the pain. They have to show us their suffering, and then we can respond to it. What that does is, you're always giving inadequate doses. You're always chasing your tail to catch up to pain, and you never do, and the patients suffer. And that's been the history of the way pain has been treated in American hospitals.

Thompson believes that "fixing suffering," which he pairs with "service to humanity," is "the thing [doctors] have always done, and have forgotten in our technological interest, and I think we've got to come back to it." He calls it "medicine's great heart."

Of course, we all know what happens to hearts.

The headline in the *Caledonian Record*, which circulates in every nook of Caledonia County, to Groton and to West Groton, to Victory, and the edge of Lunenburg and far beyond, reads, "Dr. Thompson Publicly Reprimanded." This is an action taken by the Vermont State Medical Practice Board. In the photograph Thompson stands at a podium gazing rather forlornly at something we cannot see. Perhaps he is listening to the reprimand. I wonder if he is thinking about his own death. He is dressed as he might choose to be buried. He is wearing a tweed jacket and a bow tie.

In a stipulation filed Wednesday Thompson admitted it was wrong for him to have administered the drug Norcuron to an 85-year-old patient last August. Norcuron is a drug that causes muscle paralysis.

Thompson had been treating the patient for 20 years. In August her condition deteriorated and when she suffered respiratory failure she was placed on a ventilator while at Northeastern Vermont Regional Hospital. Two years earlier she had signed a durable will which stated she did not want to be placed on any artificial life support systems but only wanted to receive care to relieve pain and maintain her dignity.

Attempts to take her off the ventilator resulted in great stress, with the woman experiencing a feeling of suffocation and panic. Her family was in the hospital room and shared this distress.

It was apparent that the woman was dying. In his statement to the board, Thompson said he wanted to make that happen as comfortably as possible. . . .

In his statement Thompson said he decided to use Norcuron because he was afraid the patient would awake and suffer just before death. He was also concerned about the family who would see this and hoped to spare them emotional pain. . . .

He said he cared for this patient for many years. "She was my friend."

Dr. Thompson will not lose his medical license. The state's attorney general says he has decided not to charge the doctor with manslaughter. He believes that Dr. Thompson's actions were well intentioned. He also notes that the family of the deceased has "strong wishes that no charge be brought against Thompson." But he adds, "The medical community should take notice that future cases may be prosecuted. Hastening death is not acceptable."

In the present instance, however, the attorney general does not see that justice would be served by prosecuting the doctor. It seems that he wants the doctor to know how carefully this was considered. The patient was so close to death that it would be difficult to prove that she died from the Norcuron. Finally, "It would be uphill sledding to convince twelve jurors in the Northeast Kingdom, where he has practiced so well for so many years, to agree."

Thompson has been advised not to talk about the case in public. He will not talk about it with me. There will be no press conference, no chance for him to say, à la Mailer, that compassion is worth a little risk, no chance for a newspaper reporter to tell him that he's full of shit. That job is left to the writers of editorials and letters to the editor. They will rise to the occasion.

All of this is happening at the time I go to see Dr. Moseley. It would seem to account for some of his weariness. He is even angry, something I have never seen him be, probably because I have usually seen him in the presence of a child. "You want to talk about help?" he says to me. "Who's helping him?"

He makes no comment on the decision of the medical board. It is the "hounding" in the press that makes him so indignant. "I wish I could protect him." He starts to tell me what he would like to say to the "casters of stones": "What a bunch of sorry, sanctimonious sons of bitches you guys are, who never have to do anything real in a real situation . . ." He doesn't finish.

But he says enough for me to hear an echo of something Norman Mailer had said to reporters at his press conference: "What did you do today to make yourselves so self-righteous?" Of course I also recall that line from Cocteau about "those intellectuals who have clean hands but who don't have any hands"—and who, in the case of editorial writers, are probably not intellectuals either.

What comes to mind most insistently, however, is a passage from a letter Florence Nightingale wrote to her long-suffering patron Sir Henry Herbert, which, if it were better known, would probably hang on posters in every teachers' room, nurses' station, and precinct house in the country:

> A great deal has been said of our "self-sacrifice," "heroism," so forth. The real humiliation, the real hardship of this place, dear Mr. Herbert, is that we have to do with men who are neither gentlemen, nor men of education, nor even men of business, nor men of feeling, whose only object is to keep themselves out of blame.

When people in my community come up to Dr. Thompson on the street and break into tears, as I am told they do, it is not only because they believe that such men as Nightingale describes have passed judgment on their physician. It is for fear that only such men will be left to attend them when they die.

"We make people two promises in hospice," Dr. Thompson told me. "We will take care of your pain, and we will not abandon you. And with that, all this talk about suicide stuff just goes away."

To profess a helping vocation is to make a promise to abide, to be *mit* the other, as the midwife is, with confidence and in humility. And in jeopardy. Perhaps with the fatal sense that *midwife* and *midlife* rhyme for a reason. "The uterus can humble any man," and so, we come to learn, does everything that issues from it.

"You get stupider every year," Dr. Moseley says. "A great number of things I once thought were amenable to cure are probably not. I guess I realize that more of what we do is not curing but just being there."

Which may explain why, on the day after September 11, he accepted an invitation to visit the elementary school in the town where he resides. "I do not like public speaking," he says. The school is very close to the Canadian border, where the guards netted in Christine Moseley's prayers were then on heightened alert. Many of the students there are his patients. "It was that sense of wanting to be around them when they were vulnerable," the doctor said. "The younger kids were especially frightened by the images of people falling from the towers."

Christine came along, with her "bigger bucket of compassion," though I think it was probably more of a Jack-and-Jill job: two bearers, one bucket. They had made a handout for parents explaining that for very young children there is no difference between the repetition of an image on television and the repetition of an event; the same building falling over and over, with the same people jumping out of it, will be for them a different building and different people each time, an endless multiplication of catastrophes. Beyond that, the program was fairly simple, as Christine explains:

> We talked about people in a bad and scary time who were doing something good and what could we notice about that. What could we see? Who was helping? Who was taking care? I think it's important to paint the helpers with as big a brush as you paint the destroyers . . . that even the smallest person can make a difference, can have something to add, some way to help. We didn't have any big-time answers. All we could say is that it wasn't so bad that it couldn't be talked about, and we were there to listen.

Probably neither of the Moseleys would have mentioned the day to me had I not asked them about it. Two years and hundreds of appointments have passed since then; their memories have started to blur. In fact, I first learned about the visit from the principal of the school, who happens to be a friend of mine. The day was still vivid for him. "It was almost like having Mr. and Mrs. Santa Claus come into your school on the day after a national tragedy and sit down in front of the blackboard and tell the kids not to be afraid."

He meant the reassurance of their authority, I suppose, but he was also making an allusion to their physical description, which I have withheld until now, not only for effect, I admit, but also because it never occurred to me to configure the details in quite that way: his whitening beard and shiny pate, the wire-framed glasses they both wear, her bright red hair and pixie face, the fact that both of them are less angular than round. The fact that, dividing their time between

pediatrics and raising pigs, they can be imagined tossing hay to rein-
deer. I find that I can scarcely tell this story to anyone without choking
up, though much of my emotion is probably tied less to the imagery of
December 25 or even to the events of September 11 than to the dates
of appointments when our baby was sick and her mother and I were
the ones who wanted to be reminded that we were not alone.

So if my retelling of this story fails to move you as it does me, that is
partly my point—not to say, "You had to be there" (I wasn't there, either), but that the Moseleys had to be there, in their community, for
their gesture to mean anything. We help by abiding, but the power of
that kind of help is cumulative. The value in William Carlos Williams's
showing up was in direct proportion to the number of times he had
shown up before. The midwife's operating room soliloquy is given
weight by her ministrations in the preceding nine months. This is not
to say that help ought to be withheld in the absence of a shared history.
There is no good Samaritan if that is true. It is only to say that shared
history all by itself can become a form of help.

That is one of the gifts that Mr. and Mrs. Santa Claus seem to have
left in my stocking—and if I'm not mistaken, I feel something else
down in there too.

There can come a time, "midway in our life's journey" and perhaps
midway to the North Pole, when you arrive at what Dante described
as a dark wood, where you are no longer sure what good can be accomplished in a world where crazy men fly airplanes into buildings
and pathetic women pledge their undying love to crazy men, even with
the cigarette burns fresh on their arms. At that point you realize that if
you are going to help anyone besides a dearly beloved few, it is going
to take something more than nobility of spirit. Even compassion may
not be enough.

In the waning of hope, in the awful fear that love is going to lose in
the end and stupidity may already have won, you look at people like
the Moseleys (or if you happen to be the Moseleys, I guess you look at
each other), sitting side by side between a blackboard and a class of
anxious children they have weighed and vaccinated and on whose
small, croupy chests they have placed their stethoscopes—or if that's a
little too Norman Rockwell for your tastes, maybe you look at another
Norman and his wife as they try desperately, comically, to make dinner

conversation with their edgy guest ("So . . . what kinds of things did you eat there in, uh, Utah?"), or if that swings too far in the opposite direction, maybe you settle on Dr. Thompson as he tries to dance alone and on point, the point being the precise hypodermic stab that puts pain to rout but does not shorten life by a nanosecond—you look at people like these and then you glance up at the sanctimonious casters of stones leaning from their reserved balcony seats (oh, but such comfortable seats), and you conclude (even with a slight groan) that if there always have to be two sides to everything in this world, then you have chosen your side.

THE DOMESTIC SAMARITAN

Help is on the way" means that relief is imminent. The fire engines have left the station. Said with a different stress, in the absence of stress, it could also mean that help is something that happens incidentally in the course of a life. It happens "on the way" to someplace else, as in the parable of the good Samaritan, who drives such a bold straight line through the moral landscape, neither seeking to do good nor shunning the opportunity, the original easy rider. We wave our hats as he roars by, bound for glory but unbounded by any mission except his own.

Larger stories of help, however, tend to fall on either side of that narrative line. In one type, the helper ventures out to meet some need. Looking for trouble, you might say. This is the story of my cousin Johanna and my younger contemporary Ben, of Doctors Farmer and Schweitzer, of Florence Nightingale and Dorothy Day, and to a lesser extent of every person who goes off to work in a place where people value his services enough to sit and wait for them.

In the other type, need comes knocking at the door, perhaps with an invitation, perhaps not. It confronts us at the place where our greatest advantage and our greatest vulnerability are perfectly matched, like a pair of slippers. In other words, it comes to us at home. And it may stay awhile.

This second story, which we could describe as one of altruistic hospitality, is often less dramatic than its more active counterpart but seldom less interesting. It is the story of Norman Mailer and Jack Abbott, of Stanley and Stella Kowalski and Stella's sister Blanche. Mythically, it is the story of Zeus and Hermes going in disguise among mortals, of Yahweh showing up at Abraham's tent and the Virgin Mary's breast. On the dark side of the archetype, it is the tale of Dracula, whose suckling is of a different order but who will enter only a house into which he has been invited.

In keeping with these extremes, the story of taking in the stranger appeals to us and appalls us both. Appeals, because of its promise of an ethical rapprochement with the dream we no longer admit. Like a mail-order catalog or a VCR, it speaks the comfortable words: *You can do this without leaving home.*

Appalls, because the threshold of one's home is where even the most dedicated of philanthropists have been known to draw the line.

Of all stories of domestic Samaritans, I know of none more beautiful than that of Le Chambon-sur-Lignon, a village on a plateau in the southeast of France where an estimated five thousand Jewish refugees, many of them children, were saved from the Holocaust. My knowledge of this place and these events comes mainly from two sources: Philip Hallie's *Lest Innocent Blood Be Shed* (1979), a book I am repeatedly giving away and replacing, and Pierre Sauvage's stirring documentary film *Weapons of the Spirit* (1989).

Sauvage himself was sheltered at Le Chambon as a child. After the defeat of Hitler, his parents took him to the United States, putting their heritage behind them along with the war, to the extent that Sauvage grew up not even knowing he was a Jew. Thus his return to the village that gave him asylum was also a return to his roots. As we watch his film or read Hallie's book, we can experience a similar sense of return, as if someone were to sit us down and tell us that, yes, we are human beings, and it is nothing to be ashamed of.

In fact, one of the things I did after first hearing the story of Le Chambon was to pull out several maps in order to determine the precise location, not only of the village, but also of the caves of Lascaux where the prehistoric paintings are. I very much wanted the one to be close to the other, the way medieval hagiographers located the Cross of Christ atop the skull of Adam. I wanted to verify the connection. Same creatures, yes? The maps were somewhat noncommittal.

I could have looked closer to home. The Chambonnais bear at least some resemblance to my neighbors here in northeastern Vermont, many of whom are also hardy farmers with French surnames, and that may be one of the reasons the story appeals to me. Hallie says that two of their favorite expressions translate as "Well, what do you expect?" and "Nine months of winter, three months of trouble." Give me one more as resonant, and the Atlantic Ocean shrinks to a lake. And I may have found it in something that André Trocmé, their charismatic minister at the time of the rescue, had written in his notes: "How could the Nazis ever get to the end of the resources of such a people."

But Europe at the time of the Holocaust was full of hardy, resourceful people, who harvested their crops in the shadows of crematoriums and who, in some cases, even murdered those Jews who managed to escape. Something happened at Le Chambon, but how it might be duplicated and under what circumstances remains an open question.

No one would dispute that a key influence on these events was the Protestant pastor and his wife, Magda. André Trocmé was a confirmed pacifist when he came to Le Chambon. He urged his flock to resist the Vichy government and their German patrons with "weapons of the spirit." It was he who told the Vichy police who came with buses to take away the Jews, "We do not know what a Jew is. We know only men."

It is important to remember that neither Trocmé nor his people knew of the extermination camps. The official word was that the Jews were to be resettled. But Trocmé did not require proof of a genocide to perceive an injustice. When asked for a list of the Jews being sheltered in the town, he replied that he had no such list (which was true) and would refuse to hand it over even if he had one. "These people have come here seeking aid and protection from the Protestants of this region. I am their pastor, their shepherd. It is not the role of the shepherd to betray the sheep confided to his keeping.'"

It was Magda, however, who encountered the first Jewish refugee at the presbytery door and called her in out of the snow with the words, "Naturally, come in, and come in," and covering her with her shawl. If there is such a thing as a domestic Samaritan, Magda comes as close as one can imagine to providing that vocation with a motto: "I do not hunt around to find people to help. But I never close my door, never refuse to help somebody who comes to me and asks for something." Hallie tells us that in the early days of their acquaintance, André had been impressed by Magda's concern for the warmth of a friend. "Go quickly and get your sweater," she had said. "In the many years to follow, he would see how poignantly Magda felt the cold in the bodies of others, and how she would spend much of their lives covering or uncovering children." For Hallie, this is an iconic image of help at its best:

> [W]hen you cover people, you are allowing their own heat to warm their bodies under that blanket or sweater; you are not intruding on their bodies. You are only permitting them to keep well by their own body heat. In this image of covering lies the essence of Magda's way of caring for others.

The Trocmés first met at the International House in New York, where André was attending Union Theological Seminary and Magda was studying to be a social worker. His proposal to her was both frank and prophetic: "I shall be a Protestant pastor, and I want to live a life of poverty. I am a conscientious objector, and that could mean prison as well as all sorts of difficulties." Magda said yes. They would have four children and remain married until Trocmé's death in 1971. Magda lived until 1996. Their relationship seems to have been marked by turbulence, deep commitment, mutual admiration, and passion. Hiding from the Gestapo at a village some distance from Le Chambon, André was subjected to the amorous attentions of the householder's grown daughter. He wrote to Magda of his distress, and at some risk to herself, she came to him on a bicycle. Help was on the way.

Le Chambon was not Trocmé's first cure. Before coming to the village, he served congregations of industrial workers and miners elsewhere in France. At Sin-le-Noble, near the Belgian border, he had been conspicuous in a religious awakening that included the conversion of a notorious proletarian drunkard named Célisse. Hallie describes him as a physically imposing man, abusive to wife and children; by the time Trocmé found him, he had sold virtually all of his household furniture to support his habit. Though Trocmé never succeeded in making Célisse a thoroughgoing pacifist—only the pastor's intervention prevented him from trouncing a heckler at one of their outdoor prayer services—the man did become an effective evangelist for sobriety and the Christian gospel among the miners of the town. But the story lacks the edifying conclusion of the stock conversion narrative. Shortly after Trocmé left for Le Chambon, Célisse returned to drinking and, presumably in despair over his lapse, committed suicide. If what happened at Le Chambon was a miracle, it is not necessarily because André Trocmé was a miracle worker.

No matter how much credit we give to Trocmé for the achievement of Le Chambon—and its chroniclers concur in giving him a great deal—his best gifts seem to have been fulfilled in partnership. He was a partner to Le Chambon, like fire to seasoned wood; to Magda, like fire to more fire; to the Quakers, who were instrumental in getting many of the refugees to Le Chambon; and to Édouard Theis, "the rock of Le Chambon," a former missionary whom Trocmé brought to the village to start a school that would include nonviolence in its curriculum. Theis participated fully in the rescue activities. After Trocmé was forced into hiding, he continued the work not only at Chambon but with the Cimade, a group of refugee smugglers, "originated and led by women alone," who moved Jews to neutral Switzerland. Yet another partnership. "I was the follower," Theis says modestly of his relationship with Pastor Trocmé, "the helper, yes!" So were they all, yes.

We often speak of help as the hand that reaches out, for obvious reasons. But what we see at Le Chambon is an activity whose best anatomical metaphor may be respiration. Trocmé and his partners breathed help like air, using it in common with each other and with those they served. "It was characteristic of him," says one of the surviving refugees, "to help you while convincing you that you were helping him." In such an atmosphere, the dangers of egoism are reduced. Who can keep track of one's breaths or divide the air into mine and yours, give and take? The pastor and people of Le Chambon fought evil, but they were also a demonstration of the kind of world they were fighting for.

●　　●　　●

I wonder that their story isn't better known. If you knew it already, you may wonder at my wondering, but almost no one to whom I have mentioned Le Chambon has ever heard of it—and I include people more widely read than I am. I wonder why, to use Nurse Moseley's words, we have not painted the helpers with as big a brush as the destroyers. Who hasn't heard of Dachau? Part of the reason is probably statistical: the destroyers destroyed so many, and the Chambonnais saved relatively few, albeit a number roughly equal to every man, woman, and child native to their village.

Perhaps we will find a clue in the parable of the good Samaritan. Not surprisingly, it was a favorite with André Trocmé, who referred to it in exhorting his congregation to their task. "We mustn't act like the priest who saw the man who had fallen among thieves and who passed by on the other side. And the Jew, truly, had fallen among thieves." By telling his parable of basic human kindness with a protagonist from a particular human tribe, Jesus calls attention to the fact that good deeds are seldom evaluated without bias. They are given a coloring that has little or nothing to do with the deed itself and everything to do with our prejudices. This goes for bad deeds as well. There are government atrocities and rebel atrocities; there are Republican philanderers and Democratic philanderers, your own party affiliation determining which are to be regarded as adorable rascals and which as despicable cheats. For all we know, the first person to name the parable was playing with oxymoron: "the *good* Samaritan"—as opposed to the usual kind. But whatever he called it, he could hardly have left *Samaritan* out of the title. You might as well leave blue out of the sky.

The people and pastor of Le Chambon are difficult to color in this way, and for that reason, I suspect, they will always remain difficult to see. Invisible. For one thing, they were deeply and conventionally religious, which immediately disqualifies them for inclusion in any secular pantheon. As for standing as heroic champions of theological faith, the Chambonnais wind up losing points there as well. They were Huguenots, French Calvinists, continental cousins of the Puritans. Hardly dashing.

Even as evangelical heroes, they turn out to be less than desirable. For one thing, they refused to evangelize. At least among their Jewish guests. Trocmé and Theis were both adamant that Jewish children were not to be proselytized. According to Sauvage's film, the only conversion in Le Chambon of any note was of a Protestant to Judaism. He wound up as an Orthodox rabbi in Jerusalem. This is probably not going to play so well with the crowd that wonders if Jews are "saved."

On top of that, some of the key players were not religious at all. Magda seems never to have had a deeply religious faith; after the untimely death of her son, she turned her back on religion altogether. André drastically revised his faith after the same tragedy. The one martyr in the story, Trocmé's nephew Daniel, appears to have been an agnostic. "I have chosen Le Chambon because I will thus be able not to be ashamed of myself." His commitment to protecting the Jews in Le Chambon was such that the Gestapo were convinced he must be a Jew himself. He was eventually murdered at the death camp of Maidanek in Poland.

The French Resistance was active around Le Chambon, and some of its members found shelter there. That at least is sexy in the postmodern sense of marketable, but Trocmé's pacifism proves to be something less than a turn-on. At one point he even refused to lend communion vessels to Resistance fighters who wanted to hold a religious service, so much did he hate violence. His hatred was not above temptation: in 1939 he had briefly considered the possibility of trying to assassinate Hitler. He spoke German, was in fact part German, and thought he might be able to get close to the Führer. In the end, however, he opted for total nonviolence. After the defeat of the Nazis, he tried to prevent retaliations against collaborators and Germans. Humane he might have been, but sexy he was not.

Finally, the story of Le Chambon may seem distracting or counterproductive to those with an understandable desire to preserve an accurate memory of the Holocaust—especially at a time when denial of that atrocity has become fashionable. But as Hallie points out on the first page of his book, "The moral brilliance of the villagers does not light up the moral darkness around the village as much as it makes that vast darkness seem darker by contrast." Nevertheless, those who prefer their world in black-and-white tend to want their darkness uncut. This is not to say that Le Chambon has gone unacknowledged; there are trees planted for both Daniel and André Trocmé at the Holocaust Memorial of Yad Vashem ("everlasting name") in Jerusalem. In 1990 the Israeli ambassador to France came to present Yad Vashem medals of righteousness to the town. (As if to show that the tradition of André Trocmé was not moribund, the current Protestant pastor used the occasion to criticize the killing of Palestinian protesters by Israeli police.) *Weapons of the Spirit* carries a glowing endorsement from Elie Wiesel. But reading through the various articles and op-ed pieces that Sauvage wrote after the release of his film, one gathers that sometimes he has had to adopt the defensive posture of a man whose loyalties are suspect.

It will not do to imply that the story of Le Chambon is politically incorrect; rather, it is politically useless. Those who try to ride it for a hobbyhorse will find it collapsing underneath them. To put it another way: the same factors that make a fertile ground for genocide will always conspire to plow the story of Le Chambon underground. The same paltry need for wearing gang colors of one sort or another that leads people to salute a Hitler will cause them to falter in repeating this story. In that sense, Le Chambon continues to bear witness against the Nazis; it bears witness by its dogged refusal to be appropriated by any group smaller than the human race.

The inability of the story of Le Chambon to take on an ideological coloring is part of what recommends it to our discussion. The truest help, the purest assistance, is useless to anyone but the person in need. It may not even allow itself to be edifying. It only insists on being completely available or, in the idiom of the Chambonnais, *toujours prêt, toujours prêt à rendre service* ("always ready, always ready to serve"). If Love ever held out a hand to desperation, it was at Le Chambon. If Truth ever gave propaganda the finger, it was in that same place, and with that same hand.

Oh, but it must have been difficult at times, for host and guest alike. I bumped quickly against the limits of my own imagination as soon as I tried to place myself in the shoes of a refugee. "It would be like having to spend *years* of your life at a *bed-and-breakfast!*"—not my favorite sort of place to spend even a night. Such horrors, right? Such a long way am I from those people and their predicament.

Exile in Le Chambon was probably both better and worse than we might think. "I have nothing but happy memories of Le Chambon," said Naomi Levi, one of those who found refuge there. "Once I arrived in Le Chambon . . . I was no longer afraid." But the danger was never far away; even in the absence of the enemy, war could still make its presence known. Next to André Trocmé's grave is a stone for Madeleine "Manou" Barraud, an eighteen-year-old Chambonnais girl who was accidentally shot by a boy staying at her house. The two of them had discovered a gun in the bedroom of a Resistance fighter. Madame Barraud found her daughter's lifeless body, and then, noticing that her young companion was missing and learning that he had run from the house in an agony of grief, she went to search for him. She is reported to have embraced him with these words: "Jean, it is not your fault. It is not your fault. It is the fault of the war. We are all a bit mad. It is not your fault." We do not hear that she ever regretted her forgiveness or having strangers in her house. But wasn't there at least a moment when she regretted being born? And the poor boy—did he regret the day he first set eyes on Le Chambon?

When the war ended, the refugees left, many never to return or be heard from again. "With a few loyal exceptions," notes Pierre Sauvage, "the Jews even appeared to have forgotten their benefactors." Of course the word *appeared* is significant. In *Weapons of the Spirit* Joseph Atlas offers this explanation of what lay behind appearances, at least in his case:

> I have something important to say to them [the Chambonnais]. When Le Chambon-sur-Lignon was liberated by the First French Army, I lived through this liberation in Le Chambon. The Jews left. And as for me, after pursuing my studies I left for South America. I forgot Le Chambon. I forgot it deliberately, because I was emerging from a nightmare. The Chambonnais may have been hurt by that. They may have thought that we didn't fully appreciate their hospitality. Such was not the case; their hospitality has remained very close to my heart. But it was necessary for me to absorb, understand, and surmount the tragedy that the Jewish people had lived through.

If you want gratitude, get a dog. Get a dog, because human beings are more complex. Human beings may find it difficult to feel gratitude without recalling the anguish of the moment in which they needed the assistance for which they are grateful. To solicit help in the way that the Jews were compelled to ask for help from the people of Le Chambon is like coming naked to the door of a stranger after having been assaulted and stripped of one's clothing. To come to that same door again, if only to say thanks for the blanket, is to be naked once more, in memory and imagination if not in fact. That many people were unable to come back to Le Chambon—that only one of ten lepers returned to Jesus after he had cured them—testifies to the fact that some of us are more comfortable than others in our own skins. It probably has little to do with gratitude itself. A forced intimacy is still forced, even when it exists with a benevolent stranger, who would never have forced it.

Why dwell on this? For the sake of those who dwell too long on ingratitude, someone else's or their own. The crowning act of help is when we assist its beneficiary in saying good-bye. *Go in peace. Your faith has saved you.*

The political scientist Norman Geras speaks of "a contract of mutual indifference," an understood agreement by which "we leave other people in peril unrescued and accept that others will do the same for us." We are familiar with that contract, and we know its disingenuousness. *If ever I wake up to find myself poor, black, and incarcerated, I won't expect anyone to help me either.* We want to know how the Chambonnais found the wherewithal to annul the contract. We want to know how they managed to live by the Golden Rule in an age that was anything but golden.

In this the Chambonnais, so helpful to their guests, are no help at all. "How can you call us 'good'?" asked Magda Trocmé. "We were doing what had to be done." Says another villager (who modestly declined to give his name to the reporter who asked), "We didn't protect the Jews because we were moral or heroic people. We helped them because it was the human thing to do." Just so—but what, after all, is "the human thing to do"? The bovine thing to do is based on norms derived from the observation of cows. One shudders to imagine the norms that might be derived from an observation of World War II.

Perhaps the best epitaph we could give the wartime generation of the Chambonnais comes from the Tao te ching:

> It is because it lays no claim to merit
> That its merit never deserts it.

If we insist on an explanation, we could start by saying that these were a people with a definite sense of history. They remembered "The Desert," a period from the sixteenth through the eighteenth century when they were a persecuted minority in Catholic France. In their book *Holocaust*, Deborah Dwork and Jan van Pelt characterize the Chambonnais as people with "a long memory and a basic principle. They remembered oppression under the Catholic rule of Louis XIV, and they believed that all men, being brothers, should be offered refuge." We would like to appropriate such an ethos. The Greek hero Achilles is supposed to have delivered his son to his pedagogue with the instructions, "Teach him to be a maker of speeches and a doer of deeds"; we can imagine delivering a similarly terse charge to the teachers of our children by saying, "Give them a long historical memory and a basic ethical principle, both in the spirit of the people of Le Chambon."

The sharper type of teacher might reply that our request was virtually a non sequitur. That is, there is no guarantee that point B (the basic ethical principle) follows inevitably from point A (the long memory). The Protestants and Catholics of Northern Ireland also have a long memory, and when it starts to get fuzzy, someone can usually be counted on to detonate a mnemonic device.

What distinguishes the Chambonnais is not so much their memory as its interpretation. Instead of construing their history as a grievance—in which case their most notable achievement might have been a tradition of virulent anti-Catholicism—they identified their sufferings with those of other oppressed people. One cannot overestimate the significance of that difference. In the previous chapter I talked about the difference between those who cite their hard backgrounds as an inspiration for benevolence and those who cite the same kind of background as a justification for remaining aloof. "Nobody ever helped me." What we are talking about here is a matter of the same difference.

If we insisted on giving a label to the distinction, I would describe the Chambonnais interpretation of history as Hebraic. Why must we care for the orphan and not put a stumbling block in front of the blind and leave the corners of our fields to be harvested by the sojourner and give the resident alien a Sabbath along with ourselves, according to the Torah? Because "you were aliens in the land of Egypt." Because your history lives whenever it is recapitulated in the experience of your neighbor. In other words, the Chambonnais gave shelter to the Jews in part because their own sense of history was markedly Jewish.

No doubt the refugees also found a welcome in Le Chambon because the Chambonnais thought of the Jews as "God's chosen people." In *Weapons of the Spirit* we are told that a villager communicated the arrival of several Jewish refugees by saying that "three Old Testaments" were at the door. I only mean to suggest that the Chambonnais were themselves steeped in the Old Testament and that this made a crucial difference.

The German theologian Dietrich Bonhoeffer, who would be executed for his part in a plot against Hitler, wrote from prison that his devotional reading was increasingly taken from the Hebrew scriptures. He also spoke of his desire for an ethics "of earth and blood." These statements are of a piece. They stand in sharp contrast to the assessment of Reich bishop Ludwif Müller, who spoke contemptuously of "the Old Testament with its Jewish money morality and . . . [its] stories of cattle dealers and pimps." I doubt that many of the Chambonnais were pimps or knew what a pimp was, but I imagine that more than one or two had done some cattle dealing in their time. They knew about earth and blood, and bread and dung. So did their pastor; he wrote that marriage to Magda had helped deliver him from "the abyss of mysticism."

It has been a commonplace since the burgeoning of the so-called New Age movement to sit down to dinner with people who say, "I'm not religious, but I am very spiritual." My reply, which I like to think is in the tradition of André Trocmé, is to say that for my own part I strive not to be overly spiritual though I am quite religious. I stop short of quoting what Martin Buber says about spirituality in *I and Thou:*

"'spiritual life' is for the most part the obstacle to a life lived in the spirit. . . . It is the obstacle; for the development of the ability to experience and use comes about mostly through the decrease of man's power to enter into relation."

The Chambonnais had not dissipated their power to enter into relation because their life was a sum total of very vivid relations—to the soil, to their neighbors, and to a God who was "the living God" of the Bible, who is known only in relationship, not in lore or rite or the nomenclature of spirituality. New Age esoterica would have made little sense to the Chambonnais. The same probably goes for this book. What need for a book about help? One might as well read a book about tying one's shoes—and in a village such as Le Chambon, no less, where many of the shoes were made of wood.

Without question religion played a large part in the achievement of Le Chambon. Philip Hallie writes, "I could not say with confidence that I believed God had worked that miracle through Trocmé, but I had to say in all certainty that Trocmé's belief in God was at the living center of the rescue efforts of the village." His view is confirmed by the villagers themselves, one of whom said, "The welcome here had a lot to do with people still believing in something." And yet, as with their sense of history, religion is an insufficient explanation by itself. There were religious people outside Le Chambon; not many of them worked for rescue. As Sauvage rightly notes, "To play up true Christian witness [in Le Chambon] is to face the magnitude of Christian apostasy."

To reckon with the religion of the Chambonnais in any meaningful way is to confront its very basis. They were a people vividly in touch either with God or with the void that human beings fill with God's imaginary existence. I am not being sarcastic; Simone Weil said that in our world God is known through absence. Present or absent, the God of the Chambonnais was no mere proposition or object of belief. In Buber's terms, their God was nothing less than Thou.

As a way of understanding what that might mean, compare the following passages. The first is taken from the Tao te ching:

A man of the highest virtue does not keep to virtue and that is why he has virtue. . . . [He] never acts yet leaves nothing undone.

... A man of the highest benevolence acts, but from no ulterior motive. A man of the highest rectitude acts, but from ulterior motive. A man most conversant in the rites acts, but when no one responds rolls up his sleeves and resorts to persuasion by force. Hence when the Way was lost there was virtue; when virtue was lost there was benevolence; when benevolence was lost there was rectitude; when rectitude was lost there were rites.

The other comes from Bonhoeffer's *Letters and Papers from Prison:*

Who stands fast? Only the man whose final standard is not his reason, his principles, his conscience, his freedom, or his virtue, but who is ready to sacrifice all this when he is called to obedient and responsible action in faith and in exclusive allegiance to God—the responsible man, who tries to make his whole life an answer to the question and call of God.

These are quotations from two different religious traditions, two different millennia. They have seemingly different valuations of action. They have different words for the supreme reality. Their authors would not be equally comfortable with a word like *supreme*. We should certainly be wary of trying to force the passages into alignment. Yet both speak of an ineluctable quality, an "obedience," a "way" of life that goes deeper than all the words we use to name laudable actions or explain them. I would suggest that both quotations apply to the people of Le Chambon. Both explain—by not explaining—why the Chambonnais had a hard time accounting for their actions or understanding "all the fuss" they inspired. Their willingness to help without stint was grounded in the Way, the Source of all Being, what righteous agnostics rightly say they cannot know for sure, even as they act with uncanny sureness.

Magda Trocmé said, "If we had been an organization, it could not have worked." As much as any statement we might venture about the role of religion or a sense of history in the actions of the Chambonnais, Madame Trocmé's statement requires the most careful qualification. On the surface it is unimpeachable. There was no formal organization in the village dedicated to the work of saving Jews. (After the war some villagers who participated were surprised to find that certain of their neighbors had been engaged in the same work.) An organization would have been easier to infiltrate than the village and easier to incapacitate by seizing its leaders. Vichy actually tried the latter by temporarily confining Pastor Trocmé, his assistant, Édouard Theis, and the public schoolmaster, Roger Darcissac, to an internment camp in 1943.

What Magda Trocmé's statement belies is the fact that there was a much deeper organization at work in the village, that is, the organic structure of the community itself. Simone Weil once noted that a phenomenon like Hitler would be inconceivable without "the existence of millions of uprooted men." Taking our cue from her, we could say that a phenomenon like Le Chambon would have been inconceivable without the existence of several thousand rooted men, women, and children. Without their connections to their place, their culture, and one another, they would have been unable to wage what Philip Hallie so memorably calls "the intimate, unglamorous kitchen struggle" to save the Jews. In his autobiography, *Confessions of an Original Sinner,* the historian Georg Lukacs says, "I believe that the foundation of decent life is permanence of residence." Surely permanence—we might rather say, *profundity*—of residence was also the foundation of the Chambonnais' ability to oppose the structures of violence with the structures of decent life.

Those structures included preexisting organizations like Boy Scouts and the church youth group, both of which Trocmé used to carry information, including warnings of approaching danger. In the midst of the crisis, it was easier and more discreet for the people of Le Chambon to transform existing cells into tools of resistance than to fashion new ones. The groundwork had already been laid—and in the most seemingly innocuous forms.

The need for qualification continues. It is far too simplistic to praise the Chambonnais as exemplars of community. Remember what I said earlier about hobbyhorses. The Chambonnais belonged to a very particular kind of community, one in which some of the very same sociable values cited in popular laments over the loss of community might have been held suspect. Our grotesque, technology-driven emphasis on communication, for example. These were not people who needed to be perpetually in the loop. In a manner of speaking, these were people capable of bowling alone. They were also capable of keeping a secret.

Hallie speaks of their talent for secrecy as a function of French village culture, one expressed even in the appearance of their houses. "Now the French, especially in the villages, are a very private people, as the windows tightly shuttered at night suggest." His depiction of "the intermingling of privacy and communion that pervaded Le Chambon during the rescue activities" seems a model not only of service in the midst of crisis but also of "decent life" in general. Even someone who could not imagine daring what the Chambonnais dared might at least aspire to living as they lived. "Though they were discreet, as silent and as separate as possible regarding the refugees, the amateurs of Le Chambon had a sense of fellowship with each other in the face of the suffering they were helping to alleviate."

If, after hearing the parable of the good Samaritan, the lawyer had turned to Jesus and said, "Yes, but this is no more than basic kindness and short-term mercy. How does one love his neighbor in the most extreme cases of need and danger?" he might have been told, "By having learned the elementary practices of neighborhood in the least extreme cases: basic kindness, as you put it, and minding one's own business."

To state it another way, if helping is an art, it derives from the same disciplines as the art of living in neighborhood. When we talk about wanting to help without smothering or wanting to be compassionate without being intrusive, we are basically talking about wanting to live under the same roof or on the same street with other persons in a decent and pleasurable manner. At their best, domestic life and civic life are not only effective instruments of help but also instructive illustrations. They illustrate how an individual life is fostered by the lives of others.

Richard Rodriguez, who has written much and well on the relationship between public and private life, faith, and language, makes this observation in his recent book, *Brown:*

Americans are so individualistic, they do not realize their individualism is a communally derived value. The American I is deconstructed for me by Paolo, an architect who was raised in Bologna: "You Americans are not truly individualistic, you merely are lonely. In order to be individualistic, one must have a strong sense of oneself within a group."

That is a sense the Chambonnais seem to have had in abundance. You see it in Sauvage's movie and in the number of distinctive individuals who emerge from the pages of Hallie's book. These are people who know who they are, both individually and as a group. They know their duties; they also know their rights. When one of the newly arrived refugees complained about having to walk from the railroad station in the rain, Magda Trocmé told her this:

A few drops of rain are bothering you? What of my friend Simone Mairesse, who found the house for you? The rain fell on her. She ran around at night, put herself in danger, and she is a widow, and she has a child, and she could have been killed, and you are saying that you can't walk this distance because of the rain?

These are the words of someone who is well beyond the posture of long-suffering servant of the human race. She is being herself in the process of extending herself—a distinguishing mark of all the best helpers I have known. In one of his articles about Le Chambon, Pierre Sauvage goes so far as to question the whole idea of selfless service, noting that Hitler and Eichmann "possessed a particularly dreadful form of selflessness—but not the people of Le Chambon," whom he sees as possessing "a very secure, very anchored sense of self—a spontaneous access to the core of their being—that resulted in a natural and irresistible proclivity to see the truth and act upon it." Not to mention an irresistible proclivity to tell the truth when someone was being a pain in the neck.

In summary, we could say that the Chambonnais could give of themselves because they had selves to give. This adds another dimension of meaning to Magda's statement "If we had been an organization, it could not have worked." What an organization or an institution most lacks is a self. For that reason it has great difficulty being authentically sacrificial. In a time of trouble, its first and only instinct is to protect itself. That is a person's first instinct too but not the only instinct. The recent sexual abuse scandal in the Catholic Church illustrates this contrast with depressing irony. The first response of the ecclesiastical hierarchy was to "protect the church," the very response that the church's founder had insisted could only doom it. "For those who want to save their life will lose it." In chambers decorated to distraction with crosses, no one appeared to remember the Cross. In starker surroundings, the people of Le Chambon never forgot it.

Among their many guests, the Chambonnais had a soon-to-be-distinguished visitor in the person of Albert Camus. He lived there while he worked on his novel *La Peste*, or as it's known in English, *The Plague*. One of the Chambonnais interviewed in *Weapons of the Spirit* recalls that the author was often observed taking a walk. The biographies I consulted make little or no mention of his sojourn in the village, though I did find one interesting and, under the circumstances, rather ironic statement from his letters. He asks to have two novels and Nietzsche's *Thus Spake Zarathustra* sent to him. "In this Protestant region, only edifying works can be found, which are instructive but make one feel anemic."

The Plague appears to be based in some ways on what was going on in Le Chambon at the time. An outbreak of bubonic plague in the fictional town of Oran places the entire community under quarantine. The citizens must battle the evil on their own with no help other than what they can and will give to one another. The protagonist, Dr. Rieux, is thought to be modeled on a quack doctor in Le Chambon (though Rieux is anything but a quack) and on the missionary doctor Roger Le Forestier, who had worked with Schweitzer in Africa and was active in Le Chambon during the war (though there is nothing of the madcap in Rieux as there surely was in Le Forestier). From Camus's terse description of Dr. Rieux, I gather that he was based on no one so much as the author himself: "The language he used was that of a man who was sick and tired of the world he lived in—though he had much liking for his fellow men—and had resolved, for his part, to have no truck with injustice and compromises with the truth."

The Plague has all the good existentialist stuff we would expect.

With the exception of a Catholic priest who finally comes around to see the situation in all its stark outline, most of the principal characters are heroes after Camus's own heart—resolute if ordinary men making their own meaning in an absurd and godless universe. I happen to love Camus very much, but given the devout people among whom he was writing, the novel really is something of a hoot. No one would miss the irony if the belief systems were reversed, say if C. S. Lewis had been with the Bolsheviks during the Russian Revolution and emerged with a manuscript for the *Chronicles of Narnia*. Aslan in wire-framed spectacles, Trotsky transformed to leonine Christ. My hunch is that either the Chambonnais were so furtive and laconic that Camus never figured out what was going on under his nose or else the sight of all these intellectually anemic Huguenots defying the Reich while thousands of their more sophisticated compatriots divided their time between reading Nietzsche and hedging their bets made him so depressed that he wrote the novel simply to keep from going out of his mind.

No matter, his story would be powerful wherever it was written; its themes could be used to outline a long and fruitful meditation on help. He shows how crisis brings out noble qualities in the most flawed people, how human beings have an intrinsic need to help, how altruism looks when extreme circumstances have stripped it of emotion. "Indeed, for Rieux his exhaustion was a blessing in disguise. Had he been less tired, his senses more alert, that all-pervading odor of death might have made him sentimental."

At the same time, the novel refuses to be grim; part of its wisdom consists of knowing that dedicated service to the physical needs of others must never preclude a celebration of the physical world. Even in the charnel house of Oran, we find the pleasure in sky and sea that the author himself found so restorative. In one of the most moving passages in the novel, Dr. Rieux and his friend Tarrou take time out for a swim. In context, their trip to the beach amounts to a cask of precious ointment poured on their heads; Judas Iscariot would have wanted the time redirected to the poor. They know better. Tarrou says:

Go for a swim. It's one of these harmless pleasures that even a saint-to-be can indulge in, don't you agree? . . . Really, it's too damn silly living only in and for the plague. Of course, a man should fight for the victims, but if he ceases caring for anything outside that, what's the use of fighting?

By the sea, under the night sky, the doctor touches some of the rocks under the water and finds that "a strange happiness possessed him."

Service cannot always be single-minded, then, although the service in this novel is virtually single-sexed. Except for Dr. Rieux's mother (his wife is away convalescing), all the principal characters are men. It is almost as if Camus cannot achieve the heroic tenor he wants without clearing the decks of women. In this he reminds us of Melville; like the whalers on the *Pequod*, the celibate heroes of Oran are a thousand miles from the nearest land. To read *The Plague* in the light of what happened at Le Chambon is to see the latter in even sharper relief, as a picture of extraordinary service grounded in ordinary domestic life. It is to envision a loaf of bread, perhaps tucked into the coat pocket of a woman pedaling fast on her bike in order to be reunited with her husband.

Just as they do without the consolations of domesticity, the men in *The Plague* are without the consolations of religion. Theirs is a bravery all too easy to extol or to dismiss. But not hard to find. I think of the agnostic Peace Corps worker that I interviewed and the agnostic pediatrician, both of whom told me they wished they could believe. I also recall reading an interview in which Christopher Hitchens said that the advantage of atheistic humanism was that it could be espoused without "wishful thinking." Hitchens is a fine writer and a smart man, but he's wrong about that. Atheistic humanism is about wishful thinking if it is about anything at all, and I'm not necessarily talking about wishing for God. The more atheistic the humanists, the more wishful their thinking, for they must believe that creatures so "deluded," and deluded for as long as human beings have been deluded, by religion can amount to something anyway. We can do without wishful thinking about as easily as we can do without help.

The characters in *The Plague* strive to believe in their fellow human beings in the absence of both God and progress. The only progressive thing in their world is disease. They have no idea when the plague will end or if it will end at all. Still, they spend themselves in helping the afflicted and each other, even when their efforts seem to have little or no point.

We forget all too easily that the architects of the Third Reich claimed it would last for a thousand years. Another Rome. We watch the newsreels of Hitler's speeches and the Panzer divisions waging blitzkrieg as though we were watching a performance of *Macbeth:* we know how everything is going to end. We foresee the tyrant's head on a sword. The people of Le Chambon knew no such thing. But they did believe that history was in the hands of God. Others, like Camus and Daniel Trocmé, were unable to find hope in that belief but still found the courage to resist—and a reason to help others do the same.

My earlier remark about Camus's novel being something of a hoot turns out to be every bit as glib and ironic as Hitchens's statement on wishful thinking. The agnostic courage that Camus portrays in *The Plague* is not so outlandish in the pious context of Le Chambon as it might appear. André Trocmé would never recover from the blow to his faith that came with the accidental death of his teenage son. After that he was no longer able to believe in an all-powerful God. In his papers he speaks of "a total resignation before nothingness." According to Hallie, "From now on, God and Jesus were to him powerless as Trocmé the father was. God could only join us in our grief, not save us from it."

In the last decade of his life, Trocmé would write of his change in belief in the last weeks of the war: "I had, without knowing it, joined Sartre and Camus, who were unknown at this time." Unknown, though for a brief interval, one of them was practically living next door in Le Chambon. I want to think that their influences met, that somehow they had helped each other, though the men themselves may only have exchanged a few words passing on the street. I want to think that on some level—or, more wishfully, in some dimension—they are swimming together, like Rieux and Tarrou, "side by side, with the same zest, in the same rhythm . . . at last free of the town and of the plague."

Where Camus's novel may be most relevant to Le Chambon, and to the subject of help, is in the way that it opens our imaginations to the possibility of an apocalypse. "There have been as many plagues as wars in history," the narrator tells us, "yet always plagues and wars take people equally by surprise." So too do the madness and the moral dislocation that accompany both. One of the Holocaust rescuers quoted in the Oliner study (not from Le Chambon, as far as I know) had this to say about the events he had survived: "It is something you cannot plan, this horrible adventure with the devil. They [the Nazis] came like a tidal wave."

Supposedly, Americans braced themselves for diabolical adventure in the wake of September 11. Our illusion of security collapsed with the towers. I have my doubts. I think rather that we saw how resilient the illusion was, how it could absorb a blow much better than any structure of concrete and steel. Already those terrible events have the look of last year's fashions, marked down and moved over to make room for this season's blockbuster movie and next fall's lackluster election.

All this may mean is that we have a hard time conceiving of a crisis when we are not affected directly. Camus describes our condition as one of vulnerability born of self-absorption.

> In this respect our townsfolk were like everybody else, wrapped up in themselves; in other words they were humanists: they disbelieved in pestilences. A pestilence isn't a thing made to man's measure; therefore we tell ourselves that pestilence is a mere bogy of the mind, a bad dream that will pass away. But it doesn't always pass away and, from one bad dream to another, it is men who pass away, and the humanists first of all, because they haven't taken their precautions. . . . [T]hey fancied themselves free, and no one will ever be free so long as there are pestilences.

He speaks of precautions. We want to know what kinds of precautions he is talking about, and what good any but the most basic safeguards can have against pestilence, be it literal or figurative. This is where Le Chambon comes to mind and the subject of help comes into play. As I read about Le Chambon, I asked myself the question most people would ask: How would I have stood up in a situation like this? If I am inclined to withhold my help when it is inconvenient, could I be counted on to offer help when it was dangerous? Perhaps I could be; there are always those who rise unexpectedly to occasions of great need. But in matters like these, I would much rather rely on a habit than a hunch. If possible, I would like to be prepared.

I took a health course in college, one of those requirements that irked me at the time, but the professor said something I never forgot. "I don't so much look at physical fitness as a matter of personal health as I do an issue of social responsibility. I never know when I might be faced with a situation of danger where someone might be dependent on me for their safety—an elderly person, for example, or someone disabled. I want to have the strength and the endurance that would be required of me at such a time." Since then, nobody's triple bypass is ever so powerful as a three-alarm fire in getting me to exercise. The analogy I'm trying to make is obvious. But had the people of Le Chambon "exercised" in preparation for their destiny?

It seems that they had. "We were used to it," said one of them. Magda Trocmé went so far as to say that the work of rescue amounted to a "hobby" among the villagers. In the 1930s they had housed refugees from the Spanish Civil War. Of course, in that case there was not the same danger of retaliation as there was with the Jews during Vichy rule and later during the German occupation. But the difficulties were probably more similar than they first appear. Many of the villagers were subsistence farmers. For some the economic risks of having additional mouths to feed were of greater moment than the fear of reprisals. In any case, Le Chambon did not become a sanctuary overnight or even over the course of a year. Its virtuosity came with a certain amount of practice.

As Hallie points out more than once in *Lest Innocent Blood Be Shed*, the crisis they faced permitted the Chambonnais little time to reflect, analyze, and consider. Situations arose in which one needed to have an answer at once. In the words of a midwife I interviewed, the Chambonnais had to "know their stuff" in order to be as attentive as possible during all the exigencies of labor. It appears that they had learned their stuff by heart.

If we stop at that, however, we have reduced the present to little more than a training ground for the future. It is not enough to recognize the possibility of crisis, the fact that "plague" can break out at any time. We also need to recognize that an apparent lack of crisis *is* our crisis. That we live in "a period which must be reckoned as an exact and pro-longed antithesis to a moment of truth" (John Berger), when "adver-tising agencies now present buying a particular model of car or acquiring a certain computer as a revolutionary gesture only slightly less radical than the storming of the Bastille" (David Rieff). We labor under the illusion of inconsequence; we're not sure if we could find our way to hell even if we were bent on going.

This is not to imply that salvation lies in crisis—what every fanatic wishes for when he blows out the candles on his cake. Camus puts it nicely in *The Plague:*

> What's true of all the evils in the world is true of plague as well. It helps men to rise above themselves. All the same, when you see the misery it brings, you'd need to be a madman, or a coward, or stone blind, to give in tamely to the plague.

Or to be nostalgic over the last outbreak. Nostalgia for the heroism of Le Chambon, which is dangerously close to nostalgia for the Holo-caust itself, amounts to a recipe for demoralization. It belittles our own potential, and it obscures our own task.

The meaningful question for a person of my generation is not "How would you have behaved during the Holocaust?" but "What is your response, right now, to the global revival of anti-Semitism and the Nietzschean 'festival of cruelty' as it gets played out at a place like Columbine High School? Or to the fact that over forty million of your fellow citizens have no public or private health insurance?" That none of these evils is of the magnitude of the Holocaust does not undermine my point; it *is* my point. How does one act in a time when the crisis is not so large or the evil so ugly as it was for Trocmé and his parish? As one of the characters says in *The Plague* when Dr. Rieux thanks him for his help: "Why, that's not difficult! Plague is here and we've got to make a stand, that's obvious. Ah, I only wish everything were as sim-ple." So do we all, but wishing is not enough. Our glory, if we are to have any, will have come from living responsibly through inglorious times, when much was amiss but little was as gross and simple as an outbreak of plague.

Unless, of course, there is an outbreak of plague.

With regard to both possibilities, I have been thinking lately about a piece of advice given by Semmy Woortman-Glasoog, a woman active in the Dutch Resistance. One night she and her husband, also a resister, met with several young men to discuss smuggling Jewish children in Amsterdam to safety.

> We had a meeting, we talked, but the boys didn't know too much because they were very young. . . . And we talked about what we could do and how it would take shape. I listened and I told them, "You have to realize that if you are going to do what you are talking about, then your life after this is a gift. If you don't want that you shouldn't go on." And they all said, yes, they wanted to do it. I think the younger boys didn't realize exactly what they did. But Jaap, he knew what he did, he knew; and Theo knew very well, and I knew.

And we know too what she meant by saying "your life after this is a gift": from this point on you will be in great danger. But do we understand all that she was saying, and might we realize it, even in the absence of a great danger, and might we help our young men and women to realize it as well: *Your life is a gift?* If the story of Le Chambon has anything to contribute to that realization, it is to show the indissoluble connection between cherishing our neighbors' lives and discovering the gift of our own. A precarious gift to be sure, even in the best days, and even at Le Chambon.

Jean-Pierre Trocmé, Magda and André's oldest son, died at the age of fourteen in August of 1944. He hanged himself in the bathroom of the presbytery.

His parents had been in the village trying to reconcile a pair of quarrelsome Swiss friends. On their way home that night Magda had said, unaccountably, "If only I do not arrive too late!" In fact, she had been restless to get back, but André had insisted that they stay to celebrate the peacemaking. Magda found Jean-Pierre hanging in the bathroom, smiling and still warm.

The village doctor's opinion was that Jean-Pierre had not intended to kill himself. The evening before he had attended an actor's public recitation of François Villon's poem "The Ballad of the Hanged." The boy had been powerfully moved by the actor's performance, which included an affecting imitation of the hanged man's movements. The doctor's theory was that the boy had taken a rope into the bathroom in order to do his own rendition in front of the mirror. During the pantomime, his foot had slipped from the stool.

On the day of his burial, the BBC announced that the Allies had landed in the south of France.

Is this another reason why the story of Le Chambon is not better known? The subtitle of Hallie's book is *The Story of the Village of Le Chambon and How Goodness Happened There*. It is also the story of how absurdity happened there. Once Jean-Pierre had told his mother,

> You know, *Maman*, Father is really a good man. When he dies, I am going to have a wonderful funeral for him—you know? And he will be in a wonderful coffin all covered with precious stones. And I am going to have made a mechanical bird, which will stand upon his tombstone, and this bird will say again and again, "Here is the pastor of Le Chambon."

He was an imaginative child and gifted. He played the piano and wrote poetry. He was brave; his mother could barely restrain him from attacking a Gestapo agent who was beating a Jewish boy with the straps of his own phylacteries. He did not like to attend services at his father's church but would go and pray with the old people in their homes when his father was too busy or away.

Might he have lived longer had his parents been less busy? Dare we ask, given the nature of their business? Did the Catholic priest in Le Chambon, who was not involved in the underground activities but who was friendly with the Trocmés, ever shake his head as he sat alone in the rectory and say, "This is why we are celibate"? Hallie writes,

[A]side from the two permanent refugee guests and the four students in the [Trocmé] house, there were almost always strangers in the dining room, preoccupied with their own terrible problems. Without ever putting their feelings into words, the children felt that their parents were not available to them. They felt that too much of their parents' lives was being given over to this one task, the helping of refugees, a task that was not that big in the lives of the children. Once Nelly [the Trocmés' daughter] said that she would not marry a minister—she did not want to be dedicated to a cause that was larger and more important than her family.

Jean-Pierre's death can be imagined in different circumstances. It could have happened on a vacation to the Riviera, at a boarding school in the Swiss Alps, in a tree house in Lake Wobegone. It is too simplistic to say that it happened because of the war and too cruel to suggest that it happened because of the helpful role the Trocmés played in their times. But why did it have such a familiar ring when I read it, as if, like Magda Trocmé herself, I had been struck by a terrible premonition, a superstitious hunch that every committed kitchen struggle includes the possibility of some tragedy occurring in another room of the house? In addition to "Oh, no!" why did I hear myself whisper, "Of course"?

I have never quite gotten my head around the fact that on either side of the hyphen in *Judeo-Christian* is the story of a sacrificed child. Isaac on the altar and Jesus on the cross. Both of them wind up all right in the end, certainly better off than the doomed children in Greek mythology, Iphigenia and the offspring of Medea and of Tantalus, all hapless instruments of their parents' propitiation, vengeance, or sheer perversity. One can argue that the tradition of the Bible represents a full-frontal assault on the notion of the expendable child, the offering to Moloch, the daughter sent to earn her keep in a brothel. Even Marx is supposed to have told his daughter Eleanor that Christianity could be forgiven much "because it taught us the worship of the child."

Still, it is hard for me to get away from the sense, born of some experience and much observation, that the altruistic demands encoded in my religion are somehow at odds with the obligations of parenthood. What father hasn't read the Sermon on the Mount, with its prohibitions against defensive violence and provision "for the morrow," without thinking of Jesus in the words of Shakespeare's Macduff: "He has no children"? What mother hasn't gone off to retrace the footsteps of the good Samaritan without imagining the question, "Where's Mommy?" in the place she has left?

In fact, one of Jean-Pierre's younger brothers found it unbearable when their father had to go into temporary hiding. Eventually he went to stay with Trocmé; they rejoiced in each other's company. Later on, in a busy train station, they were detained and nearly arrested by the Gestapo. By that time Trocmé was a wanted man. Father and son managed to slip away, but Trocmé later wrote that although he was carrying false identity papers, he had decided in those tense moments that if questioned he would not tell a lie. Face-to-face with another human being, he could not do it. In fact, he had never denied to the Vichy authorities that he and his parish were harboring Jewish refugees; he had simply refused to hand them over. His integrity defies the imagination. It may be that his insistence on truth telling was of a piece with the clear thinking that helped him and his son escape. Even so, one catches one's breath at the resolution not to deceive an agent of the Gestapo with a young child at stake. *The kid!*

"Who are these people," Katie Carr asks in *How to Be Good*, "that they want to save the world and yet they are incapable of forming proper relationships with anybody?" You cannot pin that charge on Trocmé; his relationships were far too extensive and passionate. Instead, I want to retort: Who are these people, Katie Carr included, who can overlook every excess and negligence performed in the name of personal fulfillment or creative expression but whose noses twitch like a diviner's rod at the slightest eccentricity in the struggle to save human beings? If George Sand can't find a civil word for her daughter, then "culture is worth a little risk"; if André Trocmé can't bring himself to tell a lie, then humanitarians are not fit to be parents.

But we know what lies behind Katie Carr's question, and her own conflicted sentiments don't cover it all. We have swum through the cold spots of the humanitarian heart; it may be more accurate to say we have found our own cold spots in the presence of certain humanitarians. Dr. Berman writes, "One of the more blatant paradoxes of Schweitzer's life was that, though he had such love and empathy for that huge mass of village people and patients unrelated to him, he seemed to have so little for those in his immediate family." Urged to spend more time in Paris, where his wife and daughter are currently living, Dr. Paul Farmer reportedly answers, "I don't have any patients in Paris." I'd call that an appropriately wise-ass answer to what was probably an impertinent suggestion to begin with—but still I wonder, how often does he go?

It is not only the physical or emotional absence of the Samaritan parent that can threaten his children, but the presence of strangers who want to be his children too. In her autobiography Dorothy Day tells us, "There were plenty who laid claim to my sympathy and loving care to the extent of forgetting I had personal family obligations, and there were some who were extremely jealous and found ways of showing it." By way of example, she cites a woman who stole all of the clothes belonging to Day's daughter and gave them away. She hastens to add that "this poor warped creature [was] a sufferer." No doubt. I imagine Goebbels was a sufferer too. Like Trocmé's decision not to lie to the Gestapo, Day's tolerant reflection marks the boundaries of a place I find it hard to go. There were one or two times in my tenure as a priest when that place was a church.

Yet for every saint on uneasy terms with her family we find a score of parents whose indulgence and smothering attention turn a child's heart to stone. If the Trocmé children sometimes felt neglected—as they might also have felt had their parents been teachers, doctors, corporate executives, single moms with two minimum-wage jobs—I imagine they were also having fun. I imagine what caused Jean-Pierre to be so taken with the poetry recital was something other than parental neglect—in fact, its very opposite. What happened to him was terrible, but if he'd come safely down off the stool and gone back to his Greek lesson (what he was doing when he decided to give his in-the-mirror performance of "The Ballad of the Hanged"), you would have said, "What a cool kid. I bet his parents could smack him sometimes, but what a cool kid."

My sense is that a child wants, and needs, a parent with a high degree of altruism. If the trait is biologically based, that means we have been selecting for it for millions of years; and if we find it attractive in a mate, we must also find it attractive in a parent. I spoke once with the daughter of a bishop who told me how, when she was a girl and her father was a parish priest, he would bring people home from bus stations who had no place to stay. It was clear that her "daddy," whom I knew and admired and who had not a grandiose bone in his body, was still his daughter's hero—as both the Trocmés were to all four of their children, according to Nelly, her refusal to marry a minister notwithstanding. It may be too that both daughters grew up with a constant and palpable reminder of their own status; they could gauge the difference between parental affection and Christian duty; they knew they hadn't been found in any bus station.

What may distinguish the kitchen struggle of the Trocmés from the more quixotic altruism of professionals and outgoing amateurs alike is the fact that their children were able to assist in it. They were able to help. It is so interesting to me, though not in any way surprising, that Jean-Pierre would avoid church services (he was also "not a good Boy Scout" in a community that held Scouting in high esteem) while at the same time making what amounted to pastoral calls on the old people of Le Chambon. They called him "our friend." No doubt he thought of himself as his father's assistant. Wendell Berry has written that one of the effects of our industrial economy was to separate children from the work of their parents:

> One of the most regrettable things about the industrialization of work is the segregation of children. As industrial work excludes the dead by social mobility and technological change, it excludes children by haste and danger. [In small-scale farming] children play at the grownups' work, as well as at their own play. In their play the children learn to work; they learn to know their elders and their country. And the presence of playing children means invariably that the grown-ups play too from time to time.

One can peer between the lines of Berry's quotation for a glimpse of how things might have looked some days at Le Chambon—in the fields before the war and in the woods during it—though the danger of the rescue work surely precluded much in the way of play. Still, children were intimately involved in the kitchen struggle; they had to be involved because it took place in their kitchens. They were thus made vulnerable but able to prove themselves invaluable—that is, when they weren't needing to be reminded of their value. The daily challenge of hospitality after the Chambonnais model is how to welcome a stranger into one's home without making strangers of the people already living there, in which case, the hospitality itself will be a rather cold gift.

The altruistic parent is conscious of his divided obligation; after all, his children did not ask to be born. The altruistic child may feel no such division. After all, she didn't ask to be born. Rachel Corrie, an American college student, writes to her mother from the Gaza Strip, where she has gone to protest the Israeli occupation.

> I still really want to dance around to Pat Benatar and have boyfriends and make comics for my co-workers. But I also want this to stop. Disbelief and horror are what I feel. Disappointment. I am disappointed that this is the base reality of our world and that we, in fact, participate in it. This is not at all what the people here asked for when they came into the world. This is not the world you and Dad wanted me to come into when you decided to have me.

She lies down in front of an Israeli army bulldozer about to demolish a Palestinian home. The operator either does not see her or does not care. In an instant she becomes, to select but one of the vicious epitaphs that appear on the Internet thereafter, "road kill."

Simone Weil goes to Spain to fight with the Loyalists during the Civil War, though she has no experience as a soldier and is pitifully nearsighted. In camp with her comrades (two of whom, unbeknownst to her, take turns guarding her at night while she sleeps), she steps into a pot of hot cooking oil and badly scalds herself. Contacted by a sympathetic partisan, Dr. and Mrs. Weil hurry to Spain to retrieve her. Simone, Simone. She will die in England a few years later, possibly of self-starvation, insisting that she share the privations of her compatriots in occupied France. In another decade Ethel Rosenberg will go to the electric chair just as Perpetua and her Christian companions went to the wild beasts in the arena centuries before, both impervious to parental pleas that they put aside conviction and save themselves. In a lighter vein, David Sedaris tells us about trying to help a neglected girl in his apartment building, until he finds himself in over his head and his imperious mother comes to take the matter in hand.

"What did you hope to gain by letting that girl into your apartment?" she demands of her son. "And don't tell me you wanted to make a difference in her life, please, I just ate."

Is it such a terrible blasphemy that I can imagine Saint Mary saying the same thing to her son?

She would only have been trying to help. I wasn't born for a world like this, says the child who stares down the bulldozer. Nor were you conceived for destruction, says the maternal heart, pierced with a sword. We speak too narrowly of taking in the stranger. Every family into which a child is born has taken in a stranger. What refugee ever brought as much danger, joy, or perplexity to the Trocmés' door as did their son Jean-Pierre?

The theme of the child beyond help is at the center of Philip Roth's tragic masterwork *American Pastoral*, where it is given the extra layer it often has in life: the parent not only wonders how he can help his child but what he has done or neglected to do to make the help necessary. Why has Merry Levov become a fanatic radical who blows up the town post office, killing a beloved doctor and devastating her family? Is it because her father kissed her once, too intently, when she was his adoring little girl? She goes on to kill three more people, later becoming a Jain convert who lives in filth to avoid the accidental killing of bacteria. What parental misjudgment could possibly account for these wretched extremes? I grew up in a town that contributed a member to the Symbionese Liberation Army, which kidnapped Patty Hearst—I remember that question. In time, Patty's parents must have asked it too. I heard it repeated more than once when I worked as a teacher and a priest.

Though Roth is writing about the implosion of the American dream in the affluent neighborhoods of rural New Jersey, and Camus about the outbreak of plague in a sun-bleached Algerian city, both speak a language of crisis. If anything, Roth's outlook is grimmer.

Camus tells us that a crisis may come that demands our help in extremis, that requires us to abandon almost every attachment and comfort in order to meet an apocalyptic scale of need. Roth tells us about the crisis for which there is no help; his theme is not the tidal wave but the ground opening beneath one's feet.

> He was living it out, his version of paradise. This is how successful people live. They're good citizens. They feel lucky. They feel grateful. God is smiling down on them. There are problems, they adjust. And then everything changes and it becomes impossible. Nothing is smiling down on anybody. And who can adjust then? Here is someone not set up for life's working out poorly, let alone for the impossible. But who is set up for the impossible that is going to happen? Who is set up for tragedy and the incomprehensibility of suffering? Nobody. The tragedy of the man not set up for tragedy—that is every man's tragedy.

Who is set up for a daughter who becomes a murderer? Who is set up to have a daughter lie down in front of a bulldozer in Gaza or a son hang himself in the process of trying to dramatize a poem?

The worst grief of our lives is the discovery that we are unable to help the people we love the most. Not when love is unrequited but when it proves insufficient—that is what breaks our hearts.

You want to know where we're going. You'll see in a little while. I'll give you a hint: when you get there, you will find earth and blood.

Right now we're driving the back way over to a little country town to meet with a man I know. A town not unlike Le Chambon in some ways. Plenty of French surnames. High ground. Nice scenery. "Nine months of winter, three months of trouble"—or, as people tend to say around here, "three months of poor sledding." They know all about snow. The more perverse would even drink to it. The man I'm going to see would not, however, mainly because he's done his drinking in the past, all the way to hell and back. He'd want me to italicize *and back*. He tells me he is grateful for his life every single day. It is a gift. For him, that is the essence of sobriety, which means that a lot of us must look like drunks to him.

I am going because his brother, who never managed *and back*, though he made some poignant attempts, has just committed suicide. It happens fairly often in my extended neighborhood, often during the final months of winter.

I want to stand by this fellow very much because that is my role and because I believe he would stand by me. Even in a bar. Years ago, young to my collar, I got it into my head that I ought to make a greater effort to "be among the people" in the town where my church was located, a dubious undertaking given the fact that I didn't even live there. I didn't know the story of the Trocmés then, but I suppose I was in hopes of finding my own Célisse. I would go fishing for men. There was a hole-in-the-wall bar, and I decided I should go there. "Who will come with me?" I had asked at church. The man we're driving to see said he would come.

He wasn't afraid that being at a bar would prove too much of a temptation, he told me, when I presumed to ask. I think he was afraid that kicking the crap out of someone with the cheek to walk into a bar in his clergy clothes would prove too much of a temptation for someone else.

It was kind of a funny night. There was a pool table. I took a game with another patron, all set to field the questions of where was my church and what was I doing here tonight. We racked up the balls. I forget who broke. And then a miracle occurred, like the net full of fish in the Sea of Galilee. I suddenly became Minnesota Fats. I couldn't miss. Bumper shots. Two balls at a time. Shots I took for the likelihood of missing—in they went. And something told me that I shouldn't pull back. That this was the grace of the moment.

But nothing came of it. Basically, while I cleaned the table, the other fellow drifted back to the bar and left me—I can think of no better way to put it—playing with myself. But of course I wasn't by myself. And the night wasn't as pointless as it seemed. My companion and I were practicing for a night of grief.

That other, happier night, we left the bar and walked the streets talking about whatever came to mind. He was reading about astronomy then, and he told me the humanity-dwarfing facts of deep space as we trudged through the snow. I don't think suicide occurred to us once. Or if it did, it was in that hypothetical and solipsistic way that it comes to mind during a walk when all the stars are out. You're thinking how glad you are to have made it back from hell or how glad that your companion did. Not of the brother who grows tired of letting people down or of believing he does. The person who kicks the stool from under his feet like another broken promise.

Camus says in *The Myth of Sisyphus* that the most fundamental question of philosophy is whether or not to commit suicide. The heart gives first rank to a slightly different question, though, which is what we could have done to prevent someone else from committing suicide. What we could have done to help. And it always strikes me as a totally out-of-bounds question, like asking if you might have encouraged someone to stay in the game by throwing him a touchdown pass even as he was exiting the stadium. Even if he caught your good intentions, what difference would they make? But of course that's not a thing you say out loud. And anyway, we all know or think we know that people do in some cases come in off the ledge, to answer the phone or the doorbell, thinking they'll get the job done later but procrastinating till the day when natural causes cross it off their list.

I have made visits like this one before. I have gone out in the night when the suicide was a young girl, an imaginative child like Jean-Pierre Trocmé, who fully intended to die but seemed to have no clearly formed idea of what that meant. Her farewell letter made death sound like a chapter out of Tolkien. I have seen people at the moment that "no one is set up for," and I have seen how that moment is impaled on the merciless insinuation that one "ought to have known."

It is a sad table I am invited to sit down at, such sad eyes, not only those of my friend, but his wife, his son, who loved his uncle a lot. There is nothing to say, really, but prayers, and that is all I have been asked to say. I read several from my black book. I attempt a few words besides prayer, nothing fancy, just some straight, gentle shots, the kind you ought to be able to tap right in, but this time I can't seem to sink a single ball. Nothing on the table goes where I want it to. I scratch.

The way we identify with the survivors of a suicide is by feeling as helpless toward them as they do toward the deceased. I doubt that many comforters or any mourners find solace in the comparison, but they might—to see how useless we are even when people *do* call and even when they *want* help and even when you have the authority of God and all the angels to back up what you say. You're still no help. All you can do is abide. That is why, even though this is merely the memory, and even though I can't see you, I asked you to come along.

"Help is giving part of yourself to somebody who comes to accept it willingly and needs it badly."

So says the narrator's parson father in Norman Maclean's beautiful novella, *A River Runs Through It*. He is talking to his elder son about his younger, prodigal Paul, who is heading to an early grave by gambling for stakes higher than he can afford to lose. The Reverend has more to add:

> "So it is," he said, using an old homiletic transition, "that we can seldom help anybody. Either we don't know what part to give or maybe we don't like to give any part of ourselves. Then, more often than not, the part that is needed is not wanted. And even more often, we do not have the part that is needed."

The narrator complains that his father is making things sound more difficult than they are. "Help doesn't have to be anything that big." The father remains unconvinced.

> He asked me, "Do you think your mother helps him by buttering his rolls?"
> "She might," I told him. "In fact, yes, I think she does."

Eventually the three men go fishing, which is about the only thing that seems to help in this book, though it doesn't help Paul stay alive. Maclean wrote the story when he was an old man, and it shows in this: that he has reached the age of knowing the precise importance of things like taking someone fishing and buttering his rolls. You must not place too much hope in them. And you ought not to omit them either.

Therefore, the narrator agrees to take his girlfriend's ne'er-do-well brother fishing, and even Paul begrudgingly comes along, though the expedition proves to be a minor disaster. The narrator winds up hearing from his girlfriend something similar to what his father tells him, though in a plaintive tone appropriate to her youth.

"Tell me," she asked, "if my brother comes back next summer, will you try to help me help him?"

It took a long time to say it, but I said it. "I will try."

Then she said, "He won't be back." Then she added, "Tell me, why is it that people who want help do better without it—at least, no worse. Actually, that's what it is, no worse. They take all the help they can get, and are just the same as they always have been."

I love this story, as I love trout fishing. I know people who love it just as much as I do who don't fish, though they have been fishers of men, including men of their own households, and they know what it means to get skunked. I think that is a good part of what appeals to them about Maclean's story, and another story I love, also one made popular on the screen some years back, Evelyn Waugh's *Brideshead Revisited*. It took me a while to see the resemblance. Both of the main characters, Sebastian and Paul, are alcoholic, charming, self-destructive, and in some ways running from a background of strict religion. There are striking differences, of course; a reader is amused to think what might have passed between the homosexual Oxford undergraduate and the brawling Montana reporter had they found themselves face-to-face in a bar, though probably what would have passed is a few drinks. Perhaps they would have fallen in love. They have so much in common yet plenty to prove that opposites attract.

We see each of them through the eyes of a narrator who loves and even admires a person he cannot help—and to some extent is not even sure he should help because the "trouble" is at times indistinguishable from the man's charisma. And the trouble is of a type that will suck you in if you get too close. Both Paul's brother and Sebastian's friend Charles ultimately relinquish their companions to fate. There is no question of sacrificing oneself for the other. The other is going to lie down on the altar whether in company or alone. The only choices are to lie down with him or to let him go.

Sebastian eventually finds a consolation that Paul never does: someone to take care of—in the form of a syphilitic German deserter with a wounded foot that will not heal. After Charles meets up with the pair in North Africa, Sebastian tells him, "You know, Charles . . . it's rather a pleasant change when all your life you've had people looking after you, to have someone to look after yourself. Only of course it has to be someone pretty hopeless to need looking after by *me*." The sick soldier becomes a part of Sebastian's redemption, as does the monastery where Sebastian spends his last days. Perhaps it is too simplistic to say that the novels are Protestant and Catholic versions of the same theme, that of the brother beyond help. Nevertheless, we can push the distinction at least this far: to say that Sebastian appears to be surrounded by a great company of intercessors, visible and perhaps invisible as well. He cannot leave the communion of the saints even though he wants to. He keeps running into it. Paul, on the other hand, simply keeps running until he runs into a wall. If I would have preferred to be a Protestant in Le Chambon, I think I might have liked to have a rosary stashed in my creel when I went fishing with the Macleans on the Big Blackfoot River.

At one point in *Brideshead Revisited*, Sebastian's sister Cordelia speaks of his holiness. Charles questions this, but Cordelia persists. "Oh, yes, Charles, that's what you've got to understand about Sebastian." Without resorting to the language of sanctity, the Reverend Maclean makes a similar observation in *A River Runs Through It*. His surviving son tries for a prosaic epitaph:

> "If you push me far enough, all I really know is that he was a fine fisherman."
> "You know more than that," my father said. "He was beautiful."

The beauty, or if you prefer the holiness, of Sebastian and Paul is glossed by the religion that figures so prominently in both their stories. Perhaps not only in the most obvious way of thinking about them, as lost sheep and prodigal sons beloved by God. That is indeed what they are, but it is not all they are.

When I first began to write this book, a writer friend of mine was out on tour with a book of his own. He had looked into the Gideon Bibles in a few of his motels and reported back to me that the Gospels might be summarized as the story of a man who went around helping people. In effect he was pronouncing a blessing on my project. He was also describing the mind-set of Sebastian's family and of Paul's as they tried to rescue their children; no doubt they saw themselves as doing the healing work of Christ.

But as I thought further about what my friend had said, I realized that his depiction was only part of the story—the better part, to be sure, but only a part. The Gospels are also about a man who proved nearly impossible to help. Side by side with the grand narrative of the compassionate rabbi who went about the villages casting out demons and healing the sick is the quieter if more disturbing tale of a friend and son who inspired great concern in those who loved him and who eluded their assistance. Mary, Peter, Nicodemus, the Pharisees who warn him of Herod, and Pontius Pilate all try to help him; the philanthropic women of Jerusalem who offer him drugged wine at the foot of the cross try to help him; we might be surprised to learn that Judas Iscariot was actually trying to help him—all to no avail. The Good News is laced with the more ambiguous news (though it too might be good for all we know) that the holiest persons are sometimes those who prove the most impervious to our help.

Seen in this light, the parable of the prodigal son shows flecks of autobiography. Who is this boy who goes off to keep company with harlots and squanders his inheritance on the undeserving if not an image of the Son of Man, who kept company with tax collectors and prostitutes and raised such a stir for doing so? I don't mean to twist the moral of the parable. I only mean to suggest that there is some of Jesus's own heart in the parable. He may have identified with that kid more than we realize.

I am speaking now in symbols and within the limits of a particular symbol system, which happens to be that of my religion. I don't wish to get carried away, which is what we are in danger of doing whenever we romanticize the misfit. One of Merry Levov's bomb-throwing friends tells her father, "Your daughter is divine"—mainly because of all she has suffered—and in context it sounds like crap. It is crap.

But I am too much of a materialist to dismiss a truth merely because it comes in versions that stink. The truth that Maclean and Waugh are telling us is that holiness can exist on both sides of desperation, with those who want to help and with those who are beyond help. It helps me to remember that—it helps me avoid mistaking my good intentions for the odor of sanctity.

An appreciation for what is Christlike in Paul and Sebastian also helps me appreciate why Paul's brother and Charles must cut loose from them in the end. It helps me understand why I have sometimes had to cut myself loose from someone made in the same image, just as I know I would have let go of Jesus on his way to the cross. The disciples all desert him at Gethsemane. It is a part of the story that I and my coreligionists rehearse every year, with appropriate remorse for our own apostasy and broken faith. The service for Maundy Thursday remains my favorite in the liturgy; I tell people it's where I live. But alongside my penitence I have wondered: had the disciples hung on till the bitter end, and had there been twelve extra crosses on the hill of Golgotha, would there have been thirteen resurrections on Easter? Would that have been a better ending? Is not their decision to let go of the juggernaut as it hurtles downhill part of what allows the disciples to cheer when their friend crawls from the wreckage and waves to the crowd?

What am I getting at? Again, I'm speaking within the symbol, only to say that faithfulness to a person bent on self-destruction is in some ways a profession of hopelessness, though it may feel deceptively like hope. It says, "I might as well follow my beloved to the Place of the Skull, because I'm never going to see a resurrection. He is going down, and he is never coming back." That is not martyrdom; that is a capitulation to despair. It helps to know the difference.

Finally, it helps to recognize that at least part of the holiness of a Sebastian Flyte and of a Paul Maclean consists of their inability to be helped. "What's wrong with them" is their inability to be anything other than sick in a sick world. That is not to say their sickness is actually health seen through a jaundiced eye. No, they are sick. Their health consists only of the fact that they can be nothing but sick in response to a world that is not well.

But never hopeless. Perhaps Waugh and Maclean thought it was; I can't be sure. There is an elegiac tone in both *Brideshead Revisited* and *A River Runs Through It*; both novels suggest that a better world has been lost, whether it be that of England before the Second World War or the days when you could fall asleep buck naked on the banks of the Big Blackfoot River without "half the city of Great Falls . . . standing on the shore waiting to steal your clothes." In that sense, both novels are written from a reactionary point of view. At the same time, their doomed characters protest against our complicity with the status quo. In other words, they imply that the people whom we strive in vain to help toward health and balance are, in their own unwitting way, striving to help us toward revolution. They repeat back to us the words we fling at them: "You've got to have a better plan than this!"

When the trooper called from Arizona to tell me that Kathy B. was dead and to ask if I knew of any next of kin, I asked if he knew why she had taken her life. In the days when I knew her, she had not seemed self-destructive. Eccentric, even mentally disturbed, but not suicidal. In fact, she had struck me as the quintessential survivor. A parasite, people said, but what is parasitic behavior but a time-honored strategy for survival? I didn't ask how she had done it. (I doubted she would have used a gun.) I just wanted to know why.

The trooper wasn't sure. The deceased hadn't left a note. "But people who lived nearby said she'd been pretty upset about the likelihood of a war in Iraq."

Of course she would have been. I remembered that Peace Pilgrim book she had carried around in her backpack. In the end, her tragedy was that she could not make her peace with a world where peace pilgrims have yet to make a dent.

But is this how we make peace, by killing ourselves? By starving ourselves to death? By lying down in front of a bulldozer? If this was her protest, I wanted none of it. I was glad she and I had parted company when we did. I was glad she went to Arizona. I was glad I hadn't been around to find the body. I was glad . . . to have met her.

She had none of the wayward charm of Sebastian and Paul and the Trocmés' young son, at least by the time she got to me, but I will always think of her as marching under their flag. It is too easy, too maudlin, and way too insincere for me to say that she was too good for this world. But perhaps the world is a little better for the time she spent in it.

Camus says that the first question of philosophy is whether or not to commit suicide. If that is so, then the reasons we give for committing it or not committing it amount to the most elemental philosophical argument. To date I have been spared the necessity of making such an argument, though I have gone so far as to consider the reasons I might give for choosing to live another day. I'd wager that they're the same as most people's reasons. I'd wager that a few people wouldn't mind having them repeated.

My reasons are persons who might need my help. Some of them live in my house. Others of them may be headed toward my door, refugees of a crisis that even now is building like a slow-motion tidal wave. And the truth is that I may wind up being little or no help to a single one of them. The part that is required may not be the part I give. Or not a part I have. Or else it may not be wanted. I will wait just the same.

SIX

THE DESCENT
INTO HELL

We envy the Chambonnais their moral clarity and their courage. Simply for their unstinting hospitality, we envy them. Few of us would have the candor to admit, however, even to ourselves, that we also envy them because their guests, aside from the status of being Jews under an anti-Semitic regime, were not disadvantaged people. If they came from ghettos, theirs were different ghettos from ours. If their biblical ancestors had once lived in tents, few of the descendants wound up in mobile homes.

Make the obligatory protest; then consult your mind's picture of the refugees. Is there a doctor in the house? Quite possibly. A girl whose father is also her grandfather? Such a thing never even crossed your mind.

You're not from around here, are you?

The Chambonnais were involved in the dangerous work of saving children from strangers who wanted to destroy them. They were not involved in the less dangerous but infinitely more disheartening work of saving children from the very people who had conceived them.

To put it another way: the Chambonnais were faced with the daunting prospect of waiting for the fall of the Third Reich. They were spared the more dismal prospect of waiting for the end of the world.

To put it the simplest way I know how: they didn't work for the department of social services.

"I will wait just the same," I say, at the close of the preceding chapter, attempting an affirmative moral stance. But the vigor for maintaining such a posture depends a bit on what you're waiting for, doesn't it?

Have you noticed something about this book: in the end I always try to swim toward the light? I sink myself in a tangle of contradictions and cross-references, and then, at the point where my endurance or yours is about to give out, I make (or feign) my escape and swim Houdinilike for the light.

I took a similar approach when I preached and when I taught school. I always swam toward the light. And yet, I am writing this book, and perhaps I am no longer preaching or teaching, because I began to find that approach more and more difficult to sustain. The reader ever on my mind is someone with the same difficulty, someone acutely conscious of the conundrum that to swim toward the light requires an amount of oxygen attainable only in the place where the light is.

And yet, in what other direction should you swim?

And yet, after he comes to the dark wood, Dante begins his journey toward regeneration not by climbing toward heaven but by descending into hell.

Just so you know, our subject this time around is the poor. As in *them*. If they truly are with us always, as the Bible says, then we must always be talking about them. In a book about help, we certainly must. Whom should we help if not the poor?

The word shadows them. It *becomes* them, in every sense of *becomes*. When the poor find work, they become "the help." But they remain the poor.

The poor are portrayed, and betrayed, by an ignorance of grammar. "I weren't in school today." An impression of mismatched clothing attends the disagreement of subject and verb. The shame, or the mercy, of this is that their predicament can be clarified grammatically. The difference between the haves and the have-nots can be expressed as a difference in the parts of speech given to the word *help*.

The primary moral advantage of the privileged is that for them *help* is a verb. It is what you do with your resources and skills. It does not define you. Rather, your inclinations and education define it. To help or not to help, that is the question. Pediatrics or cardiology, that is a particular subset of the question. Your father advises cardiology. It's been a gold mine for him.

The disadvantage of poverty is the disadvantage of a noun. The yards and hallways of the poor are littered with nouns: cars without engines, baby carriages without wheels, sofas without guts. The poor themselves are like nouns, jobless, hopeless, verbless.

When you are poor, you are the object of help. Like the direct object in a sentence. Which is? (I would be anything but poor had I a dollar for every time I asked that question.) Class? "A noun that receives the action of the verb." Very good. A direct object is basically a noun on welfare.

Off the dole, the noun moves from the objective to the nominative case. It remains a noun. It remains in a passive relationship to the verb. "Help wanted." Nobody cares what you want.

Those not hired as help are *not* wanted. The poorest of the poor are not exploited; they are expendable. This is where Marxist terminology becomes quaint, at the far end of the trailer park.

In a postindustrial society the poor occupy the same place as males after an Amazonian coup. We must keep a few around to pleasure us, but if the rest were to die tomorrow, Dow Jones's eyelashes would not even flutter.

It has become fashionable of late to talk about "the working poor." It is a good fashion, a laudable phrase, if for no other reason than to debunk the myth that all the poor in America are living off extravagant government entitlements. Admittedly, no one seems to cherish the prejudice as much as the working poor themselves.

But "working poor" has a different nuance for me. Like a working phone or a working toilet. The functional as opposed to the dysfunctional. When she was a little girl, our daughter heard Aretha Franklin singing on the car radio and called from the backseat, "Mommy, what is a natural woman?" "Oh, honey . . . I suppose it's a woman with all her original parts." The working poor are like a natural woman. They have all their original parts. As opposed to the others, the broken ones. Categories overlap, but you can readily intuit where my stress is going to fall: on "the help" that is not wanted.

Along with all the deprivations that come with poverty—the lack of food, shelter, medicine, education—comes the ethical deprivation of not being able "to help" in the infinitive, nondefinitive form of the verb.

No one, not even you, has ever held out a hand to help me to be a better man.

That is: no one has ever appreciated my own need to help. No one has reckoned that in the sum of my disadvantages. Even the most compassionately put together care package carries the insinuation that I am little more than an animal: I require feed, veterinary care, obedience training. Sit, boy. Can you open your mouth for me? But even a dog wants to be of use.

In one of the low-wage jobs she took to research her book *Nickel and Dimed*, Barbara Ehrenreich reflects on her desire to help an injured fellow worker: "I want to help . . . I am a 'good person' . . . but maybe I'm also just sick of my suddenly acquired insignificance." She acts on her impulse and is rebuffed.

The central paradox of helping the poor, the vortex that forms the very mouth of hell, is that our most humane gestures on their behalf serve to accentuate their dehumanization. In that sense, feeding the hungry a turkey dinner is on a par with eating it in front of them.

Hunger rightly protests that the preceding statement is a sophistry.

But I am not trying to trivialize hunger, only to point out its spiritual depths. The true heinousness of the crime. Man does not live by bread alone. To share bread with the hungry is to love one's neighbor, but to share moral agency is to love one's neighbor *as oneself.* It is to "give help" in the fullest sense—that is, to place the privilege of helping in another person's possession.

It is also to abolish hunger.

The poor you have with you always. We take that as a prophetic statement on the intransigent nature of poverty. We do not take it as a reflection on ourselves. On our intransigent smugness. On our perpetual readiness to auction off someone else's flask of perfume for the benefit of the needy.

We take it wrong, I think.

But poverty is so complex. The causes of poverty, so complex. The solutions, if solutions even exist, are bound to be phenomenally complex. So we say.

So let us talk about a more pleasant kind of complexity. Really. Something nice right here in the car, the *new* car, the one I bought with my advance for this book.

I am driving east, over the Connecticut River, to see a former student of mine, probably the most disadvantaged person I have ever known. I am bringing him a load of cedar boughs for his one-man cottage business. He builds rose arbors and trellises, lashing and screwing the branches together in intricate, hoarfrost patterns. (But that is not the complexity I intend to talk about.) He sells his creations for a song to a nearby greenhouse to buy Christmas presents and pay off his debts. He always has debts. Others owe him too but remain in perpetual default. Among these I include myself.

"Oh, I get it," someone says. (Not you, dear reader, whom I can imagine only as patient and kind. Let's say it is some pain-in-the-neck hitchhiker in the backseat.)

"This guy is really miserable; therefore, you're calling this chapter 'The Descent into Hell.' That's it, right? You're going to show us that his life is hell."

Nope, I say, we are going to hell. Where Dante visits after he enters the dark wood. The dark wood was before we picked you up. (And we'll arrive in hell after we drop him off. Let's hope so.) Right now, we are going to see a man who is poor and has always been poor, that's all. And on the way we are going to talk about complexity.

Which in this case has provided us with a certain monotony, I admit: for we have just listened for the sixth time to a song called "Central Reservation" by a recording artist named Beth Orton. All I have to do is tap this little button and it plays without ceasing. I'm impressed every time it happens. I grew up in the age of vinyl records, of turntables with arms as crude and painstakingly deliberate as those of steam shovels.

As for the song, I take it for an existential anthem on making one's own meaning in life, though according to Beth Orton—I refer you to the liner notes—it is a song about "going home with your knickers in your pocket the morning after." Not an experience I'm greatly familiar with, but I find the song fetching just the same. So we are hearing it now for the seventh time.

I have no idea how any of this works. It has something to do with laser beams and digital technology, but beyond that I'm clueless.

Clueless and amazed. When I was growing up, and something known as the custom car craze was taking place out in California and really all over the heartland, visionary mechanics were actually toying around with having record players in their cars. Big square turntables that looked as though they'd been stolen from a high school audiovisual room mounted like some Dadaist joke behind the front seats. Mustache on the Mona Lisa. Turntable in the car. Here is Big Daddy Roth (*Hot Rod* magazine, circa 1966) with his newest creation, a '38 Chevy coupe with seventy-nine coats of candy apple metal flake paint and a record player in the back. *A record player.* Hot damn.

"Good until you hit the first bump," my father said.

And here I am, thirty-seven years later, on the bumpiest Dogpatch road in Vermont logging onto "Central Reservation" for—what is it?—the eighth time.

All of this is possible because someone somewhere counted on my desire. He knew, somehow, that at the age of thirteen I looked at that record player in the backseat of Big Daddy Roth's fantastic car with almost as much longing as I looked at the sleek bare leg cocked beside the candy apple fender (Big Daddy's lovely assistant).

In the same way, this somebody-somewhere was able to anticipate that I would work to music, read to music, putter, snooze, and entertain to music—that if Ash Wednesday falls on a day when my health or responsibilities preclude fasting (say, two feet of snowfall that needs to be shoveled out of the driveway by hand), I give up recorded music and find the renunciation every bit as ascetic as going without food—sometimes more so. I tried it once for a whole Lent, and it nearly killed me.

In short, he knew that my desire to hear music and to select exactly what music I would hear was strong enough that I would pay to have it met. For his part, the auto maker wagered that this recording device and its clever little features would go a long way toward making his car attractive to me. And he was right.

Suffice it to say, the CD player is hardly a practical necessity. As a driving force in the history of peoples and their epochal migrations, it ranks rather small. As a driving force in the car, it ranks not a whit. I feel a need to mention all this because so often we speak of business and commerce as though they were matters of enormous practicality, of iron bridges spanning vast chasms and barges laden with fresh-cut wheat, of great claws digging the stuff of destiny out of the earth.

In truth, business and commerce have every bit as much to do with a girl coming home in the morning with her knickers in her pocket. They have to do with desire. Stand in the supermarket someday and ask yourself, How much of this has to do with feeding my body, and how much of this has to do with the most fickle of my desires?

The British braved the U-boats for tea. Not the stiff upper lip but the quivering nether one—that is what saved the Empire.

I will tell you something that I believe with nearly all my heart: that if I wanted (with nearly all my heart) the hungry to be fed and the diseased to be healed and the oppressed to go free—in which case I am sure that many others would want these things too, just as I am sure that I was not the only thirteen-year-old boy with one eye on Big Daddy Roth's hot rod and one eye on his lovely assistant—that I would have my desire. That if justice and mercy were as important to me as ridding myself of body odor or seeing movies or getting published, I would have what I desired. Malcolm X put it somewhat more pointedly:

> The white man—give him his due—has an extraordinary intelligence, an extraordinary cleverness. His world is full of proof of it. You can't name a thing a white man can't make. You can hardly name a scientific problem he can't solve.

If he wants to.

And I believe, furthermore, that if justice and mercy were as important to me as I like to pretend to myself they are, at least one of the white men running for president at the time I was writing this book would have used the word *poor* at least once in his campaign. Which I do not believe I have heard. I have heard about "working Americans" and "our deserving seniors" and "the struggling middle class"—you can bet I've heard all sorts of things about the middle class—but I have not heard about the poor.

Perhaps that is because I have been playing Beth Orton songs when I ought to have been listening to campaign speeches. But I have asked people less addicted and more informed than I, and they don't recall hearing the word either.

"These politicians don't care," you may say, but you will be wrong. These politicians care very much, just as the ever-vilified CEO cares very much: they care about getting elected and getting rich, respectively—and to do either, they must be able to know, and they must be able to meet, my desire. Not my official desire. Not the desire I write into a letter to the editor or take with a bottle of wine or a bowl of salsa dip to a dinner party, but my real, honest-to-God desire. What gets me to open my wallet with the reckless abandon of two necking adolescents opening their mouths—*that* desire.

Complexity, in fact, has very little to do with it. Complexity is all the stuff that a couple goes through to get a wedding ceremony up and running, the invitation for example—a whole genre unto itself, with the choices to make of paper stocks, text (traditional or contemporary), print face, colors of ink, edging, images, envelope—to say nothing of the bride's dress, the fabric, the neckline, the bodice, the sleeve, the hem, the veil, the train, along with various incidentals like the gifts for the groomsmen and the number of them required and which to pair with which bridesmaids and the dresses for those, the readings for the service, which hors d'oeuvres ought to be served at the reception and which songs the DJ needs to play for which dances, bride with groom, bride with dad, et cetera. Complex stuff indeed. An intricate coordination of experts: cooks, dressmakers, printers, jewelers, theologians, confectioners, gynecologists, notaries, musicians, photographers, pharmacists, travel agents. But desire is what gets it all done. Desire is the great "I do."

People sit down to dinner at the houses of their friends and believe, sincerely believe, that they need to understand the causes of and invent the solutions to poverty in order for the miseries of the poor to be relieved. It is completely up to them. The whole technology of justice is on their shoulders. They must put on the entire wedding by themselves. They offer tentative hypotheses. They listen with furrowed brows to the counterproposals of those on the other side of the table. They cite something they have read in the *Atlantic* or the *New York Times*. (They may still have the issue around someplace, in which case they will send it to you.) They agree that the situation is disgraceful. They go home and let out the dog and take out their earrings and brush their teeth, feeling vaguely uneasy about their own lack of grasp, the way all this complexity eludes them. We really don't know much about it, do we?

Do you know how your VCR works? How images of men and women, some of them naked in breathtaking detail, are reproduced from ribbons of shiny black tape? Or how a woman can sing the same song ten consecutive times in your car or how the car itself manages to coordinate its drive train to the conditions of the road in what the manufacturer has every reason to alleluia as "the beauty of all-wheel drive"?

It was enough that you had the desire.

Less than 0.7 percent of the GNPs of wealthy countries goes for aid to poor ones. This in a world where 1.2 billion people live on less than a dollar a day. The 0.7 percent is an estimate of our desire. Have the powers that be miscalculated? Is there disorder in the streets over spending less than 1 percent of our extremely gross national product on the abolition of hell?

I told you we were going to talk about poverty. Perhaps you expected—perhaps the pest in the backseat will go so far as to demand— "something useful" in the form of analysis, of policy; here are the causes, here are the difficulties, these are the possible remedies. But that isn't what interests me. Does it interest you?

No, what interests me is why I don't care all that much about the causes, the difficulties, the possible remedies. What interests me is why, at the end of certain days, with my face in the mirror and no one in the room but me and God, I don't seem to give a shit.

I do give a shit when I'm here, in this apartment, though if I have to shit, I will hold it until I am someplace else. My compassion does not make me any less squeamish.

We have arrived at our first destination. We have just piled several armloads of fresh cedar brush out on the sagging porch. The man who helped us is about ten years younger than I am, though if I told you he was ten years my senior you would not be surprised. Nor would you be surprised to hear that I am fifty.

He was nineteen when he entered my high school classroom, already too old. He put his head down on his desk and immediately fell asleep. Sometime during the term he woke up and we went fishing.

We would become characters in the same story, and a river runs
through it. On the last page, I am sure, it will say, "The poor you have
with you always." Perhaps it will be the very last sentence. Sometimes
I fear it will be part of a sentence passed upon my soul.

*The poor were with you always, yet you allowed them to remain poor.
Therefore . . .*

The apartment did not always look this pulled together. You should
have seen it when his mother was living here and he was her boarder.
The state took him away from her when he was a kid. After a series of
foster homes, menial jobs, job training programs (to prepare him for
menial jobs), one brief jail sentence, and a couple of marriages nearly as
brief, he was back. Like the prodigal son, except the prodigal was his
mother. It was not a happy arrangement. They fought constantly. He
mourns for her like no man I have ever known mourns for a dead parent.

To tell you his whole story would make you cry. Just to see his table
manners would make you cry—so fastidious he is, like a marquis. He
may have learned them at one of the foster homes he stayed at.
Whether or not that was the one operated by the priest-pornographer,
I do not know. He never talks with his mouth full. He hasn't a tooth in
his mouth.

When his mother was living, also toothless and one-eyed under the
watchful eye of a velvet Christ, we could not all have stood here like
this in the middle of the living room.

At the end of every rummage sale in this town, people would drop
off the unsold clothing at Lena's house, knowing it would never be refused. It piled up, box upon box, in her apartment until she scarcely
had a place to sit. The man we are visiting slept in an unheated shed
attached to the back of the apartment because her bedrooms were similarly crammed with her neighbors' benevolence.

She was as unable to say no as the purveyors of charity were unable
to take their excess to the dump (where they would have had to pay a
dollar per bag). A throwaway culture is a wicked thing, but there will
never be a Christian culture until charitably disposed Christians learn
to throw things away.

It didn't all come from churches, but I suspect that most of it came
with a feeling of righteousness. I can imagine the people bringing their
torn grocery bags of cast-off clothing and cardboard boxes of flea-

market bric-a-brac to Lena's porch, the shiver of self-congratulation as they tiptoed back to their cars. "Lena will be so tickled." Part of the sadness of all this is that she was tickled, as much as she would have been tickled, in her childbearing years, with a complimentary shot of Johnny Walker Red.

Charity seems like the wrong word for feeding an addiction. Let us call it recycling. Let us briefly review the science of waste management.

Social Darwinism was once based on a hierarchic model of evolution, one in which a human being was more evolved than a pack rat. A biologist neighbor informs me this is now passé; every species currently living on the planet has developed successful strategies for its ecological niche. We are all equals now.

In the new version of social Darwinism, *bottom-feeder* amounts to a misleading metaphor because the bottom isn't really the bottom. There is no bottom (say those at the top). Da 'hood is simply da 'hood, which from a safe and sanitary distance we are quite willing to appreciate. It may seem awful to us to find a fellow creature crawling in the dirt or hanging upside down in the dark, but to a worm or a bat, hey, that's a perfectly natural thing to do.

Haven't you ever heard the expression "happy as a pig in shit"?

It is a sentiment with a long pedigree. Thoreau said as much about the Irish laborers living in their shanties by the railroad tracks in Concord. In Montaigne it is humanized somewhat by his exasperation:

> I have picked up boys from begging, to serve me: who soon after have quitted both my kitchen and livery, only that they might return to their former course of life; and I found one afterwards, picking mussels out of the sewer for his dinner, whom I could neither by entreaties nor threats reclaim from the sweetness he found in indigence.

To say nothing of the bitterness he may have found in livery. We can see where Montaigne is a bit obtuse. But is there anyone so obtuse as not to find his own experience mirrored in Montaigne's? Only if he has very limited experience trying to help the poor. *Happy as a pig in shit*— file that among the more common reasons for not giving a shit.

Except that my former student is not happy. And he is not a pig. He is often in shit. That much is true.

American poverty is as unique and distinctly American an invention as the hot rod and the salad bar. To be sure, it shares some things in common with its counterparts in other cultures and countries. But comparisons are deceptive. By global standards the American poor are in fact rich; millions would change places with them in a heartbeat. Yet one has the sense that of all the poor in the world, the American poor are the most abject—and partly because they are so "rich." Mostly because those around them are richer still.

I do not think that Walker Evans would have photographed that woman over at checkout number eight, though anyone who sees her knows immediately that she is poor. Not a sharecropper but definitely poor. Her daughter gives her away as much as anything else, that unmistakable look of dazed, slatternly dejection. With her head bowed, she takes the groceries one by one out of the shopping cart and offers them meekly to her mother, who snatches them from her hand, as if the daughter had been apprehended in an act of shoplifting, and slams them onto the conveyor. This is not the express register ("ten items or less"), so it goes on for quite a while. Snatch, slam. Snatch, slam. It is like watching a strange penitential rite. Bless me, mother, for I have sinned: I exist. The mother is the celebrant. She speaks the liturgy in a language of jerks and scowls. *I'm not going to take it anymore. I'm in a bitching mood today. I don't know what I'm going to do with this fucking kid. I hope people are watching me, and I am furious if they are. What are you looking at, mister?*

I am looking at a case of malnutrition that weighs in excess of two hundred and fifty pounds.

An emaciated African madonna stares at you from the pages of a glossy magazine. Her condition begs, but she does not beg—she is probably too weak with hunger to make the supplicating gesture. She is dressed in articles of native clothing. It is possible she made them herself. Her breasts have no milk, her child may already be dead, but she holds him to her just the same. It is impossible to despise this woman. She is abject, but she is not absurd.

In a remote village in India, farmers have offered to sell their kidneys in order to pay the rent on their fields. It is a pathetic and shameful transaction, but its objective is not pathetic or shameful. They have not offered to sell their fields for satellite TV.

In a remote village in northern New England a little girl has been removed from her mother's custody after the woman knocked her out by lobbing soup cans at her head. (Apparently the ritual movement of what I observed in the supermarket goes two ways.) If you need to think about that for a few moments, I will understand. Take your time. You might start by imagining the Indian farmers throwing cans of soup at their children—a woman in a sari and a gold nose ring (her dowry) picking up a can of Campbell's chicken noodle and pitching it like Sandy Koufax at her daughter's head.

By Indian standards, the woman in New England is rich. She has the chicken noodle *and* both her kidneys. She has a car, for Krishna's sake. But which of the two is poorer?

They are both poor, of course. They are victims of the same systems. They are victims of the same systemic violence. It's just that, in keeping with the sophistication of a highly developed culture, the violence in America is more refined.

The final act of violence against the poor is to make them ridiculous.

If American poverty requires its own understanding, perhaps poverty requires a definition that will be especially pertinent to America. I defer to all definitions proposed by the poor themselves, who, according to David Shipler in his book *The Working Poor*, often define their condition not by a lack of money but by a lack of hope. There's no way to go one better on that. But I will venture one just below it.

Poverty is the inability to renounce anything. To live in poverty is to exist in a permanent yes relationship to the world. When you have nothing, you must say yes to everything.

Having your needs met is the prerequisite for renunciation. "No!" says the child of prosperous parents, toddling confidently across the oriental carpet with her family clambering after her like a troupe of adoring apes. The blank-eyed child of poverty tentatively opens her grimy hand. The desert knows no other response to rain than to open its mouth. In a desert that is how you obtain and retain moisture. In a consumerist culture, that is how you poison yourself to death.

The only kind of aristocracy I am willing to acknowledge belongs to those with the technical and psychic wherewithal to do without. "Why I Am Not Going to Buy a Personal Computer" by Wendell Berry, which is not nearly so illuminating as the ire it aroused, is not to my mind the manifesto of a Luddite but the testament of the last surviving duke. Here at my laptop, I doff my hat to my betters.

That is to say, I offer a definition of privilege. The template for any definition of privilege is that it be restricted to a few. The poor are not few. According to the U.S. census there were 34.6 million in 2002. My contention is that there were many more.

Conservative sociologists and the spawn of conservative think tanks speak of "the culture of poverty." If there is any humor to be had on this infernal journey, this is it. We had better pull off here because there may not be another place to stop on the highway. What, pray tell, is a culture of poverty? I would guess that it is one of waste, ignorance, substance abuse, petty squabbling, random violence, sexual irresponsibility, shabby child rearing, and a sweet tooth for scandal. I would guess it is a culture with no meaningful conception of the future and no ability whatsoever to know the proper value of anything. To borrow the eloquence of the novelist Tobias Smollett, it would manifest itself in "a mob of beings pleased with rattles, baubles, and gewgaws, so devoid of sense and distinction, that even the most acute philosopher would find it a very hard task to discover for what wise purpose of providence they were created."

In short, I assume that a culture of poverty would look exactly like the dominant culture of America, which more and more resembles that of a tenement or a trailer park. Lu Ann called Peggy Sue a slut. Monica gave Billy a blow job. The poor are with us always because the poor are us.

(Smollett, by the way, was writing about the leisured class in eighteenth-century England.)

I grew up during the building boom in housing projects. We had simultaneously declared war on poverty in America and war on the peasantry in Vietnam. I can remember overhearing the barber shop diatribes on what "those people" down in the city had done, how the spendthrift federal government had moved them out of the slums into brand-new apartments where they lost no time yanking out the faucets and the doorknobs and anything else they could pry loose to sell, probably to get money for liquor and dope. You could not help people like that.

Thus I was taught that a culture of poverty is one in which you trash a place that isn't even yours and sell whatever you can for a quick buck. In other words, you behave like a coal company in Kentucky. Or like the present administration wants to behave in Alaska. When Republicans say that theirs is the *true* party of the disadvantaged, I have no trouble keeping a straight face.

It takes a certain amount of class prejudice to grasp the ugly (and the beautiful) truths that trump all class prejudice. What do you see in the typical hour of "investigative journalism" on television? I see the *National Inquirer:* the last thing Big Mama throws onto the conveyor belt after she has yanked the last carton of sugar-coated doughnuts from her daughter's hand.

Or an SUV—which, if it were to rear up on its back tires and assume the aspect of a human being, would behave a lot like Big Mama herself. An SUV is not a middle-class person's car. An SUV is a poor person's car that only a member of the middle classes can afford. Once you grasp this, you have figured out a lot.

Look at it. Is it not the embodiment of everything we imagine poverty to be: wasteful, ill mannered, enormous, expressive of a lifelong grievance? Aimed at a set of utterly absurd eventualities: should I ever be involved in a head-on collision with a UFO. Should I ever need to go off-road in Delaware. As in: should I ever win megabucks. As in: here is a twenty-five-foot harpoon that I got in trade for a sewing machine with a busted motor belt and half a carton of smokes plus three bucks' worth of food stamps. Should I ever go whaling.

I am not worried about offending readers who drive SUVs; my hunch is that the majority will take the foregoing as a compliment. Economically we may aspire to the Trumps (itself a decidedly plebeian aspiration), but culturally we aspire to Tobacco Road. The trial lawyer's son wants to be 50 Cent. My next Beth Orton CD is going to be an album called *Trailer Park*. I can't wait to hear it. Are you getting my drift? More to the point, are you getting *the* drift?

But how can I say that we aspire to what I also say we disdain? Well, how can we help the people we also hinder? How can the same companies that invent treatments for cancer also release carcinogens into the environment? You might as well ask why we sin.

Do you remember—are you old enough to remember—that black and white and red Grove Press paperback of the *Autobiography of Malcolm X*? Malcolm with his finger pointed up, his nether lip tucked just inside his upper teeth as if he is about to say "Fire." Not the f-word you might think, because he had put that sort of language behind him. Above his face and repeated on the first page: "This is the absorbing personal story of the man who rose from hoodlum, thief, dope peddler, and pimp to become the most dynamic leader of the Black Revolution."

The man who rose . . .

College students at a nearby (and nearly all-white) university held a hip-hop-inspired Pimp 'n' Ho dance last week. Cakewalk under the aegis of diversity. Poor Malcolm. Like other poor folk, he had trouble with directions. He went swimming toward the light.

> I made the announcement: "I am going to organize and head a new mosque in New York City known as the Muslim Mosque, Inc. This will give us a religious base, and the spiritual force necessary to rid our people of the vices that destroy the moral fiber of our community."

(You have not forgotten our destination, I hope. Roll down your window and take a deep breath. Can you smell the brimstone yet?)

We talk about the most wretched of the poor as failures, as people who couldn't keep pace with the rest of us. People who fell out of the race. I suppose that's one way to see them. From a different point of view, they are the vanguard of consumerism, the swift of foot. Sugar and salt, pharmaceuticals and fat, gadgetry and grease—down the hatch. When we have spent our air, our soil, and our creativity on the equivalent of scratch tickets, we shall have arrived at the place where the poor are already waiting for us. They will ask if we have any cigarettes.

Anyone who's worked with "the disadvantaged population" realizes how many of its members are mentally ill. What fewer realize is that the mental illness is of a piece with the madness of a society in which even the cows are mad. Do sane people feed cows the ground-up carcasses of other cows? Do sane people even have to ask a question like that?

It would make a curious study to examine what conditions drive people mad over and against those that do not. After a while, I fear, the study would make casualties of the researchers. "We are all a bit mad," said Madame Barraud, forgiving the boy who accidentally shot her daughter. Was she mad, though? For that matter, was anyone reported to have arrived in Le Chambon raving? Even in those horrible times. Those who liberated the death camps found charnel houses, not madhouses.

I was a sergeant with the battalion that liberated Dachau. As the tanks tore through the gates we were shocked to find hundreds of emaciated human beings posing as Napoleon. In some of the barracks men and women masqueraded as pimps and ho's. In what was maybe the saddest scene of all, we discovered a lone mother, wildly throwing soup cans at her young child . . .

The man we visited has a computer. The result of salvage, sacrifice, and savvy trade. He does not have teeth. He does not have a functional kitchen stove. He does not have health insurance. He does not have transportation, vitamins, or a library card. He doesn't have anyone to love him and sleep with. But he has Microsoft Word. He has Windows. The landlord has forbidden him to put plastic on the outsides of the ones with the lowercase *w*. It makes the dump look too dumpy.

In the dead of winter, with the "heat on," he can see his breath in his living room. He coughs. His joints ache. He catches cold. He is cold. Grammatical distinctions begin to break down when the wind chill hits minus fifty.

The lowest circle of hell, according to the dubiously titled *Inferno*, is a sheet of windswept ice.

If he does a Google search for *cold*, he will get 27,600,000 matches.

· · ·

"So it's all somebody else's fault," says the hitchhiker, whose attempt at an audible yawn leads me to believe he has enough money to afford his own car. I wish he was riding in it.

"I didn't say that," I reply (or you reply for me, in which case, thank you). To absolve the poor of all responsibility is to maintain that poverty has degraded them to the point of total innocence, that is, to the level of animals.

I read somewhere that in a moment of pique Marx once referred to the workers as swine, an indication that he still believed they were human beings. I cannot vouch for the beliefs of his more sanctimonious descendants. When I say that we are all members of a culture of poverty, I am implying what Marx implied. I am implying a common humanity. I suppose I am also implying that Marx had a good ear for what goes oink.

As someone who lives among farmers, I trust what Wendell Berry writes about farming, not only because he is a farmer and not only because he is an insightful man, but also because his insights include this: "[I]t would be wrong, I think, to imply that the farmers are merely the victims of their predicament and share none of the blame. . . . One could argue that the great breakthrough of industrial agriculture occurred when most farmers became convinced that it would be better to own a neighbor's farm than to have a neighbor." One could also argue that the great breakthrough in a writer's career is when he can balance genuine concern with forthright disgust.

Let me tell you a little story. A way to pass the time on our slow journey through the strip-mall section of this town. Where the farms used to be. I heard the story from my mother-in-law, who, you may recall, recently came to live near us.

(And there you have another, albeit obvious, reason for the don't-give-a-shit syndrome, namely that we all have our own problems. Your concern for the hardships of the poor grows a little vague when you're rubbing morphine cream into an old woman's neck—though you are in fact at one of the best vantage points to appreciate the lives of the poor, working and otherwise. Noting the mostly African American and Hispanic nurse's aides—juxtaposed with the mostly white and Anglo patients—in the rehab center where her mother was staying before we spirited her away to Vermont, my wife asked, "Who takes care of *their* parents?")

Anyway, the story. My mother-in-law was the daughter of an Italian grocer in an immigrant community. He and his family lived over the store. Angelo's. There were bins of loose pasta that you weighed and bagged yourself, hard candies under the counter glass, salamis hanging from the ceiling. Cheeses, fruit, Italian specialties. Angelo had seen hard times. He remembered what it was like to struggle. People in the neighborhood could always come to Angelo's and get credit. He would give them their groceries and write their names in a book. Giovanni, five dollars. Viarella, dollar fifty. You paid when you could. It was a way to help one's neighbors.

When the supermarket moved in downtown, people would take their paychecks there on Friday afternoons, then walk home past Angelo's holding their grocery bags up high to block their faces. Angelo's wife, a sweet, stout Albanian woman who is reported never to have said an unkind word about anyone, would stand in the window with her hands on her hips and watch. "Look at them" was all she would say.

On Monday, if there was some money left over, the shrewd shoppers might stop by and have a little taken off Angelo's book. Otherwise, maybe next week.

Soon there was no Angelo's. Soon there was no credit. Soon there was a Wal-Mart in every state of the union.

I've heard all I want to hear about Wal-Mart, frankly. There's one on the right. We won't be stopping. But I'll tell you this: there should be a perpetually wet slab of cement on the outside corner of every Wal-Mart store where all the people alleged to be exploited and dispossessed by Wal-Mart can sign their names. Like Picasso would have signed one of his masterpieces.

In the low-income neighborhoods of Burlington, Vermont, citizens are rising up. I haven't died too soon to see it. The spark that ignited the revolution? They want their new supermarket managed by a national chain instead of by the local food co-op because the alternative types who run the latter are biased toward whole grains. In the largest city of what is arguably one of the most progressive states in the union, class struggle revolves around the right to eat bunny bread. Not over

the fact that almost twice as many workers die from work-related injuries each year as perished in the September 11 attacks or that five
million workers, few of them in white collars, I should think, are injured annually on the job or that the sentence is stiffer for "harassing a
burro on federal lands" than for causing a workplace injury by violating a federal safety standard. You couldn't get people to come to a
meeting on that, not if you served triple-decker baloney sandwiches on
Wonder Bread. No, if you want to rouse the masses, tell them that the
queers are threatening the sanctity of marriage.

The co-op has since mended its ways and begun touting its white
bread. It does not want to go the way of Angelo's. But we know that
sooner or later it will.

Progressivism is based on a faith in history, and history is a cuckold's
wife. Marie Antoinette went to the guillotine having quipped that the
Parisian poor ought to eat cake. Now their diabetic descendants sit
draped over stools at Dunkin' Donuts—eating cake.

The problem with liberation theology, a synthesis of leftist politics
and Catholic faith that quite captivated me in my thirties and still
looks like the most viable game in town for someone with my sympathies, is that it gives too much room to Marx and too short a shrift to
St. Augustine. When we absolve the poor of original sin, we absolve
them of their humanity.

On some level we need the poor to be blameless so that, in the inevitable discovery that they are not blameless, we can be free to loathe
them again. And hold ourselves blameless in our loathing. Not giving a
shit, in other words.

I'll tell you what we really need. We need them not to be poor.

This chapter, by the way, is dedicated to Angelo's granddaughter, who
is neither poor nor rich and who is not generally given to eschatological pronouncements, but who responded not long ago to yet another
report of CIA implication in the grisly doings of this dictator or that—
and I've lived with her long enough to know she was quite serious—
"Maybe everybody in this country is going to hell."

Of course she was including herself. Not to mention yours truly.

I am interested, though, in the ways that conscience establishes a
connection only to short-circuit itself, not necessarily in people as well

wired as my wife but in the mind-houses of people like me, who have problems with squirrels. So far, I have kept these ruminations on poverty close to home, close to what I know firsthand, but let us for just a moment "think globally" and try to do so with a sense of conscience.

I can stand to do it for about five minutes. The havoc that our obscene consumption and the meddling done in our names (when it is overt enough to bear a name) has wreaked in the lives of other peoples is beyond disturbing. Schoolchildren in Colombia are sprayed with toxic defoliant in our insane war on drugs, which would appear to be nothing more than an ill-disguised war on the peasantry, conducted on behalf of multinational corporations with an aim to clear them off mineral-rich lands. LSD was never so mind altering: the drug lords stay in business and the union leaders disappear. I'd love to turn you on.

But there's a faintly glowing little filament that goes dark whenever you "do a Chomsky": the acceptance of responsibility leads to an immediate abdication of hope. For if we Americans enjoy all of the fruits that global justice would bring to others—prosperity, medicine, democracy, the World Series every autumn, and the *New Yorker* every week—and the best we can manage is a second war in Iraq and a how-many-does-this-make-now coup in Haiti, where's the incentive to think globally or act locally or do much of anything besides try to find a halfway decent station on the radio? It is only to the innocent that the devil speaks of new knowledge and forbidden fruit; to the rest of us his undying refrain is "Cut your losses." The poor can't follow the directions on the ballot, and the powerful won't follow the directions in the Bill of Rights; either problem would be relatively simple to fix, but the two together in a weird kind of symbiosis start to look like a pretty unbeatable combination. To be more specific, they start to look like a hauntingly familiar mustache. If a kinder, gentler form of quasi fascism is the best we have to show for ourselves after countless strikes, demonstrations, freedom rides, pamphlets, speeches, constitutional amendments, court rulings, bloodlettings, folk songs, what exactly is the point of helping someone halfway around the world?

We had been talking about why people stop giving a shit.

You don't need to tell me that what I have just said amounts to a specious argument. It is not even an argument. A vaccinated child in a village once racked by disease—*that* is an argument, closed and ir-refutable. She does not require a predetermined historical outcome to justify her continued existence. I am not denying anyone's potential to do better with a little more sunshine than we have done with ours; nor am I suggesting that potential ought to be the prerequisite for mercy. I am trying to find out what happened to our desire. Perhaps I am trying to figure out why we are going to hell.

The worst thing we inherited from the Enlightenment is the notion that we are enlightened. It tends to paralyze us every time we discover how truly benighted we are.

But the man we visited before is not benighted. Nor should he belie anyone's belief in progress. If you wanted to argue for human per-fectibility, you could submit him with your evidence.

I had said that poverty is characterized by an inability to renounce anything. Partly I was thinking of him when I said that. And yet his life, at least a significant part of it, says that either my definition is bogus or he is not in poverty.

He has renounced the practice he calls "carving on myself," by which he means cutting into his flesh with pop-top tabs and jack-knives. To my knowledge it has been several years since he has written "I am an asshole" on the toes of his sneakers.

He has renounced cigarettes. He has kicked a habit that is suppos-edly harder to kick than heroin. He has done it by himself. True, he can't seem to get away from the dope. But he has reduced his intake, no small feat when a couple of big-time dopers are living across the hall.

He has renounced the stock pathetic pose of the creative personal-ity: the tale of what might have been. He sells his creations, and then he makes more. He works until his tools break.

He has renounced idleness, working a part-time job to supplement his disability benefits and the income from his crafts, then working for his employer on a volunteer basis when his paid hours are up.

He has renounced using the custody fight as an instrument of vengeance against women who have used him as nothing more than a pliable funding source and a free babysitter.

He has renounced using paternity testing as a ruse to avoid responsibility for sexual risk taking. When there's been a question, he gives the benefit of the doubt to the mother.

He has renounced reproductive opportunity by voluntarily having a vasectomy. He has said to me, "I don't want to bring any more children into the world that I cannot take care of." He keeps a better Lent than the Vatican.

He has renounced blame, somewhat. At least more than I ever will. He does not blame God. He does not blame his parents. He does not blame his ex-wives. He does not blame you. Did you sense any irony when he shook your hand?

He does blame the state for putting him in foster care as a child. He blames the mother of his youngest child for taking the money he voluntarily forks over for child support and spending it on scratch-off lottery tickets to the alleged tune of some sixty bucks per week.

He blames himself for nearly everything else. Scratch *else*.

He has renounced theft.

He has renounced parricide.

He has renounced murdering every clergyman who ever crossed his path. Trust me, an informed jury would ask for leniency.

He has renounced owning a gun, which as a convicted felon he cannot buy legally, no more than he can buy dope legally. No more than his landlord can operate his apartment—which I cannot fairly call a fire trap, seeing as it is probably too moldering rotten to burn—legally.

He has renounced the consolations of legality.

He has renounced volunteering to blow up buildings where his importance to the human enterprise is reckoned at something less than the dirt on the carpets.

He has renounced, thus far at least, suicide.

He has renounced more in his life than St. Anthony renounced when he went into the desert. He has renounced at a level of radicalism sufficient to balance the federal budget and study war no more. In proportion to his means, he has probably given away more money than the Gates Foundation.

It occurs to me that for all his shortcomings, he is possibly the most upright, morally heroic human being I know. Yet I have power and respect, and he has virtually none. "The way I see it," he tells me, "I'm at the bottom of society." So he *does* see it. May I be excused if I do not talk to him about the wonderful adaptive strategies of spiders, who also make things with intricate patterns and also perform a useful service and are also routinely crushed under our feet?

What separates the two of us? Is it only that my mother and father were not alcoholic shack dwellers and that I wasn't delivered to the tender mercies of state-sponsored foster care? If so, can you blame him, or should he blame his kid's mother, if the attractions of a lottery ticket should prove so irresistible—when the power of sheer dumb luck should loom so large and be so absolute?

A friend of mine says that when he was a boy, one of the nuns who taught at his Catholic school said that the sound of a coin clanging in a Salvation Army kettle was the sound that a soul makes falling into hell.

This was pre–Vatican II, so perhaps she was warning her students to keep their charity under the auspices of Mother Church. My hunch is rather that this was a nun who had mystical visions.

Yes, there was money in that envelope you saw me handing the man out on the porch where we piled the cedar boughs. It wasn't my money. The members of my church provide me with what is called a discretionary fund. I hereby confess that my discretion has sometimes crossed state lines. But my own out-of-pocket contributions have seldom crossed the lines of discretion.

Poverty is like public TV; most people don't even bother to watch it, and it depends on its subscribers for support. Contributing members like you (and me). The coins clang in the kettle. Sister cracks a knowing smile.

Robert Frost told us not to do away with the poor; "I need them in my business." Like Mailer's statement on culture being worth a little risk, Frost's is breathtaking in its candor. It suggests that we are "disturbed" by poverty in something like the same way as we are "disturbed" by certain pieces of avant-garde art. In other words, we are quite comfortable with the fact that it makes us uncomfortable. We support this kind of programming.

I sometimes have the uncanny impression that homelessness—in the *United States of America*—exists so that people "of faith" or goodwill can have something to do on the weekend. Like paintball for the pure in heart. The Habitat for Humanity Web site salutes three individuals from Northern Ireland who have joined a building team in Florida. With Belfast choking on its slums and enough capital in one block of Key West real estate to paint the Emerald Isle chartreuse, three Samaritans from over the sea are building a house in Florida. God bless every one of them, and God bless Habitat for Humanity. But *Jaysus!*

If Jesus were here in America, he would not go into churches and synagogues to overturn the tables of the moneychangers. He would walk down the streets and overturn those collection jugs sponsored by the Coalition for the Homeless. He would kick the pocket change of Wall Street brokers right off the sidewalk. To hell with this shit.

It would be a righteous action. Another would be to get down on the pavement and pick up the scattered change. And put it back in the jugs.

We have come to a well-known intersection on the way to hell. Lots of accidents here. I refer to the intersection of mercy and justice, of the apolitical approach to poverty and the piously political.

The apolitical approach says we should meet need and not concern ourselves with its ultimate causes. Perhaps Dom Helder Camara offered the best critique: "When I fed the poor, they called me a saint. When I asked why people were poor, they called me a communist." The apolitical approach sets its sights no higher than sainthood.

The advocate of the piously political approach is willing to be called a communist. In fact, he is often a little disappointed if he is not. He maintains that any mercy short of the total eradication of the systemic causes of poverty is counterproductive. Perhaps the best critique here lies in what the Jewish publisher Victor Gollancz said in response to official Allied policy toward the plight of European Jews:

> I shall be told that "the best way to save these people is to win the war." Of course: but what chance is there of winning it in time to save them? There are practical things that might be done *now*, though very soon it may be too late.

The danger—or should I say "the dodge"—in all this lies not so much with those who favor one approach over the other as with those who say that both are necessary and that, being unable to do both, they regrettably must elect to do neither.

The Hebrew prophet Micah said that what God required of mortals was to "do justice, love mercy, and walk humbly with your God." I read that to mean: seek systemic change, do not despise stopgap measures, and have the humility to realize that you are not required and probably not able to do both with equal intensity.

But do both. Paul Farmer works for changes in global health policy while still setting bones at his clinic in Haiti. For all their mistakes, the Black Panthers also seem to have grasped the double-edged sword of Micah. Have your ten-point plan and your campaign to free Huey and all the rest, but serve breakfast to children in the projects and provide them with well-baby care. If the only nurse to show up for the job is a redheaded white woman with freckles, work even harder for the cause of Black Nationalism, but hire her just the same.

Then fire her for refusing to carry a gun. The poor (excuse) you will have with you always.

As nearly as I can tell, the worst thing about being poor is having to spend most of your time with other poor people. Have you ever read that terrifying sermon in James Joyce's *Portrait of the Artist as a Young Man?* The preacher tells the boys, "[T]hings which are good in themselves become evil in hell. Company, elsewhere a source of comfort to the afflicted, will be there a continual torment."

When people are deprived and confined, they torment one another. It happens in school, it happens in prison, and it happens in poverty. To come within the orbit of the powerless is to enter a zone of constant vendettas, sniping, meanness. Poverty parodies oppression.

The second worst thing about being poor is the pull toward self-loathing that comes of meditating on the first worst thing.

My former student has been issued a restraining order by the mother of his child. She claims he threw his computer at her. Presumably he first detached all the wires. He says he kicked it over and swore at her because he caught her stealing from him again. He didn't throw anything. Of course, I am biased in his favor, but to tell you the truth, I am not sure I understand what's happening here.

"You never go over to her place, right?"

He says he doesn't. He says he keeps asking her not to spend so much time at his. She drives him nuts. But she shows up anyway, just like the dopers from across the hall, and *his problem is that he can never say no.*

"So, basically, you're being 'restrained' from opening your own door? Why doesn't she restrain herself from knocking on it?"

I advise him to obey the order and stay clear of her. He claims he's been begging her to keep clear of him. At least not to be at his door all the time. He likes to see his little boy, true. But then she leaves the kid and runs off "even when she knows I'm not good by myself with kids." He isn't. He sees his other children faithfully as part of a supervised visitation program.

He says the charges and the restraining order are simply a way to piss him off. I suspect he's right. I am not unaware of the dangers of domestic violence. I have intervened in situations of that kind. The only time I ever had to dismiss a class because I was functionally incapable of teaching it was the day after a student of mine was shot in a sand pit by her estranged husband, who then shot himself. I know that a restraining order is sometimes the only thing that stands between a woman and death. I also know what a flimsy thing it is. The man who murdered my student also had a restraining order on him. For all the good it did his wife.

Here's something else I know. I would bet money on it. This other woman is going to spend the rest of tomorrow doing drop-by visits to all her girlfriends in order to brag about her restraining order. In her circle it has a certain cachet, like a poodle on Park Avenue. You walk it around.

Within twelve hours she'll be scratching at his door. Does he have any cigarettes? Can she spare some change? For the baby, of course. He'll tell her to go away. He'll say he doesn't want to get in trouble. She'll ask him how he's going to make her go away without laying a hand on her. She'll let herself in and sit down. She'll tell him to be nice because one word from her and he's in the shit. *Mister.* She'll remind him that he has a criminal record. He'll fume and he'll sputter, and in the end he'll be nice. He'll have yet another unsaid no to loathe himself for.

It's when I start "knowing" things like this that I begin to lose my grasp of the more basic things that I'm supposed to know. Or at least believe. *Judge not, that ye be not judged.*

At this point, you may be thinking—as patient as I imagine you are, you may be thinking—"No, what you're losing grasp of is your whole subject. Because this book is supposed to be about help, and I was assuming this chapter was going to be about helping the poor, or helping one poor person at least, and to be perfectly honest, I don't see help anywhere in the picture."

Neither do I. That is my point. Neither do I. This will go on forever. That is what I keep hearing in my head on a night like tonight.

I want you to know that I was wrong about the woman. I made a promise to myself that I would finish this story regardless of its outcome. She does not show up at his place the next night. Nor does she come on the night after that. I have judged her, and I have misjudged.

She does try to phone him where he works, but let us not quibble over details.

She stays away. Perhaps because she was truly frightened by his outburst. Had I ever thought of that? She goes with her little boy to a friend's house, and they spend an evening visiting together. While they are chatting, the little boy reaffirms his yes relationship to the world. He swallows a large quantity of kerosene.

May I do the same and worse if I am making this up.

His father is on the phone to me in tears. It is close to midnight. Will I accept the charges? Yes, of course. "You always said it was okay to call late . . . if I was in trouble, remember?" Yes, of course. He is forbidden to go to the emergency room because of the restraining order. He sobs in his grief and impotence.

And I can imagine the mother sobbing too because hers is the impotence of sole responsibility whenever something like this happens. She is forbidden *not* to go to the emergency room. Her medicine is in the disapproving eyes of the medics, as bitter as the taste of kerosene.

He asks me to pray, which of course I was planning to do, but he means right then and there on the phone. He's never asked me to do anything like that before. I don't know that I've ever heard him crying before; if I have, it was never like this.

So you see, there is some help in the picture after all. You may even find it a touching picture: the distraught father reaching out to God— a reflection of that other distraught father in the Gospel of Mark who cries out to Jesus, "Lord, I believe. Help thou mine unbelief"—and the barely woken up pastor, though never this man's pastor, composing his cobwebby prayer. But it is my unbelief that needs the help. I am leaning on him, though he does not know it. I am leaning with all my tired weight.

"Do you know what the funny thing is?" he says, still crying. I'm pretty sure this is not going to be funny.

"I did the same thing when I was little."

There is a tradition that construes heaven and hell as almost identical. One crucial difference makes *all* the difference. Remember that parable of two groups of people gathered around identical pots of food with the same kinds of long spoons? Those in hell starve because they cannot reach their own mouths; those in heaven feed each other and are full.

I am thinking these days of two expressions that I heard from the time I was old enough to swallow kerosene. They sound almost alike, but for me they are as different as heaven and hell. One is "Are you saved?" and the other is "What must I do to be saved?" The difference between asking those two questions is like the difference between asking "Did you get laid last night?" and "Will you stay with me tonight?"

"Are you saved?" is a presumptuous and insinuating question. Essentially, it means, are you an evangelical Christian? Do you see your mortal predicament in the same terms as I do? Your loss if you don't.

But to ask "What must I do to be saved?" is to ask the critical question of a fully conscious human being. If there is any question that could conceivably qualify for the distinction of being the only question, this may be the one. It is not necessarily a religious question. It attracts religious answers, but if all religions were to disappear tomorrow, it would still exist. As long as a sense of mortality, culpability, and responsibility existed, it would still exist. That trinity alone would suffice to bring you to your knees.

As I said, I heard the question growing up, and as young people do, I made my escape from it as from the belly of a whale. I swam for the light. Or at least for the glare. I had help. Big Daddy Roth probably helped, by dazzling my eyes with engines of chrome, with sleek fenders and slick tires. Beatniks and Beatles, sweethearts and sweetly tempered Anglican divines all lent a hand at various stages.

Now at fifty, I find I am up against the question again. *What must I do to be saved?* And I don't think this is some midlife thing of the usual sort; I feel no inclinations to have an affair or buy a sports car. To be honest, I'd rather have an SUV (dark green). Nor do I feel poised for some religious conversion or reversion. My favorite hymn these days is Billie Holiday singing "Autumn in New York." My angels have come home to roost with their knickers in their pockets. I think it has more to do with what I find in myself when I get a phone call like the one I got the other night. Or when the person who called me says how grateful he is "for all you've done to help me."

What must I do to be saved?

I am no longer able to consider that question in a vacuum. In that sense, it is *not* an existential question for me. Existence is the least of my worries. No algebraic problem ever requires us to solve for x in existential isolation. There must be other numbers and variables. Here too. I cannot pose this question apart from the fact that I am living in the most prosperous nation ever to have thrived on the face of the earth and in a world of unprecedented suffering, much of it the price of my prosperity.

Perhaps the Apostle Paul had the option of working out his own salvation with fear and trembling. Perhaps Joan of Arc did or Kierkegaard. I don't. I want to say, "We don't," but I am determined to speak for myself. The poor are going to be with me always, at least one of them is, and I am almost more afraid of having him die poor than I am of dying myself. But if he dies poor, then, for the first time in my life, I will truly be afraid of death.

What am I saying?

I am saying that I need assistance. I am saying that for all its rhetoric, this book about helping people is essentially my own cry for help. I can't seem to swim for the light. I need to be saved.

Enough of that. I promised myself from the beginning that I was never going to let this book get too personal, and anyway, we still have to get to our destination. I have not forgotten. We have one more stop to make on the way. I want you to meet my friend Sharon.

We've already crossed one state line, so let us cross another. Sharon does not live in hell, but perhaps she has come closer than anyone I know to looking into its depths. She spent some time on the West Coast working as a counselor with the criminally insane. She was on sabbatical in Russia not long after the Chernobyl disaster and volunteered to take a secret donation of money to some of the survivors there. She swallowed the radiation pills and set off with her own supply of water. She saw. She did not turn to stone. When she got back to the States her skin turned green and peeled.

Now she works as the principal and guidance counselor of a mill town elementary school near the Canadian border. No one familiar with the territory would say she had "found something quieter."

The way I found her is rather wonderful. Quite literally, I responded to a message in a bottle. For years I had noticed a peculiar detail on an overhead lamp in the sacristy of my church, something like a small glass ampoule with a sallow core, an effect like an elongated, faded opal. One morning I happened to look closer and realized that the core was in fact a tiny rolled-up scroll. I unscrewed the fixture and discovered the message. "My name is Sharon. . . . I went to this church while I was living in the area. I loved the people here. If you find this, please get in touch with me and tell me how they are doing."

It had hung there for some fifteen years. I eventually found her among these dark satanic mills, many of them now boarded up and the lone survivor smoking like hell. I have visited her several times since. It was from her that I learned about the little girl who got knocked out with the soup cans.

I ask Sharon about the little girl and her brother. Their mother is out of the home now. The situation is "somewhat better."

I don't think their father abuses them. I just think he pays no attention to them. If they want to eat, they have to fix their own food. There's a car motor in the kitchen. They have all these dogs and cats and stray animals, and the kids are just like stray animals. They're always out in the yard.

I realize that her description resembles one of those Booth cartoons in the *New Yorker*—and that there is seldom a child in those cartoons. Would we find them funny if there was?

They're filthy, they come to school in the same clothes day after day. The school nurse and I take the boy's clothes home and wash them. They eat at school. They show up at 5 A.M. and wait for the school to open so they can have breakfast. All winter long. The cook gets there at 6, and they eat cereal. Then at 7:30 they eat the hot breakfast that the school provides. The little boy takes care of the little sister. He's like her father. He'll be in fifth grade next year.

Recently the girl tried to climb a cupboard to get something she wanted on the top of it. It fell over on top of her and scalped off the back of her head.

"Haven't we heard enough of this stuff?" the hitchhiker asks. I don't know. Have we? Because it goes on and on and on.

But I didn't come here to rub anyone's nose in tragedy. We did not come to meet the little girl. We came to meet Sharon. As much as any janitor or nurse's aide, this is someone we have hired to do our dirty work. She has a better salary and benefits package, of course. But the messes are worse. She has chosen to live apart from what Camus called "the proud egoism and injustice of happy people."

As I had asked Dr. Moseley back home, I ask Sharon what she would recommend to others who do the kind of work she does. She says, "Always make sure that you love something—even if it's not your job—and that you're living through that instead of what you hate. It's easy to give in to the hatred and start doing your job through what pisses you off." Of course, she knows the temptation all too well. I ask her to repeat a story she told me several years ago, of an interview she had had with a kindergarten child.

She described these horrible, graphic, sexual things that are al-most psychotic, talking about helping her father cut off people's penises and burying them, people kissing her on the vagina and sticking knives inside of her, how she stuck a knife inside her mother, how she and her boyfriend cut up her mother in little pieces and her boyfriend had sex with the body, talking in singsong voices as though she were telling about a trip to the park, and all the time she was jabbing the paper with her pencil, making holes in the table. It went on for forty-five minutes. . . . I can't describe how it felt. It was horrible, awful.

We do not have time for the full account of Sharon's attempt at intervention, for the mother's nonchalant reaction to Sharon's call ("Oh, she likes to make up stories"), for the political intrigue between state agencies and the school administration, for all that might contribute to an overwhelming sense of futility

One detail will suffice. Eventually the police arrested a young man who was staying at this girl's house on charges of downloading child pornography onto his computer. He had a history of sexual assault going back to grade school. He might have been incarcerated as a minor and become a state-raised criminal like Jack Abbott but for the efforts of a dedicated adult who had interceded for him, guided him through the system, and seen that he was enrolled in a treatment program.

I suspect you have already guessed who she was.

Sharon takes home the guilt, not us. She takes home the guilt for having taken her job beyond the minimal requirements. The poor are with her always. And the rest of us are more than happy to leave them there.

I am interested in how people like Sharon appear to lose their innocence. As for the child's loss of innocence, it is simply beyond my ability to fathom. I am interested in what happens to someone who becomes a social worker because she was moved by the scene at the end of *The Grapes of Wrath* where Rose of Sharon feeds a starving man from her breast, someone who leaves a message in a bottle hanging from the light in a church where some minister will find it, nosing up to it like a fish, and who trusts that she will hear from him whenever he finds it, as in a fairy tale, and does hear—but only to tell him,

I used to think that the universe was basically good and that evil came from not being able to grasp the good. I don't know if I think that anymore. . . . Sometimes it seems that the horrible stuff is just overwhelming and there's no way to get out of it and it's just fate. You're born, and you're born into whatever you're born into, and if you're lucky enough to escape it, it's luck.

Brian Cole, the young priest who works among the homeless in North Carolina, is younger and more sanguine than she, but he speaks of a comparable disenchantment.

I've always been this sort of left-leaning Democrat. Early on, something that really formed me was watching *Sesame Street*. I'm thirty-five years old; I'm first-generation *Sesame Street*. So I basically believe there's this street where different colors of people live together, and we can all count to five in Spanish, and we can all get along, and we can solve all the problems. And yet there are certain things we could never have imagined. All the structures in the world are at a loss to engage the depth of addiction to crack cocaine. The folks we work with who struggle with alcoholism are sometimes able to break through and celebrate a first, second, or third anniversary of staying clean. The folks we work with who are on crack cocaine are still on crack cocaine. When someone sat down and invented crack cocaine, we added a whole new dimension to the ways we harm each other. There are times when I bump up against the idea that it's not simply a system or a structure or a society that we have to create. It's also realizing the depth of abusive stuff we have created that we use against each other and against ourselves.

I have been reading Paul Farmer's *Pathologies of Power: Health, Human Rights, and the New War on the Poor.* It is a powerful and impressive book. It contains 256 pages of text and 124 pages of notes and bibliography. This is how Farmer chooses to conclude:

I contemplate my own loss of innocence with resentful, sometimes even tearful silence. From whom can I demand it back? As García Lorca said, "Things that go away never return—everybody knows that."

That a book so exhaustively documented, so grounded in practice, so global in scope, so authoritative in tone, so unsparing in its condemnation of inequality, should end with a doctor's lament for his own loss of innocence seems almost, as they like to say these days, over the top. That is part of its brilliance.

Farmer knows what nobody else seems to know: that the loss of innocence among those who help at the extremity of need is one of our crimes against humanity. That we are quicker to admire the good heart than to help it. That in the end we regard it as no less expendable than the poor.

Farmer *doesn't* know what everybody else knows: that he has not lost his innocence. Not entirely. If he had, he would not still be doing what he does. In fact, one proof of his innocence is his belief that he has lost it.

That is why we have made this visit to Sharon, who perhaps believes the same thing: to ask that she fashion a prayer for us out of her paradox. Maybe there is value in reading the words of a skeptic who tries to swim toward the light. But the light itself is any spark of innocence that the darkness cannot overcome.

It seems I ought to have said something about the good Samaritan by now. Especially with his descendants hovering so close in the paragraphs above. Especially when I have seen fit to mention him in nearly every chapter that comes before this one.

Luke is the only one of the four evangelists to have recorded the parable. You would think, given how beloved it has been through the generations, that Matthew, Mark, or John would have thought it worth the telling. Perhaps Jesus himself never told it. Perhaps he never told the parable of the prodigal son, which also appears only in Luke. The same goes for the parable below. It is not so well known as the other two. You will readily see why.

Yes, we have finally reached our destination.

There was a rich man who was dressed in purple and fine linen and who feasted sumptuously every day. And at his gate lay a poor man named Lazarus, covered with sores, who longed to satisfy his hunger with what fell from the rich man's table; even the dogs would come and lick his sores. The poor man died and was carried away by the angels to be with Abraham. The rich man also died and was buried. In Hades, where he was being tormented, he looked up and saw Abraham far away with Lazarus by his side. He called out, "Father Abraham, have mercy on me, and send Lazarus to dip the tip of his finger in water and cool my tongue; for I am in agony in these flames." But Abraham said, "Child, remember that during your lifetime you received your good things, and Lazarus in like manner evil things; but now he is comforted here, and you are in agony. Besides all this, between you and us a great chasm has been fixed, so that those who might want to pass from here to you cannot do so, and no one can cross from there to us."

There's more, but you've heard enough, haven't you? You don't like the story one bit. Neither do I. Tell me, though, what don't you like about it? Isn't it that Abraham sounds like such a prig? Isn't it that you are outraged by that chasm—and who put that there, God? and where the hell is he, anyway?—that cannot be bridged and that doesn't allow so small a mercy as a drop of water on a burning tongue? It's not like the man is asking for a pardon. A mere drop of water. Jesus better not have told such a story, you say. Only a monster would make up something like that.

It takes a moment for your eyes to focus and for your mind to grasp that this intolerable chasm represents the contrived separation between the rich man and Lazarus in their lives on earth. *Even the dogs licked his sores.* But the rich man would do nothing beyond the crumbs falling inadvertently off his table—as through some great galactic void—down to Lazarus's open hands. God doesn't pass sentence on anyone in this parable. God is noticeably absent. For all we know, God may not even exist. Before we realize what we are doing, we pass sentence upon ourselves.

Whether Luke is the composer or merely the editor of these stories, we recognize his signature in the theme of the small spaces that we turn into vast chasms. The priest and the Levite pass within several yards of the wounded man in the good Samaritan story; they might as well be a thousand miles away. The elder brother of the prodigal son will not join the feast that welcomes him home but stands outside, several feet from the door and as far away as the planet Neptune. It is as if Luke is saying that we come within inches of love, yet if we fail to close that small gap, it amounts to an infinity of separation. The distance between heaven and hell.

Dickens says much the same thing in *A Christmas Carol*. I would not be surprised to learn that he had the parable of Lazarus in mind. We remember the three ghosts and Bob Cratchit and all the rest, but who recalls that haunting vision of hell that Marley shows old Scrooge before the spectral visitors arrive?

> The air was filled with phantoms, wandering hither and thither in restless haste, and moaning as they went. Every one of them wore chains like Marley's Ghost; some few . . . were linked together; none were free. Many had been personally known to Scrooge in their lives. He had been quite familiar with one old ghost, in a white waistcoat, with a monstrous iron safe attached to its ankle, who cried piteously at being unable to assist a wretched woman with an infant, whom it saw below, upon a door-step. The misery with them all was, clearly, that they sought to interfere, for good, in human matters, and had lost the power forever.

I feel that you and I are at a place now where two friends might be who have driven all night and find themselves parked and wide awake at the side of the road. Perhaps they have narrowly escaped an accident a ways back and are still high on the adrenaline. Or perhaps they have just dumped a pain-in-the-neck hitchhiker and feel roused just to be rid of him at last.

They could be near the ocean, which is so dark that it exists only as a primordial sigh. Or they could be on a bluff overlooking the last town they drove out of, seeing it now as an alien vista, a Martian city on a plain. And their choice of metaphor leads them to those subjects that friends are prone to discuss on a night like this—especially when they are young, and for this moment, at least, let us be young—such things as whether there is life on other planets and if true love really exists and if you are meant to be with one special person or if there are hundreds you might love for a lifetime and if there is anything after this life and where people go when they die.

And then you ask me if I believe in it, or maybe I just say that I do without your asking.

Yes, I believe there is such a thing as hell.

The look on your face makes me want to take it back, but I don't think you will believe me if I do. "That's horrible," you say.

It's all horrible, I say. It's so horrible that you might wish for a hell even if there wasn't one. I read an article the other day about the world trade in prostitutes. Young girls kidnapped from their villages or on their way to what they have been told are jobs in other villages. Gang-raped on videotape. Their captors threaten to send copies to their parents if they don't cooperate. They live under constant threat of violence, in constant risk of disease. They live in "permanent gyneco-logical pain."

So let us say there is no hell. But what if there is a life beyond this one? What kind would you like? The sex slaves meet up with their masters on the shores of eternity. "So, like, what was that back there all about?" They reach the conclusion that it was a learning experience. Side by side they swim toward the Big Light. Pimps 'n' ho's. The girls get to wear designer bikinis. A consolation for all they've been through.

Maybe in a past life these girls were Danish sex tourists, in which case, they're just working off bad karma now. Maybe Lazarus was once a robber baron. Maybe we should go back for the cedar boughs. At least we could try to retrieve some of the money. Cut our losses.

Or maybe there's just nothing. Definitely no afterlife, maybe no God. Just luck. "The absurd," so called, a philosopher's flimsy attempt at euphemism. Absurd? I don't think so. *Waiting for Godot* is absurd. Sitting through a whole performance without nodding out once is absurd. But a world in which some of us get to be sex slaves and some of us get to live on Sesame Street is not absurd. It is horrible.

Hell is merely the least horrible in a set of horrible possibilities. I'm saying things to you that I have never said to my daughter, and she'll be twenty next month. I'm saying things I never said in that many years of preaching from a church pulpit. I'm saying things that, frankly, I'm not even sure I believe, and yet I hear myself saying them.

Do you know what I imagine the torments of hell to be? Not the wrath of a sadistic God, that's for sure. Not even the anguished reaching out to the needy on earth that Dickens talks about. The torments of hell are nothing but an eternal sting of remorse for the missed pleasure that would have been ours had we made a more just world.

I said *the pleasure*. Your surprise at that statement is like a brief, metallic foretaste of hell. It's what that nun heard in the Salvation Army kettle. We like to tell ourselves that we may have to forfeit some future paradise because we find the joys of the here and now too good to resist. We are unable to enter that gray cloistered gloom of delayed gratification that is the monastic life and the socialist state. Such a bunch of old sensualists we are. Such reprobates, such irrepressible rascals. There is bound to be hell to pay.

It's all a crock. A crock with two nickels and a dime. That we had too little fun, not that we had too much—that will be our damnation. No hangovers in the hereafter. If we are punished, it will not be for our indulgence but for our rigid self-denial, our disciplined refusal to have a better time with one another. We would have had a better time had we been more willing to share. You probably expected me to say, "had we been more willing to help." At the end of the day—at the end of the world—the difference is one of synonyms.

But that is not all I believe. You got me going on this, and now I can't stop. I want to slide off the hood first. I need to say this part standing up. If they could hear me down in that Martian city, I'd tell them too.

I also believe that we can abolish hell. I am not talking about building a heaven on earth, which has been tried and seems only to lead to more hell. I am talking about abolishing hell, in all the ways it exists, because as long as it exists in even one of these ways, it *might as well exist* in all the others—as an apt metaphor, a psychological state, a metaphysical reality. All the way down the line. I am talking about another way of saying "on earth as it is in heaven." In hell as it is on earth.

It is precisely because I believe in hell that I believe it can be abolished. A justice so dreadful calls for some justification, and the only possible justification is that we could have gotten rid of it if we wanted to. We could have stood before our Judge and said, "We got rid of ours. What are you going to do with yours?"

Imagine waking up early on a Monday, and in those first gray moments when your drowsy mind asks itself, "So what goddamn thing is on my agenda today?" you remember that the agenda has recently been revised. The business of the day, of everybody's beautiful, purposeful day, is to abolish hell. To destroy *the goddamn thing* once and for all.

And what might that involve? It would involve what political scientist Judith Shklar called "putting cruelty first," that is, first among the things that have to go. If help, as Philip Hallie defined it, is like covering someone with a blanket and allowing her body to create its own heat, then cruelty is the act of turning a body against itself. Its nerves and reflexes, against itself. Its inability to hold back from shivering, shitting, or screaming. Cruelty is the antihelp.

Consumerism is a soft form of cruelty. It too takes advantage of the body's naive devices. Its atavistic desire to store sugar and salt. Its hardwired need for neural stimulation. Its long-evolved predisposition for rhythm, acquisition, display. Its snuffling, burrowing drive to meet its perceived needs, even when they are not, in fact, its real needs.

I said we could abolish hell. I didn't say we would.

Even if we did, there would still be volcanoes. There would be earthquakes and diseases we could not cure. Dogs, mosquitoes, and snakes would still bite. We would still die. But no one would die in needless torment or alone. No one would be without help.

We would still have to work, probably harder than ever before. There could be no abolition of hell without the reformation of work, without the reclamation of work from mere toil. For the poor that would mean some other fate than being the expendable "help" of a service economy. Simone Weil began to grasp this when she went to work in the factories. The liberation of the worker must be found in the shaping of the work itself. The pleasure of the worker might be found there too.

When I asked Brian Cole what he did to keep the sadness of his ministry from getting the better of him, he told me of an antique store in Asheville where he sometimes goes on his lunch hour.

People make beautiful things. They make beautiful rugs, beautiful pieces of furniture. I need to remember that not everything is broken, not everything is destroyed, not everything is lost—that some folks made things that worked and lasted and held together.

I wonder if he has ever sensed a connection between the broken lives of the "folks at the shelter" and the fact that these beautiful objects in which he takes such comfort and delight are *antiques*. That is to say, that human beings are unmade whenever they are divorced from making. And it has been a long and rancorous divorce.

When my former student makes his arbors and trellises, he is transformed. He thinks of himself no longer as a loser but as a maker. An artisan. He is still poor. If anything, his poverty seems like more of a crime when he is able to achieve these rare moments of transcendence. They excuse nothing. But, like Cole's antique shop, they help me to remember that not everything is in pieces. Something still works even in those who may not always qualify as "the working poor."

In another month I will return and find his porch lined with rustic archways, set side by side along the railing, ready to sell. He will drag each one forward and turn it so I can admire the designs. They are built to stand as doorways to a garden. Perhaps one of them will be wide enough for both of us to walk through.

Only the sound of crickets now. The car engine is too cold to accompany them with its ticking or singe the long grass underneath. A red flare, or perhaps a meteor, flashes like a brief exclamation point in the sky. *I saw Satan fall like lightning from heaven.* Or did you just flick your cigarette over the embankment?

"It's getting pretty late," you say.

It is in fact very late. I never meant for us to stay out this long. All I meant to say was, maybe it is not too late. Maybe even at our age—for it seems as though we have grown old in a matter of hours—we are not past help.

Come on. I'll take you home.

SEVEN

A BETTER PLAN
THAN THIS

I was thinking the other day of a visit I had some years ago with the intake clerk at a Job Service office in northeastern Vermont. Hers was a smaller branch than the one in Burlington where I had worked for the same agency and met Debbie Sunn. The diversity of her clients was likely to be smaller too. The clerk was well into middle age, efficient, maternal, "from around here." I would be willing to wager a fairly good sum that she had at least one dish that was a favorite at the local church supper and at least one son or grandson who was an avid deer hunter and that, on a prearranged weekend in November, she went "up to camp" to cook for her men. All of these would be safe bets. An even safer bet would be that she had never in her career had a request quite like the one I took to her that afternoon.

I was seeing her on behalf of a young man from out of state, soon to graduate from high school, who planned to move to northeastern Vermont in the hopes of finding a job and making a fresh start. He had been referred to me by his parish priest. He had no appreciable skills, though he was intelligent, affable, and in my experience honest to a fault. He was also, by his own report, in the wrong body. That is to say, he had been convinced since early childhood that he had been born with the wrong genitals. Eventually, he hoped to rectify the confusion through surgery. That would require some money and probably another move. In the meantime, he wanted to present himself as a woman, in women's clothes and with a woman's name. If hired, he expected to use the ladies' restroom at his place of work. Of course, all of this would be at variance with his legal name as it appeared on his diploma and driver's license.

The meeting at the employment agency was meant to test the waters. I expected, I suppose I even hoped, that it would lead the kid to modify his approach. In other words, I was expecting to hear something along the lines of "Girl, you got to have a better plan than this."

To my surprise, there was no such reaction, no double take. The woman did see difficulties in the boy's requirements. It took me several minutes simply to explain them. He wasn't interested in trying to pass for a woman in the sense of duping his employer, nor was he willing to dress like a man, which to his mind was just another way of passing.

She thought for a moment. Then, in the tone an Avon lady might use to recommend a certain shade of lipstick to a neighbor, she said, "What if he were to obtain something like a silk camisole and wear it underneath his regular clothes? Maybe that would allow him to feel more feminine and still manage to land a job."

If I asked myself why this has come to mind after lying dormant in my memory for so long, I would answer, first of all, that it stands as a good symbol of how far from the mark our helpfulness is likely to fall. A camisole didn't come anywhere near what this young person envisioned for himself, and what I had in fact seen in the form of opulent wigs and voluptuous padding. I knew even before conveying her suggestion that it would strike him as the most paltry thing he had ever heard.

But mostly it comes to mind for being such an intelligent, empathetic response to his predicament. The interviewer may not have understood what it means to be a transgendered person, but she did understand what it means to be a woman, and on the basis of that understanding she tried to be of help to someone who thought of himself as a woman too. In a strange way, her suggestion made me more aware of the femaleness of them both. I was suddenly demoted from messenger to meek witness of their sorority.

I would not recognize that woman today. Nor would I be able to distinguish her by some mark in a crowd. She was a so-called ordinary person, as was the storekeeper who provided an apartment where that same young man would sequester himself for much of a summer before returning home to work out a better plan. Sometimes when I'm visiting a friend of mine, I stop into the store to buy a coffee. You can get grinders from the cold case, live bait from the shed out back, and there's usually a brand of beer for sale. Locally grown pumpkins in the fall. Small-town bellyachers at the counter. "Goddamn school budget up again." "Christ, these teachers." "Christ, these kids today." Would any of them believe that for a short interval Christ himself wept and slept upstairs in a lavender dressing gown? For hadn't he said that whatever we do for the least of his brothers and sisters, we do for him? Down-country leaf peepers stop in to ask directions, perhaps thinking what someone passing through Le Chambon without reading his tour guide might say out loud to his companion: "Well, dear, I guess this is what they mean by 'the provinces.'"

Farther down the road they may refuel at a gas station whose proprietor has taken one after another of troubled young men under his wing, dropouts and misfits, providing job, training, uniform (name stitched in red), and sometimes lodging as well. Even after one of the harder cases defecated in all his dresser drawers by way of saying "thanks and so long," he continued to help on. As far as I know, he still does. He doesn't advertise. I know what I know by word of mouth, the way of most knowledge in this community. I will not give his name, but I will give you his metaphor. He keeps a tow truck, and he is always on call.

All these numinous places—the store, the service station, and the employment office—are within twenty miles of a notorious house, once a parsonage, into whose walls night riders fired bullets in the late 1960s. The minister was a black man. His female companion was white. It made *Life* magazine. By local reckoning it was a long time ago. But just last week as I write, and within the same twenty-mile radius, a mother complained to her neighbor that demons were carving Stars of David into her child's feet because "one of the teachers up at the graded school" had read her class a picture book about a dreidel.

This is where I live. This is my birthplace, though the certificate says I was born someplace else. "Nothing human is alien to me," Terence said. He lived here too, neither in Jerusalem nor in Jericho but at some point in between, where good Samaritans and robbers appear and vanish like tin targets in a shooting gallery, where plague can break out any minute, where in the gloom of the same summer night a refugee finds asylum and a bullet comes through the wall. In short, where every contrast we can draw between help and harm exists within the same human breast.

I have a mental snapshot from another place, conjured from something I read in a book called *Humanity*. A white South African policeman is chasing after a black demonstrator in the days of apartheid. His club is raised. In her rush to get away, the woman's shoe comes off. Suddenly there is a woman's shoe in the road. He turns—the word *repent* literally means "to turn"—and picks up the shoe. He hands it to her. He helps.

Philip Hallie speaks of an "unbridgeable difference between those who can torture and destroy children and those who can only save them" and goes on to assert that "no verbal bridges may be erected connecting these two kinds of people." I believe that. I also believe there is an unbridgeable difference between knowing that for a truth and knowing how we will sort ourselves out should children appear crying and cold at the door. Between those who can torture children and those who can only save them are multitudes who will simply do nothing. All we know for sure is that in the moment of danger we will have to choose.

It has occurred to me lately that the thief on the cross who turns to Jesus and asks, "Remember me when you come into your kingdom," may be taken on some level for one of the robbers who assaulted the man helped by the good Samaritan. Same man, different circumstances. Or, we might say, different men, same humanity—same potential for hurt and harm.

And it has also occurred to me that the thief may not have believed that the one he addressed was coming into any kingdom whatsoever, that all he foresaw was a dark void looming ahead of him—and in his peripheral vision, a wannabe messiah with a low threshold for pain and tears running down his cheeks, and that he offered his plea without any hope or faith at all, only a crude, robberly kind of love, acting a part not unlike Steinbeck's George telling Lenny about the farm with the rabbits just before executing the mercy of blowing out his brains, and when Jesus said, "Today, you will be with me in Paradise," the thief's only comfort came from the thought that Jesus had taken the bait and that maybe in this moment of fantastical largesse the nails were a little less sharp for him. So, if there is a paradise, the joke would be on them both, as I suspect it is in any number of relationships between helper and helped. As I suspect it will be on any number of believer and agnostic combinations, on André Trocmé and Albert Camus. My faith consists of daring to believe that the joke is not cruel. In fact, the joke may be Paradise itself.

Sometimes we hear faint traces of its laughter.

I get a call, not a wrong number, from the young man who was in the wrong body. He is almost not young. I cannot be certain if he is still a man. He is living in a city now, far away, though he will be passing through my neighborhood in another day or so. He and his partner are starting up a safe house and counseling service to help young people with questions about their sexual identity. "So kids like I was will have someplace to turn." He invites me to hear more about the project.

We arrange to meet at a diner. He is even taller than I remember, at least a head above me. He is not dressed like a woman. I don't ask if he ever does that now. I don't ask if he gave up on the operation. I don't ask or even think to ask what he might be wearing underneath his clothes. I look into his eyes, which were always warm and a bit dubious—as if he were asking, "Are you really able to follow this, Reverend Keizer, or are you simply trying to be tolerant?"—and I ask to whom I should make out the check. The donation is my idea. It's one of the last things I'll do with my priest's discretionary fund before closing the account and moving my black clergy shirt to the far left side of the closet.

I suppose that before you close this book, I might do you the favor of recalling some of its main points. Just before a friend gets out of your car, you ask, "Do you have all your stuff?"

Help is a part of our humanity; it is what human beings do. If it is complicated, inconclusive, that is because we are. Its paradoxes define us. Alone in the universe, I am as helpless as a stone. But with my disappearance, or the turning of one stone into bread, the universe is bereft. In the Bolivian jungle, after Che Guevara's little band suffers its first casualties, he records in his diary what amounts to the only manifesto I am willing to sign: "The human loss of the three is incalculable."

As may be the human value of our ministrations. In my first chapter, I distinguished help from altruism by saying that altruism is what it is but that help, being an action, must always submit to a verdict. I ought to have added that the jury is often out. As the nurse said, we plant seeds, and some take a long time to mature.

Anything beyond that is subject to argument. Give me a statement about help that purports to be definitive, and I will give you a situation that makes it sound ridiculous. Philip Hallie and Norman Maclean, trustworthy writers of markedly different sensibilities, both define help as giving a part of oneself. Hallie goes further: "When you give somebody a thing without giving yourself, you degrade both parties by making the receiver utterly passive and by making yourself a benefactor standing there to receive thanks." True enough, but not always true. If I'm drifting fast towards the falls, I don't want you to give me a part of yourself. I want you to throw me a rope. Trust me, I won't feel degraded. The neurologist Oliver Sacks was asked by the husband of a patient suffering from a rare form of dementia when he ought to help his wife and when it would be better to let her sort out her own dilemmas. "I could suggest no rule, I said to Josef, except that of fact; each situation would call for its own solution." Any other approach, and Josef becomes The Man Who Mistook His Wife for a Categorical Imperative. Better to mistake her for a hat.

But indefiniteness has its own way of becoming dogmatic, so if there is anything we can say for sure, we will want to say it now. I believe that I did say it, fairly early on, when I said that if we choose to act on Dr. Rony Brauman's assertion that human beings were not made to suffer, we must paradoxically assume a willingness to suffer ourselves. That strikes me as fairly self-evident.

Less clear is the situation in which the costs of our compassion are likely to be borne by a third party. The biblical commandment to "love your neighbor as yourself" is a dubious ethic unless the neighbor is taken both individually and collectively. To love a neighbor who means only to harm the neighborhood is not love; it's misanthropy. When Timon of Athens was asked why he, the least benevolent of men, spent so much time entertaining an arrogant young upstart, he said, "Because I know that one day he will do much mischief to the Athenians."

We can also state with assurance that no program, however utopian, will ever abolish the need for individual acts of kindness. For that reason, we need not fear that progressive changes in our society will make us progressively less human. And I think that people do fear that. When ramps for the disabled became mandatory at public buildings, a local clergyman wrote a letter to the newspaper lamenting how simple neighborliness was being lost through our misguided attempts to legislate compassion. He fondly recalled a familiar scene from his childhood when the deacons of his church would meet a disabled man at the foot of the steps every Sunday and carry him up to the door. I never heard a more persuasive argument—for mandatory ramps. Had the paraplegic lacked the use of his hands, I'm sure these same good people would have fed him with a long spoon. What I'm less sure of is how much he would have enjoyed the meal.

If we fear that systemic justice will abolish mercy, then something insidious has already abolished our imaginations. So the man in the wheelchair no longer needs our help getting into church; what if the service is his mother's funeral? Tell the deacons not to worry. They will never be dismissed.

The complement to this is obvious: no act of personal service, no association of right-minded volunteers, no constellation of altruistic superstars can replace a society's need for the political will to take care of its own. We cannot privatize justice. Tending our own gardens in the manner of Candide will never get us closer to the Garden. The dream we no longer admit, if pursued in isolation, soon becomes the dream we can no longer dream.

Perhaps the altruistic hero's greatest social value is as an *object* of compassion. The good Samaritan is a lame excuse and a middling example as long as he fails to inspire as much sympathy as the man he picks off the road. The Samaritan is our neighbor no less than the victim is his. Yes, I want the world's hungry to be fed. I also want Paul Farmer to have a few more free weekends with his daughter. The two desires are linked. If I am content to watch a great humanitarian beat his head against the wall, should I be surprised to discover that I am also content to let a less admirable person starve?

Help can never serve as a talisman to ward off all temptation because help itself can be a temptation. It can be an escape from responsibility. It can be a vain attempt to place oneself beyond reproach.

I have a friend who is in seminary studying for the Episcopal priesthood. When she first went to talk to her bishop about her call, the bishop gave her what I regard as a wise piece of advice. "Try to locate the sin in your calling," she said. I realize that some of my readers may balk at the mention of sin, but their scruple is largely a matter of terminology. Everyone believes in sin, the people who charge their peers with political incorrectness and the people who regard political incorrectness as the bogey of a little mind. What everyone does not believe in, as nearly as I can tell, is forgiveness.

Making any necessary allowances for the bishop's language, we would have to give her credit for much good sense. She was not saying that locating the sin would invalidate the call. She didn't say, if you find a sin in your calling, you shouldn't become a priest. She did say, locate the dark side of your aspiration. Then you will be able to aspire in earnest. As the sibyl Liesl tells Dunstable Ramsay in Robertson Davies's novel *Fifth Business:* "You must get to know your personal devil."

In some ways, this book has been about making the devil's acquaintance, about locating the sin in altruism. To a lesser extent, it has been about locating the sin that can exist in neediness. But those aims are incomplete and even insincere unless I also try to locate the sin in this book. It isn't all that hard to do.

The sin of this book resides in its invitation to readers to think too much about actions that in some cases are best not thought about at all. It involves tempting people to be clever when cleverness is the least thing required. Qualifying Socrates, Iris Murdoch said, "An unexamined life can be virtuous." If, as we kept company together, you were sometimes impatient with my ruminations, thinking to yourself, "It's not like that at all! It's simpler, something much more basic," I'm inclined to think you were right. But if my book has renewed your appreciation for basic instincts, then its sin is in some ways redeemed. The English mystic Julian of Norwich said, "Sin is behoovable"—and we had better hope so, given the fact that in books of more than three words, it is also inevitable.

To say that "we are here to help" falls short of the mark in my view; we are also here to help in conjunction with other helpers. We are here to delight in *we*. Doctor and Nurse. At its best, social action is sociable in the same way that the best demonstration for peace is peaceful. The good Samaritan is alone, of course, and has to make do. But he wastes no time getting to the inn.

The example of shared help that means the most to me is a marriage. Love moving between two partners, and from them to the world—that is what moves me. André and Magda Trocmé will always be high on my list of heroes. I am not suggesting that a long-term committed relationship is the only authentic way to help; it is merely the only authentic way to be married. The world has been blessed repeatedly through the ministrations of individuals who chose to remain solitary. It has probably been the most blessed, the most spectacularly blessed, by such individuals. I am only saying that marriage remains the best source, sustenance, and simile for what I know about help. It reminds me of help, it reminds me to help, and it reminds me of a few things that helpers forget to their peril.

One of these things is that not every relationship is a marriage. The union of two people in body and mind for the duration of their lifetime is an instrument, and sometimes an inspiration, for helping others; it is not the standard. A person who comes to believe he must exercise the same fidelity and show the same passion toward his clients, patients, or students as he would to a spouse turns out to be a monster or an accident waiting to happen. We are meant to help in partnership; we are not meant to be intimate partners to every person we help.

If marriage is all I think it is and can be—and if the world can be as cruel as we know it to be—we had better think twice about denying people the right to marry. It would be humorous were it not so very sad that at a time of catastrophic social damage, much of it caused by marital disaffection and most of it borne by children, we should be so leery of lending our support to any earnest public pledge of love. It is like slowing the evacuation of Dunkirk with an argument about harbor privileges. No queer skippers. No pink boats.

It may seem that I'm veering off to the shoulder of the road, but in fact I am coming around to a place we have already passed several times. I want to be sure you have seen the view. We were here when we spoke of medicine. In fact, we passed this way whenever we spoke of pain. The Right in this country talks about protecting life and protecting tradition, but on some level—the level, let's say, where someone like Dr. Thompson can be threatened with prosecution—I think it is mostly interested in protecting pain. For two reasons.

The first is theological: the belief that pain holds the meaning of life. Mother Teresa: "The suffering of the poor is beautiful." We are not so rhapsodic as all that, though we do prefer our suffering to be done, as much as possible, by the poor. And we remain convinced, no less than the Aztec priest who held up a captive's butchered heart, that somebody has to do it. Earlier I said that we may have to suffer in order to help; this is something else—the idea that suffering is beyond help, as God is beyond time, that it is ordained and holy. Supposedly, this is a Christian idea, though if Jesus had believed it he would have told the lepers to find meaning in their sores.

The second reason is political: the belief that pain is integral to justice, which of course makes sense if justice is conceived of as nothing more than a system of punishments and rewards. The essence of punishment is pain. Whoever owns pain owns power. Saint Peter and his successors may claim the keys to heaven and hell, but in the kingdom of Caesar, authority belongs to those with keys to the medicine cabinet. The mystic, the suicide, the addict, the woman who seeks an abortion are all roundly condemned for their escape from responsibility; they are truly feared for their escape from jurisdiction. The first thought of power is to make that escape impossible; love would rather work to make a world in which escape is undesirable.

I am reminded of this every time we jump through a succession of hoops to refill my mother-in-law's prescription for pain medicine. The patch she applies to her skin is a regulated substance: the doctor and the pharmacist are included in the "we" who must jump. I have to drive thirty-five miles in order to retrieve the script in person. God forbid that it fall into the wrong hands. With far less trouble, and far less official anxiety about wrong hands, we could relieve Grandma's discomfort by buying a gun and shooting her. That, at least, would involve some pain all around.

The other thing we learn from helping "two by two" is the vacillation of strength, the flux of need, that exists in any exchange of help that lasts longer than a brief encounter on the road. Today's helper is tomorrow's applicant for help; unexpectedly, the shoe is on the other foot. We learn this in a marriage or a friendship; we recognize it whenever help that seemed one-sided turns out to be something else.

I get a call from Loretta. When I had my discretionary fund, she would occasionally call when she was in a pinch with one of her bills. Now that the fund is gone, she calls me even more often. It was never about the money. She calls me Garner. "Hey, Garner, how you doing? You keeping warm over there?" She is calling to share the good news that her cancer is in remission—for about the third time this year. I am skeptical of much that she tells me, yet I am continually discovering that something she told me is true. "This is wonderful news," I say.

I am not sure how old she is—I'd guess around sixty, she says thirty-eight—but something ancient comes through her mountain speech, like wood smoke curling through what she calls a "chimbley." She tells me I am in her prayers. In fact, her phone calls work like prayers, my prayers anyway: I seldom hear her say hello without thinking, "I don't have time for this," and I never hang up without feeling I have just been lifted above time. How is it that I must always be reminded? It occurs to me that for all intents and purposes she is now my priest.

"Well, sweetheart, I'll let you go. You tell your wife and your daughter I'm praying for them too. God bless you, Garner." That evening I tell my wife that I hope God really is omniscient, knowing all thoughts, desires, and mispronunciations, else there may be some son of a bitch named Garner who's got more grace and good luck than he knows what to do with. But of course I am that son of a bitch. And I know it. I may turn out to be the only mortal who gets into heaven under a false name.

I had a dear friend once tell me something about help that I will never forget, though had I remembered it when I most needed to, he might be my dear friend still.

I believe we were talking about the art of teaching, an art we were both trying to learn, but I cannot be sure. He said to me, "Lately I have been thinking about the story of Christ in the Garden of Gethsemane. He says to his disciples, 'Watch with me for an hour.' He doesn't say, 'Save me from the trouble ahead,' or, 'Give me an answer to the riddle of existence,' or, 'Show me a better way to bear my pain.'

He doesn't ask them for any advice. All he wants is their companionship in a time of anguish."

The book of Job was often on my friend's mind, and though I don't recall his making any such comparison, I am sure that he had thought much about the contrast between what Jesus asks of Peter, James, and John at Gethsemane and what poor Job gets from Bildad, Zophar, and Eliphaz, who offer Job comfort in the form of insinuation masquerading as advice. In circumstances of extreme suffering, advice easily reduces to insinuation. The disciples may have fallen asleep during their friend's dark night of the soul, but at least they were not talking.

One night a young woman I had taught in high school called me up from her college dorm. She sounded awfully depressed. I thought she had called for a good word, and I tried to give her one. In fact, she had called to tell me that she had just swallowed several bottles of Tylenol. She waited patiently for me to pause in my monologue before saying so. Thankfully, I was able to call the campus police in time to save her. But I could have helped her much sooner had I simply known when to shut up.

A teacher might be able to learn that. It is harder for a writer, who is more accustomed to talking without interruptions.

Still, it is a point well taken. Sometimes the only help we can give a friend or even a reader is to keep watch, not in the sense of gawking at someone's difficulties, but in the sense of sharing the same guard. Mother Jones to the striking coal miners: "I will be with you at midnight." We build a small fire on the battlements and warm our hands. It will be a long stretch, but between the two of us we'll manage to stay awake. And I happen to have brought a sandwich. I hope that at least some of these pages worked that way for you. In any event, let this be the last point of my summation, the final thing I have learned about help: the thing I am still trying to learn.

This fall my wife and I drove our only child to college. We crossed two state lines and a threshold. We brought her to a place where we would be less able than ever before to give her our help. From now on all the dosages will be up to her.

It was a sunny day with a sunny group of resident advisers waiting to welcome us and help in the moving. Like angels in running shorts, they swooped down from the steps, fluttering all around us, taking up pillows and suitcases, computer printers and portable TVs from the hands of parents and freshmen only too happy for the help. No one offered to help me. Perhaps it was my sunglasses, which both my wife and daughter maintain give me a sinister appearance. Perhaps the help I received was commensurate with the face I deserved, which Orwell said we all have by the age of fifty. After about my second or third trip into the dorm, I began to feel strangely charmed. It was as if I were only dreaming the move, from a vantage point of invisibility, whereas the people in my dream were all visible to one another.

The truth was, I didn't want anyone's help, and it may be that I managed to communicate that somehow. I wanted this to take time. I wanted to be sure that every item I had fitted so painstakingly into the hatchback of the car made it safely to my daughter's room. I needed to be able to vouch for that. Maybe too I needed some excuse to escape from the emotions of imminent separation that I could sense were coming to the surface up in her room where she and her mom were unpacking. Mothers give comfort, you see; fathers were made to haul baggage up flights of stairs. That is why women have fuller bosoms and men have bigger feet.

I wondered if the young people around me were able to sense any of this, if they had learned so early in their lives to intuit when help is not going to be helpful. If so, they are better than I was at their age. I suspect that is true. I suspect that their altruism tends to be a little less flamboyant and a lot more informed than it was for the youth of my generation. "Ask not what you can do for your country"—just do what you can.

I wondered too if I had become one of those people who give help more graciously than they receive it. An ophthalmologist had recently told me about his work with people who have lost their sight. "Often it's the ones who have been most helpful in their own lives who are the most loath to accept help when they go blind." Perhaps I fit the description, right down to the dark glasses.

"I ask them to think about the pleasure they have experienced when they could be of help. I say, 'Don't you want other people to know that same enjoyment?'"

I do. I resolved that if someone asked to carry one of my cartons, I would not refuse. And on my next-to-last trip from the car, someone did.

It will be a familiar story to many my age, our drive home to the empty nest. Those desolate first days. The renewed partnership that comes of sharing desolation. By homecoming weekend, desolation is starting to feel like adventure. You're looking forward to seeing your kid; you're also looking forward to the ride. Two warm coffees rim to rim in the cup holder. I discover that I am as happy in the passenger seat as I ever was behind the wheel.

We take more rides together now. We drive over one evening to see Sonny and his wife. He opens a can of the gourmet nuts. He asks if we'd like a beer. "Do you remember that trip we took?" he says to me, as if we had once been two sailors on leave. The exasperation of our night in the dark wood has the patina of nostalgia now. He shakes his head at the craziness of it. "I hope you know," he says, "that you can always call on me if you need some help." I think he means that we might try a stunt like that again. I have a feeling we will, perhaps with a better plan than we had the last time. Perhaps not.

But if there is a better plan, I'm ready to hear it. I'm at the crossroads, and I know I am, because I am not even intimidated by the cliché. I also know that being at the crossroads is the luxury of people with enough to eat.

I made my annual pilgrimage to New York City not long ago, when all these transitions were imminent—the end of priesting, at least for a while, the start of this book, the beginning of a time when I would no longer hear my daughter's voice singing through the wall in unison with some screaming Ophelia, when I would have neither a father's excuse nor a Levite's for passing the man lying in the road. I walked with the aim of finding a cathedral spire, down Forty-second Street and up Fifth Avenue to what turned out to be Saint Patrick's. A mass was in progress. It was the Feast of Saint James.

I knelt in the pew. The deacon stepped from behind the altar. "The mass is over," he announced. I had arrived just in time for the dismissal, which struck my ears as dismissive. The mass is over. "Go in peace." But I had just gotten there. So I found a place off to the side, with a great pillar between me and the rest of the nave, where I might pray in peace. I knelt again.

No sooner had I done so than a sacristan came and threw open the wide doors beside me, like Noah might have done on the grounded ark, revealing the plains of Armenia to a pair of sun-blinded zebras. I found myself in full view of a busy New York street—exposed, on my knees, as if curtains had opened to discover me in my bathtub on a Broadway stage. Taxis drove through the puddles, past street vendors and pedestrians on cell phones, dappled with the shadows of departing wings. The mass is over. And this is where your work is now and will be from now on. Out there.

And that would have been such a nice epiphany with which to close this book—I thought so even then, with the book barely begun—but in fact I cannot end there, because number one, I am sick of epiphanies and the smug spirituality of epiphanies, and number two, God wouldn't let me. If I wanted to construct a narrative out of epiphanies, there was to be one more.

For as I approached Port Authority, with an editor's encouragement and a cab driver's heavily accented benediction still warm on my ears, I saw a young woman in black shorts and tank top sitting on the side-walk—first the white flash of her flesh, then the dark bruises on her thighs, the livid fingerprints on her upper arms. There it is, I said, your first assignment under the new dispensation. On the Feast of Saint James, patron saint of good works: *Behold.*

I hesitated for no more than half a step. What would she think to have a middle-aged man bending down to inquire after her welfare? Even if he removed his sunglasses. "I couldn't help but notice the bruises on your thighs, my dear." And why her, and not the male derelict a few yards away? Good question.

But what if she were your daughter?

I kept walking. Like the priest and the Levite and probably a thou-sand other commuters, I made my way to the numbered gate where the buses were now running every quarter hour. Roy Orbison switched genders in my head: "Is he walking back to me?" This time it was the pretty woman who got to ask. Nope, he's not. He's going home.

Would Dr. Johnson have stopped, I wondered, or Dr. Farmer or the Reverend Trocmé? Or would they not even have noticed, their eyes being less wayward than mine?

You can bet that William Carlos Williams would have noticed. Earthy fellow. But how responded, as doctor or scribe?

What if I had bent to her and she had said, Yeah, I'm in a heap of trouble, help me. What would I have done then? Taken her home? Found her an inn? Missed my bus? And what if she had a friend named Eddie, because they always have a friend named Eddie, or Bruce or Butch or Slash, who may or may not have been the person responsible for those bruises? And Eddie would need a favor too, of course. Because she could never leave Eddie in a million years and hasn't for the past ten thousand at least.

What a rube I was even to entertain such thoughts. This was Manhattan, for God's sake. The navel of the civilized world, the center of art, business, diplomacy—where every section of the Sunday *New York Times* is opened up and magically folded into giant structures of stone and steel, the origami of the gods. (A bit much, that, but jot it down anyway.) Did you see anyone else hesitate? These people know the score. That's how they have managed to survive, all of them, even that girl on the sidewalk: they know the score. The *plan*. And it has nothing to do with the libel of their supposed coldness because you have found assistance in this city whenever you asked for it—but only when you asked. *When help ain't asked for, it ain't help.* There is no better plan than that. Right?

For what would happen to the world—really, when you stop to think about it, what would happen to this world—if every ambulatory man and woman on earth were to stop dead in his or her tracks right now and for no other reason than that someone who might be construed as a neighbor lies wounded and left for dead by the side of the road?

You tell me.

NOTES

CHAPTER 1. THE DARK WOOD

2 *"If you can't find"* Joni Mitchell, "Just Like This Train," *Court and Spark* (Asylum Records, 1974).

2 *"I lost my tenderness"* Paul Kelly and the Messengers, "Careless," *So Much Water So Close to Home* (A & M Records, 1989).

2 *Winston Churchill* Varying forms of the quotation have been attributed to François Guizot, Georges Clemençeau, Benjamin Disraeli, Bertrand Russell, and George Bernard Shaw. See Ralph Keyes, *Nice Guys Finish Seventh: False Phrases, Spurious Sayings, and Familiar Misquotations* (New York: HarperCollins, 1992), 51.

3 *Anna Freud* Cited in Robert Coles, *The Moral Life of Children* (Boston: Atlantic Monthly Press, 1986), 169.

3 *I and Thou* Martin Buber, *I and Thou*, trans. Ronald Gregor Smith, 2nd ed. (New York: Scribner's, 1958).

4 *"Noble let man be"* Johann Wolfgang von Goethe, "The Divine" (1783), *Selected Poems*, trans. John Whaley (London: J. M. Dent, 1998), 45.

6 *"until the grass"* Huston Smith, *The Religions of Man* (New York: Harper & Row, 1965), 137.

6 *"I saw that for us"* Julian of Norwich, *Revelations of Divine Love*, trans. Elizabeth Spearing (London: Penguin, 1998), 7.

6 *Einstein* A number of sources quote Einstein's remark on the question of a friendly or unfriendly universe; however, I have yet to locate one that can be considered authoritative.

7 *children of baby boomers* "From 2000 to 2002 alone, the household income of those under 35 dropped 14%—the biggest decline of any age group." "[N]o generation since the Great Depression has had the odds so stacked against it, notes New York University economist Edward Wolff." Michelle Conlin, "For Gen X, It's Paradise Lost," *Business Week*, 30 June 2003, 72ff.

8 *Habitat for Humanity* "By the age of twenty-nine, [Habitat founder Millard] Fuller was a millionaire but began to lose the things that were most important to him. His marriage, integrity, and health soon began to fade, which caused him to re-evaluate his life and make significant changes. . . . Millard and wife Linda decided to sell their possessions, give the money away, and find a new purpose for life." Tether M. Coppock, "Historic Roots," Habitat for Humanity International Web site, http://www.learningtogive.org/papers/organizations/habitat-humanity.html.

9 *"Midway in our life's journey"* Dante Alighieri, *The Inferno*, trans. John Ciardi (New York: Mentor, 1954), 28.

9 *"Why have I not found favor"* The Oxford Annotated Bible with Apocrypha (NRSV) (New York: Oxford Univ. Press, 1991); Numbers 11:11–12. Except for several places where the language of the King James Bible proved irresistible, all subsequent biblical references are to this translation.

9 *"You faithless generation"* Mark 9:19.

10 *"Who has ever had a sadder"* Sue M. Goldie, ed., *"I Have Done My Duty": Florence Nightingale in the Crimean War, 1854–1856* (Iowa City: Univ. of Iowa Press, 1987), 165.

10 *"Do you think I enjoy"* Dr. Edgar Berman, *In Africa with Schweitzer* (New York: Harper & Row, 1986), 62.

13 *as much as God does* But see Etty Hillesum, *An Interrupted Life: The Diaries, 1941–1943, and Letters from Westerbork*, trans. Arnold J. Pomerans (1981; New York: Henry Holt, 1996), 178. A Dutch Jew at the time of the Holocaust, she prays, "I shall try to help You, God, to stop my strength from ebbing away, though I cannot vouch for it in advance."

13 *"Teach us to care"* T. S. Eliot, "Ash Wednesday," *Collected Poems, 1909–1962* (New York: Harcourt, Brace & World, 1970), 95.

CHAPTER 2. THE DUBIOUS SAMARITAN

24 *parable of Good Samaritan* Luke 10:29–37.

25 *"To choose a beloved"* Søren Kierkegaard, "Works of Love" (1847), in *A Kierkegaard Anthology*, ed. Robert Bretall (New York: Modern Library, 1946), 289.

26 *"wagon train morality"* Joan Didion, "On Morality," *Slouching Towards Bethlehem* (New York: Dell, 1968), 158.

26 *"The true place of God"* Cited in John Berger, *A Fortunate Man: The Story of a Country Doctor* (1967; New York: Vintage, 1997), 78.

28 *Samaritans* See *The Oxford Companion to the Bible*, ed. Bruce M. Metzger and Michael D. Coogan (New York: Oxford Univ. Press, 1993), 671–73.

28 *woman at the well* John 4:3–42.

29 *Trotsky had more* Leon Trotsky, *Their Morals and Ours* (New York: Pioneer, 1942), 10–13.

29 *Doctor Schulz* Karl Stern, *The Pillar of Fire* (New York: Harcourt Brace, 1951), 130.

29 *Himmler* Jonathan Glover, *Humanity: A Moral History of the Twentieth Century* (New Haven: Yale Nota Bene, 2001), 404.

29 *"human responses"* Glover, *Humanity*, 404.

30 *Saddam Hussein* Mark Bowden, "Tales of the Tyrant," *Atlantic Monthly*, May 2002, 51–52.

30 *moved by pity* "The Samaritan approached the injured man on the side of the road not because of some cold religious obligation, but because 'his heart was melting' (this is literally what the verb *splankhnizein* means in Luke 10:33)." Gustavo Gutierrez, *A Theology of Liberation* (Maryknoll, NY: Orbis, 1973), 199.

30 *"Unable to comprehend"* Samuel P. Oliner and Pearl M. Oliner, *The Altruistic Personality: Rescuers of the Jews in Nazi Europe* (New York: Free Press, 1988), 251.

30 *"The Way is empty"* Lao-tzu, Tao te ching, trans. D. C. Lau (Harmondsworth, UK: Penguin, 1963), 60.

30 *"Deep, it is"* Lao-tzu, Tao te ching, 60.

30 *"Highest good"* Lao-tzu, Tao te ching, 64.

30 *"I only did my duty"* Oliner and Oliner, *Altruistic Personality*, 228.

31 *"It all happened"* Weapons of the Spirit, written and directed by Pierre Sauvage (First Run Features, 1989), 16. A transcript of the documentary can be obtained from Friends of Le Chambon, 8033 Sunset Boulevard, Los Angeles, CA 90046. Subsequent quotations from the film refer to this transcript.

31 *"not a hero"* Michelle R. McCann, *Luba: The Angel of Bergen-Belsen*, as told by Luba Tryszynska-Frederick (Berkeley: Tricycle Press, 2003), back cover. With illustrations by Ann Marshall, this is a beautiful book to share with a child.

31 *John Stuart Mill* Cited in Philip Hallie, *Lest Innocent Blood Be Shed: The Story of the Village of Le Chambon and How Goodness Happened There* (1979; New York: Harper-Collins, 1994), 284.

31 *"are adamant in their feelings"* Kathleen B. Brehony, *Ordinary Grace: An Examination of the Roots of Compassion, Altruism, and Empathy, and the Ordinary Individuals Who Help Others in Extraordinary Ways* (New York: Riverhead, 1999), 96.

31 *"If we pass along a legacy"* Pierre Sauvage, interview with Bill Moyers, Public Broadcasting System, 12 December 1990.

32 *the Gestapo files* Oliner and Oliner, *Altruistic Personality*, 8.

33 *"feeling personally potent"* Oliner and Oliner, *Altruistic Personality*, 226. See also 241 on the tendency of bystanders to emphasize "their own impotence and victimization at the hands of external circumstances."

33 *"occupational advantage"* Oliner and Oliner, *Altruistic Personality*, 226.

33 *In matters of health* Oliner and Oliner, *Altruistic Personality*, 246. The Oliners report that only 32 percent of the rescuers they interviewed described themselves as in good or excellent health as opposed to 56 percent of nonrescuers, a challenge to any easy assumption that altruism is "good for you" simply because it is *good*. Still, it is no surprise to find good health and good deeds in conjunction. See Allan Luks and Peggy Payne, *The Healing Power of Doing Good: The Health and Spiritual Benefits of Helping Others* (New York: Fawcett, 1992).

33 *"I would look out"* Elliott J. Gorn, *Mother Jones: The Most Dangerous Woman in America* (New York: Hill and Wang, 2001), 42.

33 *"I'm a hell-raiser"* Gorn, *Mother Jones*, 3.

34 *a study showing* K. E. Matthews and L. K. Cannon, "Environmental Noise Level as a Determinant of Helping Behavior," *Journal of Personality and Social Psychology* 32 (1975): 571–77.

35 *"When I was a child"* Edward Hoagland, "The Problem of the Golden Rule," in *The Courage of Turtles* (1968; San Francisco: North Point, 1985), 6.

36 *"In illness many connexions"* Berger, *Fortunate Man*, 69. Compare Berger's observation with what John Donne writes in *Devotions upon Emergent Occasions* (1624): "As sickness is the greatest misery, so the greatest misery of sickness is solitude, when the infectiousness of the disease deters them who should assist from coming; even the physician dares scarce come." *Seventeenth-Century Prose and Poetry*, ed. Alexander M. Witherspoon and Frank J. Warnke, 2nd edition (New York: Harcourt Brace, 1982), 62.

37 *"Things changed that horrible day"* Deborah Dwork and Robert Jan van Pelt, *Holocaust: A History* (New York: Norton, 2002), 344.

37 *"What is a human being?"* Cited in David Rieff, *A Bed for the Night: Humanitarianism in Crisis* (New York: Simon & Schuster, 2002), 92.

37 *"deep radicalism"* Rieff, *Bed for the Night*, 28.

38 *"meant for happiness"* Dorothy Day, *The Long Loneliness* (1952; San Francisco: HarperSanFrancisco, 1997), 113.

38 *"I request that it be arranged"* Glover, *Humanity*, 379–80.

39 *"Whoever saves a single soul"* *Schindler*, dir. John Blair (Thames Video Collection, n.d.).

40 *"take him by force"* John 6:14.

40 *"Touch me not"* John 20:17.

40 *For a contrasting portrait* Richard Price, *Samaritan* (New York: Knopf, 2003).

41 *"Nerese got it"* Price, *Samaritan*, 215.

41 *"Ray says . . . a dent"* Price, *Samaritan*, 125.

42 *"one long unbroken cavalcade"* Price, *Samaritan*, 265.

42 *the essence of all great art* "The whole of beautiful art and of great art belongs here: their common essence is gratitude." Frederick Nietzsche, *The Case of Wagner* (1888), trans. Anthony M. Ludovici, vol. 8, *The Complete Works of Frederick Nietzsche*, ed. Oscar Levy (New York: Russell & Russell, 1964), 50.

43 *"Master, speak to my brother"* Luke 12:13–15.

44 *"I've been busting my butt"* Rieff, *Bed for the Night*, 184.

45 *average duration of rescue* Oliner and Oliner, *Altruistic Personality*, 6.

45 *the maddening habit* Hallie, *Lest Innocent Blood*, 18. For a stark and affecting depiction of ordinary people hiding fugitives at the risk of their lives, see Rink van der Velde's short novel *The Trap*, trans. Henry J. Baron (1966; Grand Rapids: Redux, 1995).

45 *"I don't want him bleedin'"* *To Have and Have Not*, dir. Howard Hawks (MGM, 1944).

46 *Socrates would not* "Is it not obvious that those who are ignorant of their nature do not desire [evils]; but they desire what they suppose to be goods." Plato, *Meno*, in *The Dialogues of Plato*, trans. Benjamin Jowett, The Great Books of the Western World 7 (Chicago: Britannica, 1952), 178.

46 *"realizing that everyone wants"* Jeffrey Hopkins, *Cultivating Compassion: A Buddhist Perspective* (New York: Broadway, 2001), 22.

47 *"The appeal of the practice"* Hopkins, *Cultivating Compassion*, 40.

47 *Harriet Tubman* M. W. Taylor, *Harriet Tubman: Antislavery Activist* (New York: Chelsea House, 1991), 49.

48 *her life was her argument* See Dr. Edgar Berman, *In Africa with Schweitzer* (New York: Harper & Row, 1986), 106.

48 *part about the gun* See *Camilo Torres: His Life and Message*, ed. John Alvarez Garcia and Christian Restropo Calle, trans. Virginia M. O'Grady, intro. Dorothy Day (Springfield, IL: Templegate, 1968). Torres was a Colombian Roman Catholic priest who abandoned his ecclesiastical position in order to join with leftist guerrillas in his country. "I have stopped offering Mass to live out the love for my neighbor in the temporal, economic, and social orders. When my neighbor no longer has anything against me, and when the revolution has been completed, then I will offer Mass again, if God so wills it" (74). He was killed by government soldiers in 1966.

49 *"When help ain't asked for"* Rita Mae Brown, *Six of One* (New York: Bantam, 1979), 230.

49 *"Well, I'd rather my man"* Porter Grainger and Everett Robbins, "T'ain't Nobody's Bizness if I Do," *The Best of Billie Holiday* (Universal Music Enterprises, 2002).

50 *St. Augustine* Cited in Day, *Long Loneliness*, 255.

51 *"A few screams evoke"* Cited in Lacey Baldwin Smith, *Fools, Martyrs, Traitors: The Story of Martyrdom in the Western World* (New York: Knopf, 1997), 313.

CHAPTER 3. THE DREAM WE NO LONGER ADMIT

54 *"What do you want"* Mark 10:51. In this connection, see the documentary film *Sound and Fury*, directed by John Aronson (Artistic License/Docurama, 2000), which raises interesting questions about help and handicap. A deaf child's hearing grandparents want him to have a cochlear implant so that he can hear; his deaf parents fear this will effectively alienate him from his household and from deaf culture. The theme is not without relevance to the discussion of missionary activity that follows.

55 *Sigmund Freud* "A General Introduction to Psycho-Analysis" (1917), trans. Joan Riviere, in *The Major Works of Sigmund Freud*, The Great Books of the Western World 54 (Chicago: Britannica, 1952), 623–25.

56 *a religion of . . . self-reliance* Huston Smith, *The Religions of Man* (New York: Harper & Row, 1965), 107.

56 *"Self is the lord of self"* *The Dhammapada*, trans. Irving Babbitt (New York: New Directions, 1965), 26.

56 *"Let no one forget"* Dhammapada, 27.

56 *"Make thyself an island"* Dhammapada, 38.

56 *"relying on myself alone"* E. A. Burtt, ed., *The Teachings of the Compassionate Buddha* (New York: Mentor, 1955), 50.

56 *"Therefore, O Ananda"* Burtt, *Compassionate Buddha*, 49.

57 *"Nobody can counsel"* Rainer Maria Rilke, *Letters to a Young Poet*, trans. M. D. Herter Norton (1934; New York: Norton, 1963), 18.

57 *Theravada and Mahayana* See Huston Smith, *Religions of Man*, 132–39, and Burtt, *Compassionate Buddha*, 83–204.

57 *The crux of their argument* Burtt, *Compassionate Buddha*, 125.

57 *St. Paul and burdens* Galatians 6:2, 6:5.

58 *"If you meet the Buddha"* Wing-Tsit Chan, comp. and trans., *A Source Book in Chinese Philosophy* (Princeton: Princeton Univ. Press, 1969), 447.

58 *Augustine and Pelagius* See Henry Chadwick, *The Early Church* (Harmondsworth, UK: Penguin, 1967), 225–35.

58 *Arminius* The Concise Oxford Dictionary of the Christian Church, ed. E. A. Livingstone (New York: Oxford Univ. Press, 1977), s.v. "Arminianism."

60 *"There has always been [a] divergence"* Joan Didion, "7000 Romaine, Los Angeles 38," *Slouching Towards Bethlehem* (New York: Dell, 1968), 71–72. See also Albert Camus: "Unlike many of my . . . contemporaries, I do not think that man is by nature a social animal. To tell the truth, I think the reverse. But I believe . . . that he cannot live henceforth outside society, whose laws are necessary to his physical survival"; "Reflections on the Guillotine" (1957), in *Resistance, Rebellion, and Death*, trans. Justin O'Brien (New York: Vintage, 1995), 178.

60 *parable of heaven and hell* Barbara Kingsolver, *The Bean Trees* (New York: Harper & Row, 1988), 107–8. Kingsolver identifies the story as South American Indian; Brehony (see *Ordinary Grace*, below) identifies it as Hasidic.

61 *"Do not tell me"* Ralph Waldo Emerson, "Self-Reliance" (1841), in *Emerson: Essays and Lectures*, ed. Joel Porte, Library of America 15 (New York: Literary Classics of the United States, 1983), 262–63.

61 *"Nature suffers nothing"* Emerson, "Self-Reliance," 272.

61 *"the praise that is due"* Henry David Thoreau, *Walden*, ed. Owen Thomas (1854; New York: Norton, 1966), 52.

61 *"You must have a genius"* Thoreau, *Walden*, 49

62 *"I want the flower and fruit"* Thoreau, *Walden*, 52.

62 *"If I knew for a certainty"* Thoreau, *Walden*, 50.

62 *"teenage wasteland"* The Who, "Baba O'Riley," *The Kids Are All Right* (MCA, 1979).

63 *"The Solitude of the Self"* Elizabeth Cady Stanton, *The Elizabeth Cady Stanton–Susan B. Anthony Reader*, ed. Ellen Carol DuBois, rev. ed. (Boston: Northeastern Univ. Press, 1992), 246–54. "There is a solitude which each and every one of us has always carried with him, more inaccessible than the ice-cold mountains, more profound than the midnight sea." Stanton delivered the address in 1892.

63 *"rucksack revolution"* Jack Kerouac, *Big Sur* (1962; New York: Penguin, 1992), 44–48.

64 *"a harkening back to the old days"* Kathleen A. Brehony, *Ordinary Grace: An Examination of the Roots of Compassion, Altruism, and Empathy, and the Ordinary Individuals Who Help Others in Extraordinary Ways* (New York: Riverhead, 1999), 119.

65 *"I don't believe in Heaven"* Nick Hornby, *How to Be Good* (New York: Riverhead, 2001), 154.

65 *"All my life"* Hornby, *How to Be Good*, 293.

66 *"I suspect"* Hornby, *How to Be Good*, 251.

66 *"Maybe I can't live"* Hornby, *How to Be Good*, 303.

66 *"need the Discman"* Hornby, *How to Be Good*, 303–4.

67 *"The virtues are penances"* Emerson, "Self-Reliance," 263.

67 *"It struck me as incomprehensible"* Albert Schweitzer, *Out of My Life and Thought: An Autobiography* (New York: Henry Holt, 1933), 84.

67 *As a child he had refused* Dr. Edgar Berman, *In Africa with Schweitzer* (New York: Harper & Row, 1986), 259.

67 *"Those who receive beauty"* Berman, *In Africa*, 263.

67 *"Rarely could I ever"* Berman, *In Africa*, 263.

68 *He also told him* Berman, *In Africa*, 237.

68 *St. Francis and lepers* Omer Englebert, *St. Francis of Assisi: A Biography* (Ann Arbor: Servant Books, 1979), 32.

68 *Dorothy Day* Cited in Robert Coles, *The Moral Life of Children* (Boston: Atlantic Monthly Press, 1986), 190.

69 *"I believe he is a god"* Tracy Kidder, *Mountains Beyond Mountains: The Quest of Dr. Paul Farmer, A Man Who Would Cure the World* (New York: Random House, 2003), 27.

69 *"We need stories"* Simon Blackburn, *Being Good: A Short Introduction to Ethics* (Oxford: Oxford Univ. Press, 2001), 2.

70 *"Rescue allowed them"* Samuel P. Oliner and Pearl M. Oliner, *The Altruistic Personality: Rescuers of the Jews in Nazi Europe* (New York: Free Press, 1988), 227.

72 *"Who are these people"* Hornby, *How to Be Good*, 275.

73 *all the reasons . . . for helping* Samuel Johnson asserts that acts of help are even more numerous. "To enumerate the various modes of charity, as it is difficult, would be useless. They are as extensive as want, and as vacuous as misery." Henry Darcy Curwen, ed., *A Johnson Sampler* (Boston: David R. Godine, 2002), 210.

73 *Anna Freud* Cited in Coles, *Moral Life of Children*, 168.

73 *"Letter to Lord Chesterfield"* W. Jackson Bate, *Samuel Johnson* (New York: Harcourt Brace Jovanovich, 1977), 256–57.

74 *After one of Chopin's* Benita Eisler, *Chopin's Funeral* (New York: Knopf, 2003), 85–86.

74 *"I'm trying to help you"* *The Beatles Anthology*, dir. Geoff Wontor, vol. 8 (Apple, 1996).

74 *On Johnson and Boswell's . . . tour* Samuel Johnson and James Boswell, *A Journey to the Western Islands of Scotland and The Journal of a Tour of the Hebrides* (New York: Penguin, 1984), 331. The account is from Boswell (1785).

75 *"the most pestilential . . . habit"* John Lukacs, *Confessions of an Original Sinner* (New York: Tickner & Fields, 1990), 5.

75 *"the dispiriting view"* Blackburn, *Being Good*, 35–37.

75 *"Have you thrown"* Coles, *Moral Life of Children*, 161.

76 *communists and Christian missionaries* David Rieff, *A Bed for the Night: Humanitarianism in Crisis* (New York: Simon & Schuster, 2002), 47.

77 *"I'm very proud"* The Good Fight: The Abraham Lincoln Brigade in the Spanish Civil War, dir. Noel Buckner, Mary Dore, and Sam Sills (Kino, 1984).

78 *"dragging themselves"* Allen Ginsberg, "Howl," *Howl and Other Poems* (San Francisco: City Lights, 1956), 9.

78 Johanna Veenstra, *Pioneering for Christ in the Sudan* (Grand Rapids: Smitter, 1926). As this book is long out of print, I have not troubled to document individual quotations.

80 *"Just recently a TB patient"* Kidder, *Mountains Beyond Mountains*, 36.

81 *"It's the same culture"* I have been unable to locate the source of this quotation, though it seems consistent with Mary Daly's views as expressed in *Gyn/Ecology: The Metaethics of Radical Feminism* (1978; Boston: Beacon Press, 1990), 153–77. See also Simon Blackburn's comment on "the idea that we are just 'imposing' parochial western standards when, in the name of universal human rights, we oppose oppression of people on grounds of gender, caste, race, or religion." He notes that "it is typically only the oppressors who are spokespersons for *their* culture or *their* ways of doing it. It is not slaves who value slavery, or the women who value the fact that they may not take employment, or the young girls who value disfigurement." *Being Good*, 27.

82 *Cocteau's wonderful line* Cited in Frederic Vitoux, *Celine: A Biography*, trans. Jesse Browner (New York: Paragon House, 1992), 379.

82 *Jesuits in China* See Stephen Neill, *A History of Christian Missions* (Harmondsworth, UK: Penguin, 1964), 162–65; 188–94.

82 *Schweitzer . . . would play* Berman, *In Africa*, 149.

83 *"the kind of naïveté"* Peter N. Carroll, *The Odyssey of the Abraham Lincoln Brigade* (Stanford: Stanford Univ. Press, 1994), 4.

88 *Schweitzer had to build* Berman, *In Africa*, 87.

88 *"the brotherhood of all"* Berman, *In Africa*, 61.

88 *"Love diversifies them"* Cited in Lukacs, *Confessions*, 29.

88 *"a book begun in despair"* Rieff, *Bed for the Night*, 1.

89 *"a world too sad"* Rieff, *Bed for the Night*, 274.

89 *"we delude ourselves"* Rieff, *Bed for the Night*, 87.

89 *"vertebral nonbeliever"* Rieff, *Bed for the Night*, 3.

89 *"the horror of the cost"* Rieff, *Bed for the Night*, 56.

89 *"the language of oppressor"* Rieff, *Bed for the Night*, 14.

89 *"They . . . desperate to help"* Rieff, *Bed for the Night*, 297.

89 *"lose if you stay"* Rieff, *Bed for the Night*, 249.

90 *"to front only . . . life"* Thoreau, *Walden*, 61.

90 *"vulgar shitbags"* Vitoux, *Celine*, 421. Celine's paradoxical (but by no means unique) combination of compassion and misanthropy informs his masterpiece *Journey to the End of the Night*, trans. John H. P. Marks (1932; New York: New Directions, 1960), in which his narrator says, "People are so bad perhaps only because they suffer; but it takes a long time after they have ceased suffering for them to become a little better" (70).

90 *"in an era that"* Rieff, *Bed for the Night*, 1.

95 *swords into plowshares* Isaiah 2:4.

96 *shade of . . . fig tree* Micah 4:4.

96 *"To be happy"* Samuel Johnson, "The Rambler" (No. 68, 1750), vol. 1, *Select Essays of Dr. Johnson*, ed. George Birbeck Hill (London: J. M. Dent, 1889), 113.

96 *Dr. Paul Farmer* Tracy Kidder, *Mountains Beyond Mountains*, 189–90.

96 *"a pint of porter a day"* Sue M. Goldie, ed. *"I Have Done My Duty": Florence Nightingale in the Crimean War 1854–1856* (Iowa City: Univ. of Iowa Press, 1987), 75.

97 *Mary of Bethany* Matthew 26:6–13.

CHAPTER 4. THOSE WHO HAVE HANDS

99 *"The sustained effort"* Dorothy Day, *The Long Loneliness* (1952; San Francisco: HarperSanFrancisco, 1952), 11.

101 *The patron saint of helpful writers* Walter Jackson Bate, *Samuel Johnson* (New York: Harcourt Brace Jovanovich, 1975), 208–18; John Wain, *Samuel Johnson* (New York: Viking, 1974), 102–13, 120–24.

101 *A well-known painting* Bate, *Samuel Johnson*, plate 17.

101 *And not to writers only* Bate, *Samuel Johnson*, 501–4.

101 *"so they might beg"* on" Bate, *Samuel Johnson*, 501.

102 *Joseph Mitchell* "Professor Seagull" and "Joe Gould's Secret," in *Up in the Old Hotel* (New York: Pantheon, 1992), 52–72; 623–716.

103 *William F. Buckley* John B. Judis, *William F. Buckley: Patron Saint of Conservatives* (New York: Simon & Schuster, 1988), 257. For Buckley's own analysis and a comparison of his project with Mailer's, see William F. Buckley Jr., *Overdrive: A Personal Documentary* (Garden City, NY: Doubleday, 1983), 186–87. "I thought [Edgar] Smith innocent, Mailer knew Abbott to be guilty—indeed, Abbott never said he was not."

103 *Norman Mailer* My account of Norman Mailer and Jack Abbott is derived from the following sources: Mary V. Dearborn, *Mailer: A Biography* (Boston: Houghton Mifflin, 1999), 357–63; Peter Manso, ed., *Mailer, His Life and Times* (New York: Simon and Schuster, 1985), 620–51; Hilary Mills, *Mailer: A Biography* (New York: Empire Books, 1982), 13–37; Carl Rollyson, *The Lives of Norman Mailer* (New York: Paragon House, 1991), 304–18.

103 *William Styron* James L. W. West III, *William Styron: A Life* (New York: Random House, 1998), 320–23, 398–400. Also see 428–29 for an account of Styron's support of Mailer at the height of the Abbott controversy. At a PEN conference Styron said, "My heart goes out to him. I have an Abbott in my life."

104 *"state-reared" convict* Dearborn, *Mailer*, 360.

105 *"[Adan] was the type"* Manso, ed., *Mailer*, 642.

105 *"culture worth . . . risk"* Mills, *Mailer*, 17.

105 *"class enemies"* Mills, *Mailer*, 32.

107 *"I was so egocentric"* Dearborn, *Mailer*, 360.

107 *"You wrote the book"* Manso, ed., *Mailer*, 625.

108 *"He was very sweet"* Rollyson, *Lives*, 310.

108 *"At thirty-seven I am"* Rollyson, *Lives*, 307.

108 *"Whoever does not receive"* Mark 10:15.

108 *The Baal Shem Tov* Cited in Samuel P. Oliner and Pearl M. Oliner, *The Altruistic Personality: Rescuers of the Jews in Nazi Europe* (New York: Free Press, 1988), xii–xiii.

108 *"was playing [Norman]"* Rollyson, *Lives*, 306.

109 *"I wouldn't say [Mailer]"* Manso, ed., *Mailer*, 635.

109 *"I had read Abbott's book"* Manso, ed., *Mailer*, 636.

109 *"[Abbott] also told me* Manso, ed., *Mailer*, 626.

110 *"He who would do good"* William Blake, "Jerusalem" (1804–20), *Blake: The Complete Writings*, ed. Geoffrey Keynes (New York: Oxford Univ. Press, 1979), 687.

110 *"No one, not even you"* Rollyson, *Mailer*, 307.

110 *Peter Maurin* Cited in Dorothy Day, *The Long Loneliness* (1952; San Francisco: HarperSanFrancisco, 1997), 280.

111 *"One way or another"* Mills, *Mailer*, 17.

111 *Rabbi Moses ben Maimon* Julie Salamon, *Rambam's Ladder: A Meditation on Generosity and Why It Is Necessary to Give* (New York: Workman, 2003), 20, 148. On this point, certain Islamic authorities seem to agree with Rambam. They "maintain that lending is more meritorious" than giving because the obligation to repay will prompt someone to find work. See Sachiko Murata and William C. Chittick, *The Vision of Islam* (New York: Paragon House, 1994), 23.

113 *"I'm willing to gamble"* Rollyson, *Lives*, 315.

117 *Zen story* Adapted from Paul Reps, comp., *Zen Flesh, Zen Bones: A Collection of Zen and Pre-Zen Writings* (New York: Anchor, 1989), 10.

118 *"Norman, can we help?"* Manso, ed., *Mailer*, 648.

118 *"The hidden forces of goodness"* Albert Schweitzer, *Out of My Life and Thought: An Autobiography*, trans. C. T. Campion (New York: Henry Holt, 1933), 93.

119 *"Perfect action is called"* The Bhagavad Gita, trans. Franklin Edgerton (Cambridge, MA: Harvard Univ. Press, 1972), 161.

120 *"We don't need no"* Pink Floyd, "Another Brick in the Wall, Part II," *The Wall* (Columbia Records, 1979).

122 *"All I do know"* John Berger, *A Fortunate Man: The Story of a Country Doctor* (1967; New York: Vintage, 1997), 165.

124 *"My own conception"* William Carlos Williams, *The Autobiography of William Carlos Williams* (New York: New Directions, 1967), 291.

125 *"I don't tan"* *Play It Again, Sam*, dir. Herbert Ross (Paramount, 1972).

128 *Balanchine and Farrell* Francine Prose, *The Lives of the Muses: Nine Women and The Artists They Inspired* (New York: HarperCollins, 2002), 308. Of this relationship, Prose says, "Perhaps uniquely in the lives of the muses, the partnership of Suzanne Farrell and George Balanchine suggests that the roles of inspired and inspirer, artist and muse, *can* be divided and shared between a man and a woman, two artists collaborating to produce work that neither could accomplish alone" (9).

131 *"die miserably every day"* William Carlos Williams, "An Asphodel," *Selected Poems* (New York: New Directions, 1963), 150–51.

131 *"Let us help you"* Day, *Long Loneliness*, 89.

133 *Socrates's chosen metaphor* Plato, "Theaetetus," in *The Great Dialogues of Plato*, trans. Benjamin Jowett, The Great Books of the Western World 7 (Chicago: Britannica, 1952), 515–17. "Well, my art of midwifery is in most respects like theirs; but differs, in that I attend men and not women, and I look after their souls when they are in labour, and not after their bodies: and the triumph of my art is in thoroughly examining whether the thought which the mind of the young man brings forth is a false idol or a noble and true birth." Socrates also says that his mother was a midwife.

133 *obstetrical establishment* See Peggy Vincent, *Baby Catcher: Chronicles of a Modern Midwife* (New York: Scribner, 2002), 332. Using birth statistics complied by Dr. Marsden Wagner, a consultant to the World Health Organization, Vincent notes that while only 4 percent of U.S. births are attended by midwives, as opposed to 75 percent of European births, no European country has a perinatal mortality rate higher than that of the United States.

133 *"when to speak"* Vincent, *Baby Catcher*, 135.

134 *"Sometimes birth"* Vincent, *Baby Catcher*, 296.

134 *absorbed "in the process"* Vincent, *Baby Catcher*, 293.

142 *"Thompson . . . Reprimanded"* Jeanne Miles, *Caledonian Record*, 3 July 2003, A1.

144 *"A great deal has been said"* Sue M. Goldie, ed., *"I Have Done My Duty": Florence Nightingale in the Crimean War, 1854–1856* (Iowa City: Univ. of Iowa Press, 1987), 107. For an illuminating (and, in this context, qualifying) portrait of a physician willing to take risks, see Atul Gawande, "Desperate Measures: A Doctor Who Would Try Anything," *New Yorker*, 5 May 2003, 70–81.

CHAPTER 5. THE DOMESTIC SAMARITAN

150 *Sauvage . . . a child* Connie Louise Katz, "Weapons of the Spirit," *Lifestyles*, pre-spring, 1991, 28.

151 *two of their . . . expressions* Philip Hallie, *Lest Innocent Blood Be Shed: The Story of the Village of Le Chambon and How Goodness Happened There* (1979; New York: Harper-Collins, 1994), 78.

151 *"How could the Nazis"* Hallie, *Lest Innocent Blood*, 270

151 *"weapons of the spirit"* *Weapons of the Spirit*, written and directed by Pierre Sauvage (First Run Features, 1989), 18. Page numbers refer to the script, which is available from Friends of Le Chambon, 8033 Sunset Boulevard, Los Angeles, CA 90046.

151 *"We know only men"* Hallie, *Lest Innocent Blood*, 103.

151 *"These people have come"* Hallie, *Lest Innocent Blood*, 108.

151 *"Naturally, come in"* Hallie, *Lest Innocent Blood*, 120.

151 *"I do not hunt"* Hallie, *Lest Innocent Blood*, 152–53.

152 *"get your sweater"* Hallie, *Lest Innocent Blood*, 64–65.

152 *His proposal to her* Hallie, *Lest Innocent Blood*, 66.

152 *Their relationship* Hallie, *Lest Innocent Blood*, 19.

152 *He wrote to Magda* Hallie, *Lest Innocent Blood*, 224.

152 *At Sin-le-Noble* Hallie, *Lest Innocent Blood*, 69–71.

153 *The Quakers* Hallie, *Lest Innocent Blood*, 119–38.

153 *Édouard Theis* Hallie, *Lest Innocent Blood*, 27–28, 47–48, 176.

153 *"It was characteristic"* Hallie, *Lest Innocent Blood*, 159.

154 *"We mustn't act"* *Weapons of the Spirit*, 27.

154 *they refused to evangelize* Hallie, *Lest Innocent Blood*, 54–55.

155 *the only conversion* *Weapons of the Spirit*, 40.

155 *Daniel . . . agnostic* *Weapons of the Spirit*, 45. "He had no interest in religious dogma and great wariness about all narrow religious beliefs."

155 *"I have chosen Le Chambon"* *Weapons of the Spirit*, 45.

155 *Daniel's death* Hallie, *Lest Innocent Blood*, 203–17.

155 *The French Resistance* Hallie, *Lest Innocent Blood*, 184.

155 *assassinate Hitler* Hallie, *Lest Innocent Blood*, 265.

155 *to prevent retaliations* Hallie, *Lest Innocent Blood*, 261.

155 *"The moral brilliance"* Hallie, *Lest Innocent Blood*, xiii.

156 *Yad Vashem medals* Rone Tempest, "Jews Thank the French Town That Saved Them," *Los Angeles Times*, 15 October 1990.

156 *"always ready to serve"* Hallie, *Lest Innocent Blood*, 196.

156 *"nothing but happy memories"* Deborah Dwork and Robert Jan van Pelt, *Holocaust: A History* (New York: Norton, 2002), 335.

157 *Madeleine Barraud* Hallie, *Lest Innocent Blood*, 252–53.

157 *"With a few loyal exceptions"* *Weapons of the Spirit*, 46.

157 *Joseph Atlas* *Weapons of the Spirit*, 46.

158 *"contract of mutual indifference"* Cited in Jonathan Glover, *Humanity: A Moral History of the Twentieth Century* (New Haven: Yale Nota Bene, 2001), 393.

158 *"How can you call us"* Hallie, *Lest Innocent Blood*, 20.

158 *"We didn't protect"* Alexandra Tuttle, "Marking a Blessed Conspiracy," *Time*, 5 November 1990, 9.

159 *"It is because"* Lao-tzu, Tao te ching, trans. D. C. Lau (Harmondsworth, UK: Penguin, 1963), 58.

159 *"They remembered"* Dwork and van Pelt, *Holocaust*, 335.

159 *Achilles* H. D. F. Kitto, *The Greeks* (Harmondsworth, UK: Penguin, 1957), 172.

160 *"you were aliens"* Exodus 22:21 and 23:9. See also Deuteronomy 10:19 and 24:17.

160 *"three Old Testaments"* *Weapons of the Spirit*, 17.

160 *The German theologian* Dietrich Bonhoeffer, *Letters and Papers from Prison*, ed. Eberhard Bethge (1950–51; New York: Macmillan, 1972), 156–57.

160 *"of earth and blood"* Cited in Lacey Baldwin Smith, *Fools, Martyrs, Traitors: The Story of Martyrdom in the Western World* (New York: Knopf, 1997), 327.

160 *Ludwif Müller* Smith, *Fools*, 324.

160 *"the abyss of mysticism"* Hallie, *Lest Innocent Blood*, 67.

161 *"spiritual life"* Martin Buber, *I and Thou*, trans. Ronald Gregor Smith, 2nd ed. (New York: Scribner's, 1958), 38.

161 *"I could not say"* Hallie, *Lest Innocent Blood*, xxi.

161 *"To play up true Christian"* Pierre Sauvage, "Learning Hope from the Holocaust" (paper presented at Remembering for the Future: Jews and Christians During and After the Holocaust International Scholars Conference, Oxford University, 10–13 July 1988). Available from Friends of Le Chambon.

161 *God known through absence* Simone Weil, *Gravity and Grace*, trans. Emma Craufurd (1947; London: Routledge & Kegan Paul, 1952), 99.

161 *"A man of the highest virtue"* Lao-tzu, Tao te ching, 99.

162 *"Who stands fast?"* Bonhoeffer, *Letters and Papers*, 5.

162 *"an organization"* Hallie, *Lest Innocent Blood*, 199.

163 *internment camp in 1943* Hallie, *Lest Innocent Blood*, 15–44.

163 *"millions of uprooted men"* Simone Pétrement, *Simone Weil: A Life*, trans. Raymond Rosenthal (New York: Schocken, 1988), 511. See also Simone Weil, *The Need for Roots* (1949; London and New York: Routledge, 2002), 47. "The Germans, at the time Hitler assumed command over them, were really—as he was never tired of repeating—proletarians, that is to say, uprooted individuals."

163 *"unglamorous kitchen struggle"* Hallie, *Lest Innocent Blood*, 91. See also 8 and 204–5.

163 *"foundation of decent life"* John Lukacs, *Confessions of an Original Sinner* (New York: Tickner & Fields, 1990), 276.

163 *Boy Scouts* Hallie, *Lest Innocent Blood*, 108.

164 *their talent for secrecy* Hallie, *Lest Innocent Blood*, 200.

164 *"Though they were discreet"* Hallie, *Lest Innocent Blood*, 198.

164 *"Americans are so"* Richard Rodriguez, *Brown* (New York: Viking, 2002), 200.

165 *one of . . . refugees complained* Hallie, *Lest Innocent Blood*, 155.

165 *the idea of selfless service* Pierre Sauvage, "Ten Things I Would Like to Know About Righteous Conduct in Le Chambon and Elsewhere During the Holocaust," *Humboldt Journal of Social Relations* 13, nos. 1, 2 (1985–86): 256.

166 *Camus at Le Chambon* Hallie, *Lest Innocent Blood*, 248–49. See also Oliver Todd, *Albert Camus: A Life*, trans. Benjamin Ivry (New York: Knopf, 1997), 167.

166 *"In this Protestant region"* Todd, *Albert Camus*, 160.

166 *The protagonist, Dr. Rieux* Todd, *Albert Camus*, 161.

166 *"The language he used"* Albert Camus, *The Plague*, trans. Stuart Gilbert (1947; New York: Vintage, 1991), 12.

167 *"Indeed, for Rieux"* Camus, *Plague*, 192–93.

167 *"Go for a swim."* Camus, *Plague*, 256.

168 *"wishful thinking"* Matt Cherry, "Christopher Hitchens on Mother Theresa (Interview)," *Free Inquiry Magazine* 16, no. 4 (Fall 1996): 12. Available at the Council for Secular Humanism Web site, http://www.secularhumanism.org/library/fi/hitchens_16_4.html, 29 April 2004.

169 *blow to Trocmé's faith* Hallie, *Lest Innocent Blood*, 256–59.

169 *"side by side"* Camus, *Plague*, 257.

170 *"There have been . . . plagues"* Camus, *Plague*, 37.

170 *"this horrible adventure"* Samuel P. Oliner and Pearl M. Oliner, *The Altruistic Personality: Rescuers of Jews in Nazi Europe* (New York: Free Press, 1988), 229.

170 *"In this respect"* Camus, *Plague*, 37.

171 *"We were used to it"* *Weapons of the Spirit*, 10.

171 *rescue a "hobby"* Hallie, *Lest Innocent Blood*, 195.

171 *the economic risks Weapons of the Spirit*, 23.

171 *little time to reflect* Hallie, *Lest Innocent Blood*, 292.

172 *"a period which must"* John Berger, *A Fortunate Man: The Story of a Country Doctor* (1967; New York: Vintage, 1997), 162.

172 *"advertising agencies"* David Rieff, *A Bed for the Night: Humanitarianism in Crisis* (New York: Simon & Schuster, 2002), 289.

172 *"What's true of all the evils"* Camus, *Plague*, 125–26.

172 *"festival of cruelty"* From Nietzsche's *Genealogy of Morals* (1887). "Without cruelty, there is no festival. . . ." Cited (and opposed) in Glover, *Humanity*, 17.

172 *"Why, that's not difficult!"* Camus, *Plague*, 134.

173 *"We had a meeting"* Dwork and van Pelt, *Holocaust*, 343.

173 *Jean-Pierre Trocmé* Hallie, *Lest Innocent Blood*, 254–60.

174 *"You know, Maman"* Hallie, *Lest Innocent Blood*, 146–47.

174 *the Catholic priest* Hallie, *Lest Innocent Blood*, 188.

175 *"[A]side from the two"* Hallie, *Lest Innocent Blood*, 141–42.

175 *Even Marx is supposed* Erich Fromm, *Marx's Concept of Man* (New York: Frederick Unger, 1961), 252–53.

176 *in a busy train station* Hallie, *Lest Innocent Blood*, 225–31.

176 *"Who are these people"* Nick Hornby, *How to Be Good* (New York: Riverhead, 2001), 275.

177 *"One of the more blatant"* Dr. Edgar Berman, *In Africa with Schweitzer* (New York: Harper & Row, 1986), 67.

177 *"I don't have any"* Tracy Kidder, *Mountains Beyond Mountains: The Quest of Dr. Paul Farmer, A Man Who Would Cure the World* (New York: Random House, 2003), 23.

177 *"plenty who laid claim"* Dorothy Day, *The Long Loneliness* (1952; San Francisco: HarperSanFrancisco, 1997), 237.

178 *"not a good Boy Scout"* Hallie, *Lest Innocent Blood*, 252.

178 *"One of the most regrettable"* Wendell Berry, "Economy and Pleasure," in *What Are People For?* (New York: North Point, 1990), 142–43.

179 *"I still really want"* Rachel Corrie, "This Happens Every Day," *Harper's Magazine*, June 2003, 19.

179 *"road kill"* Joshua Hammer, "The Death of Rachel Corrie," *Mother Jones*, October 2003, 70.

179 *Simone Weil . . . Spain* Simone Pétrement, *Simone Weil*, 272, 276–77.

179 *Ethel Rosenberg* Smith, *Fools*, 362.

179 *Perpetua* Smith, *Fools*, 89–115. Obviously I have chosen to focus here on the difficulties involved in trying to "help" idealistic daughters. For a study of the difficulties involved in trying to help elderly fathers, compare Phillip Lopate's essay "The Story of My Father," in *Portrait of My Body* (New York: Anchor, 1997), Philip Roth's memoir

Patrimony (New York: Touchstone, 1991), and Joel Meyerowitz's film, *Pop* (First Run Features, 1998).

180 *"What did you hope"* David Sedaris, "The Girl Next Door: How Much Trouble Could a Nine-Year-Old Be?" *New Yorker*, 18 and 25 August 2003, 57.

181 *"He was living it out"* Philip Roth, *American Pastoral* (Boston: Houghton Mifflin, 1997), 86.

183 *to commit suicide* Albert Camus, *The Myth of Sisyphus and Other Essays*, trans. Justin O'Brien (1942; New York: Vintage, 1955), 3.

184 *"Help is giving part"* Norman Maclean, *A River Runs Through It, and Other Stories* (Chicago: Univ. of Chicago Press, 1976), 81.

184 *"So it is"* Maclean, *River*, 81.

184 *"He asked me"* Maclean, *River*, 81.

185 *"Tell me"* Maclean, *River*, 77.

186 *"You know, Charles"* Evelyn Waugh, *Brideshead Revisited* (Boston: Little, Brown, 1945), 215.

186 *Sebastian's "holiness"* Waugh, *Brideshead Revisited*, 305–6.

186 *"If you push me"* Maclean, *River*, 103.

187 *parable of the prodigal son* Luke 15:11–32.

187 *"Your daughter is divine"* Roth, *American Pastoral*, 176.

189 *"half the city of Great Falls"* Maclean, *River*, 67.

189 *she could not make her peace* As of this writing, 23 American soldiers have committed suicide while stationed in Iraq. Erin Emery and Eileen Kelley, "GI Remembered for His Life, Not His Suicide," *Denver Post*, 19 March 2004, A14.

CHAPTER 6. THE DESCENT INTO HELL

194 *"I want to help"* Barbara Ehrenreich, *Nickel and Dimed: On (Not) Getting By in America* (New York: Henry Holt, 2001), 99.

195 *"going home . . . knickers"* Liner notes from Beth Orton's *Pass in Time* (London: BMG, 2003).

197 *"The white man"* Malcolm X, *The Autobiography of Malcolm X* (New York: Grove, 1964), 268.

199 *Less than 0.7* Paul Farmer, *Pathologies of Power: Health, Human Rights, and the New War on the Poor* (Berkeley: Univ. of California Press, 2003), 250.

199 *1.2 billion people* "2.4 billion people have no access to basic sanitation; and 854 million adults, 543 million of them women, are illiterate"; David Rieff, *A Bed for the Night: Humanitarianism in Crisis* (New York: Simon & Schuster, 2002), 46–47.

201 *Thoreau said as much* "Often the poor man is not so cold and hungry as he is dirty and ragged and gross. It is partly his taste, and not merely his misfortune." Henry David Thoreau, *Walden*, ed. Owen Thomas (New York: Norton, 1966), 51.

201 *"I have picked up boys"* Michel Eyquem de Montaigne, "Of Experience," in *The Essays of Michel Eyquem de Montaigne*, trans. Charles Cotton, ed. W. Carew Hazlitt, The Great Books of the Western World 25 (Chicago: Britannica, 1952), 525.

203 *remote village in India* Vandana Shiva, "Globalization and the War Against Farmers and the Land," in *The Agrarian Reader,* ed. Norman Wirzba (Lexington: Univ. Press of Kentucky, 2003), 125–26. Shiva gives the names of nine farmers in Rentichintala Mandal who sold their kidneys for this purpose.

203 *a lack of hope* David K. Shipler, *The Working Poor* (New York: Knopf, 2004), 10.

204 *"Why I Am Not"* Wendell Berry, *What Are People For?* (New York: North Point, 1990), 170–77.

204 *34.6 million* "Americans Living in Poverty," *Christian Century,* 9 March 2004, 7.

204 *"culture of poverty"* For a summary and critique, see Cynthia Duncan, *Worlds Apart: Why Poverty Persists in Rural America* (New Haven: Yale Univ. Press, 1999), 187–91.

204 *"a mob of beings"* Tobias George Smollett, *The Expedition of Humphry Clinker* (1771; New York: Rinehart, 1950), 338.

206 *"I made the announcement"* Malcolm X, *Autobiography,* 316.

208 *"[I]t would be wrong"* Wendell Berry, "In Defense of the Family Farm," *Home Economics* (New York: North Point, 1987), 173.

209 *the right to eat bunny bread People Like Us: Social Class in America,* produced and directed by Louis Alvarez and Andrew Kolker (Center for New American Media, 2001).

210 *almost twice as many workers* Luke Mitchell, "A Run on Terror: The Rising Cost of Fear Itself," *Harper's Magazine,* March 2004, 79. Fatal workplace injuries numbered 5,431 in 2001; 2,978 Americans died from terrorist attacks that same year. Since 1995, 2,250 migrants have died trying to cross the U.S.-Mexico border. See Bob Moser, "Samaritans in the Desert," *Nation,* 26 May 2003, 13. As its title suggests, this article gives us an idea of how the Good Samaritan might appear in twenty-first-century garb.

210 *five million workers* Molly Ivins, "The Uncompassionate Conservative," *Mother Jones,* November-December 2003, 47.

210 *"harassing a burro"* "The Harper's Index," *Harper's Magazine,* March 2004, 11. As cited: "Maximum prison sentence in months for causing the death of a U.S. worker by willfully violating federal safety regulations: 6. Maximum prison sentence in months for harassing a wild burro on federal lands: 12."

210 *liberation theology* See Gustavo Gutiérrez, *A Theology of Liberation* (Maryknoll, NY: Orbis, 1973).

211 *Schoolchildren in Colombia* Hector Mondragon, talk on Colombia, Lyndonville, Vermont, 30 January 2003. Mondragon is a Colombian economist and human rights activist.

214 *Robert Frost . . . the poor* Cited in *The Norton Anthology of Modern Poetry,* ed. Richard Ellman and Robert O'Clair (New York: Norton, 1973), 191.

215 *three . . . from Northern Ireland* Rebekah Graydon, "A Long Way from Home," Habitat for Humanity Web site, http://www.habitat.org/hw/dec-jan01/Feature/fla-irishframe.html.

215 *Dom Helder Camara* Alex Bellos, "Helder Camara, Brazilian Cleric Who Eschewed Pomp in His Battles Against Injustice and Inequality," *The Guardian*, 31 August 1999, 24.

215 *Victor Gollancz* Cited in Deborah Dwork and Robert Jan van Pelt, *Holocaust: A History* (New York: Norton, 2002), 323.

216 *"do justice, love mercy"* Micah 6:8.

216 *that terrifying sermon* James Joyce, *Portrait of the Artist as a Young Man* (1914–15; New York: Viking, 1968), 130–31.

219 *"Lord, I believe"* Mark 9:24.

219 *There is a tradition* See Alan W. Watts, *Myth and Ritual in Christianity* (Boston: Beacon Press, 1968), 43. "Above and below, and around on every side, [the devils] rushed towards darkness and found—always—the inescapable Light, the hated Love which began to burn them like a raging fire."

222 *"the proud egoism"* Albert Camus, *The Plague*, trans. Justin O'Brien (1947; New York: Vintage, 1991), 297.

224 *"I contemplate my own loss"* Paul Farmer, *Pathologies of Power*, 250.

225 *"There was a rich man"* Traditionally known as the parable of Lazarus and Dives, Luke 16:19–31.

227 *"The air was filled"* Charles Dickens, "A Christmas Carol," vol. 1, *The Christmas Books* (Harmondsworth, UK: Penguin, 1971), 65.

228 *world trade in prostitutes* Karen Long, "Sex Trafficking Runs Rampant, Expert Says," *Christian Century*, 27 January 2004, 17–18: "Somewhere between 700,000 and 2 million women and girls are taken beyond their national borders and forced into prostitution each year." It is naïve to assume that none of these crimes take place inside U.S. borders.

230 *"putting cruelty first"* Judith N. Shklar, "Putting Cruelty First," in *Ordinary Vices* (Cambridge, MA: Harvard Univ. Press, 1984), 7–44. Shklar claims that Montaigne was the first to do so. For an illuminating discussion of cruelty in art and politics, see Gerald Marzorati, *A Painter of Darkness: Leon Golub and His Times* (New York: Penguin, 1990).

230 *Simone Weil* Simone Pétrement, *Simone Weil: A Life*, trans. Raymond Rosenthal (New York: Pantheon, 1976), 240: "She thought in fact that the liberation of the worker must be accomplished in the work itself, and the work, in order to become that of a free man, must be pervaded by thought, invention, and judgment."

231 *I saw Satan fall* Luke 10:18.

CHAPTER 7. A BETTER PLAN THAN THIS

235 *night riders fired* H. Moffett, "Ruckus in Irasburg: The Case That Had the Gossips Buzzing in Vermont, *Life*, 4 April 1969, 62–64.

236 *white South African policeman* Jonathan Glover, *Humanity: A Moral History of the Twentieth Century* (New Haven: Yale Nota Bene, 2001), 38.

236 *"unbridgeable difference"* Philip Hallie, *Lest Innocent Blood Be Shed: The Story of the Village of Le Chambon and How Goodness Happened There* (1979; New York: Harper-Collins, 1994), 275.

236 *thief on the cross* Luke 23:39–43.

237 *"The human loss"* *The Bolivian Diary of Che Guevara,* dir. Richard Dindo (Fox Lorber, 1997).

238 *"When you give somebody"* Hallie, *Lest Innocent Blood,* 72.

238 *"I could suggest no rule"* Oliver Sacks, "The Case of Anna H," *New Yorker,* 7 October 2002, 72.

238 *Timon of Athens* Plutarch, "Alcibiades," in *The Lives of the Noble Grecians and Romans,* trans. Dryden, The Great Books of the Western World 14 (Chicago: Britannica, 1952), 774.

239 *Perhaps the altruistic* Tracy Kidder puts this quite succinctly: "Lives of service depend on lives of support"; see *Mountains Beyond Mountains: The Quest of Dr. Paul Farmer, A Man Who Would Cure the World* (New York: Random House, 2003), 108.

240 *"You must get to know"* Robinson Davies, *Fifth Business* (1970; New York: Penguin, 1977), 226.

240 *Iris Murdoch* Cited in Samuel P. Oliner and Pearl M. Oliner, *The Altruistic Personality: Rescuers of Jews in Nazi Europe* (New York: Free Press, 1988), 9.

240 *"Sin is behoovable"* Cited in F. C. Happold, *Mysticism* (Harmondsworth, UK: Penguin, 1970), 328.

242 *Mother Teresa* Christopher Hitchens, *The Missionary Position: Mother Teresa in Theory and Practice* (London: Verso, 1995), 11.

244 *"I will be with you"* Elliot J. Gorn, *Mother Jones: The Most Dangerous Woman in America* (New York: Hill and Wang, 2001), 179.

245 *our faces at fifty* George Orwell, *In Front of Your Nose (1945–1950),* vol. 4, *The Collected Essays, Journalism and Letters of George Orwell,* ed. Sonia Orwell and Ian Angus (New York: Harcourt Brace Jovanovich, 1968), 515. "At 50, everyone has the face he deserves." These were the last words Orwell wrote in his journal.

BIBLIOGRAPHY

Alighieri, Dante. *The Inferno.* Trans. John Ciardi. New York: Mentor, 1954.

"Americans Living in Poverty." *Christian Century,* 9 March 2004, 7.

Bate, Walter Jackson. *Samuel Johnson.* New York: Harcourt Brace Jovanovich, 1975.

Bellos, Alex. "Helder Camara, Brazilian Cleric Who Eschewed Pomp in His Battles Against Injustice and Inequality." *The Guardian,* 31 August 1999, 24.

Berger, John. *A Fortunate Man: The Story of a Country Doctor.* 1967. New York: Vintage, 1997.

Berman, Dr. Edgar. *In Africa with Schweitzer.* New York: Harper & Row, 1986.

Berry, Wendell. *Home Economics.* New York: North Point, 1987.

———. *What Are People For?* New York: North Point, 1990.

The Bhagavad Gita. Trans. Franklin Edgerton. Cambridge, MA: Harvard Univ. Press, 1972.

Blackburn, Simon. *Being Good: A Short Introduction to Ethics.* Oxford: Oxford Univ. Press, 2001.

Blake, William. *Blake: The Complete Writings.* Ed. Geoffrey Keynes. New York: Oxford Univ. Press, 1979.

Bonhoeffer, Dietrich. *Letters and Papers from Prison.* Ed. Eberhard Bethge. 1950–51. New York: Macmillan, 1972.

Bowden, Mark. "Tales of the Tyrant." *Atlantic Monthly,* May 2002, 35–53.

Brehony, Kathleen A. *Ordinary Grace: An Examination of the Roots of Compassion, Altruism, and Empathy, and the Ordinary Individuals Who Help Others in Extraordinary Ways.* New York: Riverhead, 1999.

Brown, Rita Mae. *Six of One.* New York: Bantam, 1979.

Buber, Martin. *I and Thou.* Trans. Ronald Gregor Smith. 2nd ed. New York: Scribner's, 1958.

Buckley, William F., Jr. *Overdrive: A Personal Documentary.* Garden City, NY: Doubleday, 1983.

Burtt, E. A., ed. *The Teachings of the Compassionate Buddha.* New York: Mentor, 1955.

Camus, Albert. *The Myth of Sisyphus and Other Essays.* Trans. Justin O'Brien. 1942. New York: Vintage, 1955.

———. *The Plague*. Trans. Stuart Gilbert. 1947. New York: Vintage, 1991.

———. "Reflections on the Guillotine" (1957). In *Resistance, Rebellion, and Death*. Trans. Justin O'Brien. New York: Vintage, 1995.

Carroll, Peter N. *The Odyssey of the Abraham Lincoln Brigade*. Stanford: Stanford Univ. Press, 1994.

Celine, Louis-Ferdinand. *Journey to the End of the Night*. Trans. John H. P. Marks. 1932. New York: New Directions, 1960.

Chadwick, Henry. *The Early Church*. Harmondsworth, UK: Penguin, 1967.

Chan, Wing-Tsit, comp and trans. *A Source Book in Chinese Philosophy*. Princeton: Princeton Univ. Press, 1963.

Cherry, Matt. "Christopher Hitchens on Mother Teresa (Interview)." *Free Inquiry Magazine* 16, no. 4 (Fall 1996). Available at the Council for Secular Humanism Web site, http://www.secularhumanism.org/library/fi/hitchens_16_4.html, 29 April 2004.

Coles, Robert. *The Moral Life of Children*. Boston: Atlantic Monthly Press, 1986.

Conlin, Michelle. "For Gen X, It's Paradise Lost." *Business Week*, 30 June 2003, 72ff.

Coppock, Michelle, "Habitat for Humanity International: Historic Roots, Habitat for Humanity Web site, http://www.learningtogive.org/papers/organizations/habitat_humanity.html.

Corrie, Rachel. "This Happens Every Day." *Harper's Magazine*, June 2003, 15–20.

Curwen, Henry Darcy, ed. *A Johnson Sampler*. Boston: David R. Godine, 2002.

Daly, Mary. *Gyn/Ecology: The Metaethics of Radical Feminism*. 1978. Boston: Beacon Press, 1990.

Davies, Robertson. *Fifth Business*. 1970. New York: Penguin, 1977.

Day, Dorothy. *The Long Loneliness: The Autobiography of Dorothy Day*. 1952. San Francisco: HarperSanFrancisco, 1997.

Dearborn, Mary V. *Mailer: A Biography*. Boston: Houghton Mifflin, 1999.

The Dhammapada. Trans. Irving Babbitt. New York: New Directions, 1965.

Dickens, Charles. "A Christmas Carol." 1843. Vol 1, *The Christmas Books*. New York: Penguin, 1971.

Didion, Joan. *Slouching Towards Bethlehem*. New York: Dell, 1968.

Donne, John. Selections from *Devotions upon Emergent Occasions*. In *Seventeenth Century Prose and Poetry*. Ed. Alexander M. Witherspoon and Frank J. Warnke. 2nd ed. New York: Harcourt Brace Jovanovich, 1982.

Duncan, Cynthia. *Worlds Apart: Why Poverty Persists in Rural America*. New Haven: Yale Univ. Press, 1999.

Dwork, Deborah, and Robert Jan van Pelt. *Holocaust: A History*. New York: Norton, 2002.

Ehrenreich, Barbara. *Nickel and Dimed: On (Not) Getting By in America*. New York: Henry Holt, 2001.

Eisler, Benita. *Chopin's Funeral*. New York: Knopf, 2003.

Eliot, T. S. *Collected Poems, 1909–1962*. New York: Harcourt, Brace & World, 1970.

Ellman, Richard, and Robert O'Clair, eds. *The Norton Anthology of Modern Poetry*. New York: Norton, 1973.

Emerson, Ralph Waldo. "Self-Reliance" (1841). In *Emerson: Essays and Lectures*. Ed. Joel Porte. Library of America 15. New York: Literary Classics of the United States, 1983.

Emery, Erin, and Eileen Kelley. "GI Remembered for His Life, Not His Suicide," *Denver Post*, 19 March 2004, A14.

Englebert, Omer. *St. Francis of Assisi: A Biography*. Ann Arbor: Servant Books, 1979.

Farmer, Paul. *Pathologies of Power: Health, Human Rights, and the New War on the Poor*. Berkeley: Univ. of California Press, 2003.

Freud, Sigmund. *A General Introduction to Psycho-Analysis*. 1917. Trans. Joan Riviere. In *The Major Works of Sigmund Freud*. The Great Books of the Western World 54. Chicago: Britannica, 1952.

Friends of Peace Pilgrim, comps. *Peace Pilgrim: Her Life and Work in Her Own Words*. Santa Fe: Ocean Tree Books, 1982.

Fromm, Erich. *Marx's Concept of Man*. New York: Frederick Unger, 1961.

Gawande, Atul. "Desperate Measures: A Doctor Who Would Try Anything." *New Yorker*, 5 May 2003.

Ginsberg, Allen. *Howl and Other Poems*. San Francisco: City Lights, 1956.

Glover, Jonathan. *Humanity: A Moral History of the Twentieth Century*. New Haven: Yale Nota Bene, 2001.

Goethe, Johann Wolfgang von. *Selected Poems*. Trans. John Whaley. London: J. M. Dent, 1998.

Goldie, Sue M., ed. *"I Have Done My Duty": Florence Nightingale in the Crimean War, 1854–1856*. Iowa City: Univ. of Iowa Press, 1987.

Gorn, Elliott J. *Mother Jones: The Most Dangerous Woman in America*. New York: Hill and Wang, 2001.

Graydon, Rebekah. "A Long Way from Home." Habitat for Humanity Web site, http://habitat.org/hw/dec-jan01/Feature/fla-irishframe.html.

Gutiérrez, Gustavo. *A Theology of Liberation*. Maryknoll, NY: Orbis, 1973.

Hallie, Philip. *Lest Innocent Blood Be Shed: The Story of the Village of Le Chambon and How Goodness Happened There*. 1979. New York: HarperCollins, 1994.

Hammer, Joshua. "The Death of Rachel Corrie." *Mother Jones*, September-October 2003, 69–75, 98–102.

Happold, F. C. *Mysticism: A Study and an Anthology*. Harmondsworth, UK: Penguin, 1970.

"The Harper's Index." *Harper's Magazine*, March 2004, 11.

Hillesum, Etty. *An Interrupted Life: The Diaries, 1941–1943, and Letters from Westerbork*. Trans. Arnold J. Pomerans. 1981. New York: Henry Holt, 1996.

Hitchens, Christopher. *The Missionary Position: Mother Teresa in Theory and Practice*. London: Verso, 1995.

Hoagland, Edward. "The Problem of the Golden Rule." In *The Courage of Turtles*. 1968. San Francisco: North Point, 1985.

Hopkins, Jeffrey. *Cultivating Compassion: A Buddhist Perspective*. New York: Broadway, 2001.

Hornby, Nick. *How to Be Good.* New York: Riverhead, 2001.

Ivins, Molly. "The Uncompassionate Conservative." *Mother Jones,* November 2003, 45–47.

Johnson, Samuel. "The Rambler (No. 68, 1750)." In *Select Essays of Dr. Johnson.* Ed. George Birbeck Hill. Vol 1. London: J. M. Dent, 1889.

Johnson, Samuel, and James Boswell. *A Journey to the Western Islands of Scotland and The Journal of a Tour of the Hebrides.* 1775; 1785. London: Penguin, 1984.

Joyce, James. *A Portrait of the Artist as a Young Man.* Ed. Chester G. Anderson. 1914–15. New York: Viking, 1964.

Judis, John B. *William F. Buckley: Patron Saint of Conservatives.* New York: Simon & Schuster, 1988.

Julian of Norwich. *Revelations of Divine Love.* Trans. Elizabeth Spearing. London: Penguin, 1998.

Katz, Connie Louise. "Weapons of the Spirit." *Lifestyles,* Pre-spring 1991, 28–31.

Kerouac, Jack. *Big Sur.* 1962. New York: Penguin, 1992.

Keyes, Ralph, *Nice Guys Finish Seventh: False Phrases, Spurious Sayings, and Familiar Misquotations.* New York: HarperCollins, 1992.

Kidder, Tracy. *Mountains Beyond Mountains: The Quest of Dr. Paul Farmer, a Man Who Would Cure the World.* New York: Random House, 2003.

Kierkegaard, Søren. "Works of Love" (1847). In *A Kierkegaard Anthology.* Ed. Robert Bretall. New York: Modern Library, 1946.

Kingsolver, Barbara. *The Bean Trees.* New York: Harper & Row, 1988.

Kitto, H. D. F. *The Greeks.* Harmondsworth, UK: Penguin, 1957.

Lao-tzu. Tao te ching. Trans. D. C. Lau. Harmondsworth, UK: Penguin, 1972.

Long, Karen. "Sex Trafficking Runs Rampant, Expert Says." *Christian Century,* 27 January 2004, 17–18.

Lopate, Phillip. "The Story of My Father." In *Portrait of My Body.* New York: Anchor, 1996.

Lukacs, John. *Confessions of an Original Sinner.* New York: Tickner & Fields, 1990.

Luks, Allan, and Peggy Payne. *The Healing Power of Doing Good: The Health and Spiritual Benefits of Helping Others.* New York: Fawcett, 1992.

Maclean, Norman. *A River Runs Through It and Other Stories.* Chicago: Univ. of Chicago Press, 1976.

Malcolm X. *The Autobiography of Malcolm X.* New York: Grove, 1964.

Manso, Peter, ed. *Mailer, His Life and Times.* New York: Simon & Schuster, 1985.

Marzorati, Gerald. *A Painter of Darkness: Leon Golub and His Times.* New York: Viking, 1990.

Matthews, K. E., and L. K. Cannon. "Environmental Noise Level as a Determinant of Helping Behavior." *Journal of Personality and Social Psychology* 32 (1975): 571–77.

McCann, Michelle R. *Luba: The Angel of Bergen-Belsen.* Berkeley: Tricycle, 2003.

Metzger, Bruce M., and Michael D. Coogan. *The Oxford Companion to the Bible.* New York: Oxford Univ. Press, 1993.

Miles, Jeanne. "Dr. Thompson Publicly Reprimanded." *Caledonian Record,* 3 July 2003, A1.

Mills, Hilary. *Mailer: A Biography*. New York: Empire, 1982.

Mitchell, Joseph. "Professor Seagull" (1942) and "Joe Gould's Secret" (1964). In *Up in the Old Hotel*. New York: Pantheon, 1992.

Mitchell, Luke. "A Run on Terror: The Rising Cost of Fear Itself." *Harper's Magazine*, March 2004, 79–81.

Moffett, H. "Ruckus in Irasburg: The Case That Had the Gossips Buzzing in Vermont." *Life*, 4 April 1969, 62–64.

Mondragon, Hector. Talk on Colombia. Lyndonville, Vermont, 30 January 2003.

Montaigne, Michel Eyquem de. "Of Experience." In *The Essays of Michel Eyquem de Montaigne*. Trans. Charles Cotton. Ed. W. Carew Hazlitt. The Great Books of the Western World 25. Chicago: Britannica, 1952.

Moser, Bob. "Samaritans in the Desert." *Nation*, 26 May 2003, 13–14, 16, 18.

Murata, Sachiko, and William C. Chittick. *The Vision of Islam*. New York: Paragon House, 1994.

Neill, Stephen. *A History of Christian Missions*. New York: Penguin, 1964.

Nietzsche, Frederick. *The Case of Wagner*. 1888. Trans. Anthony M. Ludovici. Vol. 8, *The Complete Works of Frederick Nietzsche*. Ed. Oscar Levy. New York: Russell & Russell, 1964.

Oliner, Samuel P., and Pearl M. Oliner. *The Altruistic Personality: Rescuers of Jews in Nazi Europe*. New York: Free Press, 1988.

Orwell, George. *In Front of Your Nose 1945–1950*. Vol. 4, *The Collected Essays, Journalism and Letters of George Orwell*. Ed. Sonia Orwell and Ian Angus. New York: Harcourt Brace Jovanovich, 1968.

Oxford Annotated Bible with Apocrypha (NRSV). New York: Oxford Univ. Press, 1991.

Pétrement, Simone. *Simone Weil: A Life*. Trans. Raymond Rosenthal. New York: Pantheon, 1976.

Picon, Gaeton. "Notes on *The Plague*." In *Camus: A Collection of Critical Essays*. Ed. Germaine Bree. Englewood Cliffs, NJ: Prentice-Hall, 1962.

Plato. *Meno* and *Theaetetus*. In *The Dialogues of Plato*. Trans. Benjamin Jowett. The Great Books of the Western World 7. Chicago: Britannica, 1952.

Plutarch. "Alcibiades." In *The Lives of the Noble Grecians and Romans*, Dryden Translation. The Great Books of the Western World 14. Chicago: Britannica, 1952.

Price, Richard. *Samaritan*. New York: Knopf, 2003.

Prose, Francine. *The Lives of the Muses: Nine Women and the Artists They Inspired*. New York: HarperCollins, 2002.

Reps, Paul, comp. *Zen Flesh, Zen Bones: A Collection of Zen and Pre-Zen Writings*. New York: Anchor, 1989.

Rieff, David. *A Bed for the Night: Humanitarianism in Crisis*. New York: Simon & Schuster, 2002.

Rilke, Rainer Maria. *Letters to a Young Poet*. Trans. M. D. Herter Norton. 1934. New York: Norton, 1963.

Rodriguez, Richard. *Brown: The Last Discovery of America*. New York: Viking, 2003.

Rollyson, Carl. *The Lives of Norman Mailer*. New York: Paragon House, 1991.

Roth, Philip. *American Pastoral.* Boston: Houghton Mifflin, 1997.

———. *Patrimony.* New York: Touchstone, 1991.

Sacks, Oliver. "The Case of Anna H." *New Yorker,* 7 October 2002, 63–73.

Salamon, Julie. *Rambam's Ladder: A Meditation on Generosity and Why It Is Necessary to Give.* New York: Workman, 2003.

Sauvage, Pierre. Interview with Bill Moyers. Public Broadcasting System, 12 December 1990.

———. "Learning Hope from the Holocaust." Speech delivered at International Scholars' Conference on Jews and Christians During and After the Holocaust, Oxford University, 10–13 July 1988. Available from Friends of Le Chambon, 8033 Sunset Boulevard, Los Angeles, CA 90046.

———. "Ten Things I Would Like to Know About Righteous Conduct in Le Chambon and Elsewhere During the Holocaust." *Humboldt Journal of Social Relations* 13, nos. 1, 2 (1985–86): 252–59.

Schweitzer, Albert. *Out of My Life and Thought: An Autobiography.* Trans. C. T. Campion. New York: Henry Holt, 1933.

Sedaris, David. "The Girl Next Door: How Much Trouble Could a Nine-Year-Old Be?" *New Yorker,* 18 and 25 August 2003, 50–57.

Shipler, David K. *The Working Poor.* New York: Knopf, 2004.

Shiva, Vandana. "The War Against Farmers and the Land." In *The Essential Agrarian Reader.* Ed. Norman Wirzba. Lexington: Univ. Press of Kentucky, 2003.

Shklar, Judith N. "Putting Cruelty First." In *Ordinary Vices.* Cambridge, MA: Harvard Univ. Press, 1984.

Smith, Huston. *The Religions of Man.* New York: Harper & Row, 1965.

Smith, Lacey Baldwin. *Fools, Martyrs, Traitors: The Story of Martyrdom in the Western World.* New York: Knopf, 1997.

Smollett, Tobias. *The Expedition of Humphry Clinker.* 1771. New York: Rinehart, 1950.

Stanton, Elizabeth Cady. "The Solitude of the Self" (1892). In *The Elizabeth Cady Stanton–Susan B. Anthony Reader.* Ed. Ellen Carol DuBois. Rev. ed. Boston: Northeastern Univ. Press, 1992.

Stern, Karl. *The Pillar of Fire.* New York: Harcourt Brace, 1951.

Taylor, M. W. *Harriet Tubman: Antislavery Activist.* New York: Chelsea House, 1991.

Tempest, Rone. "Jews Thank the French Town That Saved Them." *Los Angeles Times,* 15 October 1990.

Thoreau, Henry David. *Walden.* Ed. Owen Thomas. 1852. New York: Norton, 1966.

Todd, Oliver. *Albert Camus: A Life.* Trans. Benjamin Ivry. New York: Knopf, 1997.

Torres, Camilo. *Camilo Torres: His Life and Message.* Ed. John Alvarez Garcia and Christian Restropo Calle. Trans. Virginia M. O'Grady. Intro. Dorothy Day. Springfield, IL: Templegate, 1968.

Trotsky, Leon. *Their Morals and Ours.* New York: Pioneer, 1942.

Tuttle, Alexandra. "Marking a Blessed Conspiracy." *Time,* 5 November 1990, 9.

van der Velde, Rink. *The Trap.* Trans. Henry J. Baron. 1966. Grand Rapids: Redux, 1995.

Veenstra, Johanna. *Pioneering for Christ in the Sudan*. Grand Rapids: Smitter, 1926.

Vincent, Peggy. *Baby Catcher: Chronicles of a Modern Midwife*. New York: Scribner, 2002.

Vitoux, Frederic. *Celine: A Biography*. Trans. Jesse Browner. New York: Paragon House, 1992.

Wain, John. *Samuel Johnson*. New York: Viking, 1974.

Watts, Alan W. *Myth and Ritual in Christianity*. Boston: Beacon Press, 1968.

Waugh, Evelyn. *Brideshead Revisited*. Boston: Little, Brown, 1945.

Weil, Simone. *Gravity and Grace*. Trans. Emma Craufurd. 1947. London: Routledge & Kegan Paul, 1952.

———. *The Need for Roots*. 1949. London: Routledge, 2002.

West, James L. W., III. *William Styron: A Life*. New York: Random House, 1998.

Williams, William Carlos. *The Autobiography of William Carlos Williams*. New York: New Directions, 1967.

———. *Selected Poems*. New York: New Directions, 1963.

Young, Steve. "Burlington, Vermont, in Midst of Controversy over Who Should Provide City with Its Only Downtown Grocery Store." National Public Radio, 11 February 2000.

MUSIC AND FILMS

The Beatles Anthology. Dir. Geoff Wonfor. Vol. 8. Apple, 1996.

The Bolivian Diary of Che Guevara. Dir. Richard Dindo. Fox Lorber, 1997.

The Good Fight: The Abraham Lincoln Brigade in the Spanish Civil War. Dir. Noel Buckner, Mary Dore, and Sam Sills. Kino, 1984.

Orton, Beth. *Pass in Time*. London: BMG, 2003.

People Like Us: Social Class in America. Dir. Louis Alvarez and Andrew Kolker. Center for New American Media, 2001.

Pop. Dir. Joel Meyerowitz. First Run Features, 1998.

Schindler. Dir. Jon Blair. Thames Video Collection, n.d.

Sound and Fury. Dir. John Aronson. Artistic License/Docurama, 2000.

Weapons of the Spirit. Dir. Pierre Sauvage. First Run Features, 1989.

ACKNOWLEDGMENTS

The subject of this book would have reminded me, had I ever been in danger of forgetting, that I wrote it with a good deal of help. I am indebted to Peter Matson of Sterling Lord Literistic for his representation, to Gideon Weil at HarperSanFrancisco for his patience and editorial guidance, to the Valparaiso Project for a generous grant in support of my work, and to its director, Dorothy Bass, for offering me the opportunity and for respecting my freedom in all things.

I was greatly helped by the insights of the men and women I interviewed, some named in these pages and others anonymous or in disguise—all much appreciated.

I showed my first drafts to James Doyle, Kathy Keizer, and Howard Frank Mosher. They have my warmest thanks for their responses.

I also wish to thank Dr. John Ajamie, who saw to my health during a time of exertion, and my brother, Henry Keizer, whose advice on practical matters has helped me stay afloat in a precarious business.

The librarians at Lyndon State College and the Cobleigh Public Library, along with Ellen Doyle at Green Mountain Books and Prints, were invaluable in helping me track down certain books. Claire Gutierrez helped me track down details that those books did not contain. Amy Leal brought her old English teacher up to speed on a few matters of form, her husband, David Yaffe, kindly assisting. Toward improving and producing the text, Karen Stough, Priscilla Stuckey, and Lisa Zuniga made painstaking contributions.

I am deeply grateful to two publications that have given me a place to shape my ideas over recent years and to my principal editors there:

Debra Bendis at *Christian Century* and Ellen Rosenbush at *Harper's Magazine*.

The writing of this book began in earnest just as my daughter, Sarah, was looking to start college and came to completion just as my mother-in-law, Theresa, was finishing her life. She died two weeks after I sent in the final chapter. It is no exaggeration to say that the courage of these two women sustained me in tasks less daunting than either of theirs, though daunting enough for me.

Even more was I sustained by the loving strength of my wife, Kathy, who managed to shore up all three of us while continuing to help the young children she teaches and heals. "Let her own works praise her in the gates."